A Comprehensive English Grammar

Raj Kumar Sharma
Bhushan Singh

ATLANTIC
PUBLISHERS & DISTRIBUTORS (P) LTD

ATLANTIC
PUBLISHERS & DISTRIBUTORS (P) LTD
7/22, Ansari Road, Darya Ganj, New Delhi
Tel.: +91-11-4077 5252, 2327 3880
E-mail: orders@atlanticbooks.com
Web: www.atlanticbooks.com

Published by Atlantic Publishers & Distributors (P) Ltd.

Reprinted in 2018, 2019, 2023, 2025

Printed & bound in India by Atlantic Print Services

Dedicated to

Our parents, who sacrificed immeasurably to provide us with the best they could to inculcate in us all that we need for ideal nature, and nurture as human beings

Acknowledgements

Bringing out a book involves a lot of assignments that cannot be completed without the support of others. The book is a product that enfolds the inspiration, encouragement and support of our well-wishers. We sincerely acknowledge the support of our friends—Dr. Samir, Dr. Afroz, Dr. Mukul, Dr. Asra, Prof. Niranjan, Dr. Ramkumar, and Prof. Deoraj—who went on encouraging us to come out with this work. We are extremely indebted to Prof. S.S. Haider, Prof. Amarendra Kumar, and Prof. B.P. Majumdar, whose scholarly inspirations keep on guiding us.

We are equally grateful to the members of our family who spared us from domestic responsibilities during the writing of the book that enabled us to complete the work within the stipulated time.

Our sincere thanks are due to all the colleagues and students who stand as valuable resources as the constant interactions with them contribute meaningfully to our academic maturity manifested in the book.

Raj Kumar Sharma
Bhushan Singh

Preface

This book deals comprehensively with all the fundamental aspects of English grammar in a very simple language and scientific manner. The emphasis has been laid on simplicity of language and scientific presentation so that it may help the learners assimilate the grammatical concepts with ease and facility. A descriptive and analytical approach has been adopted in dealing with the grammatical concepts. Though grammar intends to describe the ways a language should be used to fulfill the communicative needs, an additional effort has been made to explain the role of different grammatical constituents and underlying patterns among them that result into acceptable grammatical structures. It will certainly infuse a fresh interest among the learners, enhancing their inquisitiveness, and help them in developing scientific attitude towards analysis of this language.

The book is meant for all those who are interested in developing their competence in English in all possible ways, i.e. language skills, pedagogy, philosophic insights into grammatical operations, etc. Every possible attempt has been made to update the book by introducing latest terminologies helpful in describing and explaining English language. All the chapters are almost all-inclusive as they hardly leave any aspect untouched related to the topic dealt with. Each chapter contains sufficient examples and exercises that will facilitate learning and boost the confidence of learners. Certain new ways of description, explanation and analysis of the complex grammatical concepts have been introduced in order to enlighten the learners about the inherent link between grammar and linguistics. As description deals with whats and explanation with whys of grammatical nuances, both of these components have been adequately covered in handling the topics. The descriptive (what aspect) component will be useful for those who wish to master how to use English language in different contexts, whereas the explanatory (why aspect) component may effectively be used by those who want to have command of reasons involved in the framing of grammatical constructions along with their usage. Thus, the book has been designed to suit the needs of learners as well as teachers.

The emergence of English language as the global language has made it reasonably flexible, and so is the case with its grammar that has shifted its focus from prescriptivism to descriptivism. Keeping this in view, an attempt has been made to include and justify many alternative English structures which have made inroads with the expansion of this language in terms of usage across the globe. In spite of taking all precautions to bring out the book in the best possible way, the scope of further improvement can never be ruled out. Therefore, all the suggestions intending to improve its quality are always welcome.

Raj Kumar Sharma

Bhushan Singh

Contents

1

Noun

What is a Noun?

A noun is the name of a person, place, thing or an idea. It means anything of this universe which has a name is treated as a noun. It is an extensive entity that includes abstract as well as concrete elements of nature.

Examples: Ram, book, team, water, love, etc.

Kinds of Noun

There are five kinds of nouns.

(i) Proper Noun—A proper noun refers to the name of a particular person, place, river, mountain, etc.

Ramesh, Delhi, Ganga, Everest, etc.

Note: Proper nouns always begin with capital letters.

(ii) Common Noun—A common noun refers to the people or things of the same class:

boy, country, river, peak, town, etc.

Common Nouns	Proper Nouns
Boy	Pratyush (the name of a boy)
Country	India (the name of a country)
River	Ganga (the name of a river)
Peak	Everest (the name of a peak)
Town	Patna (the name of a town)

(iii) Collective Noun—A collective noun refers to a group of people or collection of things belonging to the same class:

team, family, class, library, fleet, etc.

(iv) Material Noun—A material noun refers to materials (substances) or articles of day-to-day use:

bread, water, soda, juice, iron, stone, gold, etc.

(v) Abstract Noun—An abstract noun refers to quality, state or idea:

love, joy, beauty, poverty, childhood, strength, softness, etc.

But all kinds of nouns have basically two sub-classes: concrete and abstract. That is to say, all nouns can be realized in either concrete or abstract form.

Concrete	Abstract
girl	beauty
honey	sweetness
chilly	bitterness
lion	strength
man	courage

Here, the difference between concrete and abstract nouns should be made clear. Concrete nouns are those which can be seen or touched but abstract nouns are those which are only felt.

Nouns and the Concept of Countability

Nouns are of two kinds on the basis of countability: countable and uncountable.

Countable nouns are those which may be counted, i.e. numeral in nature but uncountable nouns cannot be counted.

We can say:

one cow, two cows, five cows, etc.
one book, two books, five books, etc.

But we can't say:

one milk, two milks, five milks, etc.
one gold, two golds, five golds, etc.

Note: Common and collective nouns are by and large countable and the rest are uncountable.

Sometimes proper nouns are used as countable nouns in special situations:

There are four Ashoks in this class.
(four students with the name Ashok)

Certain nouns are used as countable (common nouns) in one context and as uncountable (material or abstract nouns) in another context.

Look at some of the examples.

Countable (common)		Uncountable (material or abstract)	
art	a skill	art	creation of beauty
chicken	a young cock or hen	chicken	flesh/meat
iron	an instrument	iron	metal
stone	a small chip	stone	substance
paper	a newspaper	paper	the thin material
beauty	a beautiful girl/woman	beauty	the combination of good qualities
fish	an animal that lives in water	fish	flesh/meat
love	a person one is in love with	love	strong liking or affection

Nouns and Number System

The number system of nouns is not uniform. It varies from language to language. In Arabic and Sanskrit, for example, there are three numbers: singular, dual and plural. But there are only two numbers in English language: singular and plural.

A singular number refers to only one person or thing.
one boy, one pen, one bag, one car, etc.

A plural number refers to more than one person or thing.

I lived in Allahabad for one and a half months.
She bought two and a half kilos of sugar.
She bought two kilos and a half of sugar.
Five students have got above 90% marks.

Formation of Plural Nouns

(i) Most plural nouns are formed by adding an 's' to the singular nouns.

Singular: book, school, cow, page, house, bag, etc.
Plural: books, schools, cows, pages, houses, bags, etc.

(ii) Nouns ending in 'ch, sh, s, ss, and x' form their plurals by adding 'es' to the singular.

Singular: watch, dish, gas, kiss, box, fox, bench, etc.
Plural: watches, dishes, gases, kisses, boxes, foxes, benches, etc.

(iii) Nouns ending in 'consonant + o' form their plural by adding 'es' to the singular.

Singular: potato, echo, hero, mosquito, mango, banjo, etc.
Plural: potatoes, echoes, heroes, mosquitoes, mangoes, banjoes, etc.

Notes:

1. Some nouns like mango, banjo, halo, cargo, etc. can be made plural by adding [s] only.
2. buffalo is either buffaloes or buffalo in plural form.

(iv) Nouns ending in 'vowel + o' form their plural by adding 's' to the singular.

Singular: radio, studio, zoo, cuckoo, portfolio, etc.
Plural: radios, studios, zoos, cuckoos, portfolios, etc.

(v) Words of foreign origin or abbreviated words ending in [o] take [s] to form their plural.

Singular: piano, photo, kilo, tempo, dynamo, solo, etc.
Plural: pianos, photos, kilos, tempos, dynamos, solos, etc.

(vi) Nouns ending in consonant letter form their plural by dropping 'y' and adding 'ies' to the singular.

Singular: baby, copy, duty, fly, lady, story, etc.

Plural: babies, copies, duties, flies, ladies, stories, etc.

Note: A proper noun ending in 'y' takes 's' not 'ies'.

Singular: Johny, Harry, Germany, Henry, Mary, etc.

Plural: Johnys, Harrys, Germanys, Henrys, Marys, etc.

(vii) Nouns ending in 'vowel + y' form their plural by adding 's' to the singular.

Singular: boy, day, key, monkey, guy, storey, etc.

Plural: boys, days, keys, monkeys, guys, storeys, etc.

(viii) Nouns ending in 'f or fe' form their plural by dropping 'f or fe' and adding 'ves' to the singular.

Singular: calf, half, knife, leaf, wife, thief, wolf, etc.

Plural: calves, halves, knives, leaves, wives, thieves, wolves, etc.

(ix) But there are many words ending in 'f or fe' that form their plural by adding 's' to the singular.

Singular: cliff, belief, roof, gulf, proof, chief, etc.

Plural: cliffs, beliefs, roofs, gulfs, proofs, chiefs, etc.

(x) Nouns ending in 'ful' take 's' in the plural.

Singular: handful, spoonful, mouthful, cupful, etc.

Plural: handfuls, spoonfuls, mouthfuls, cupfuls, etc.

(xi) The plural of numerals or abbreviated words is formed by adding [s] or apostrophe s ['s].

Singular: 2010, 1857, MA, etc.

Plural: 2010s/2010's 1857s/1857's MAs/MA's, etc.

Note: Usually only [s] is used to express the plural form of acronyms in possessive case.

Many BAs are looking for a good job.

Several MLAs attended the condolence meeting.

(xii) Numbers written in words take [s/es] in their plural.

Singular: three, two, seven, four, six, etc.

Plural: threes, twos, sevens, fours, sixes, etc.

(xiii) The plural of *pages* and *lines* in abbreviated form is [pp] and [ll].

(xiv) The plural of letters is formed by adding ['s].

Singular: p, t, b, g, etc.

Plural: p's, t's, b's, g's, etc.

(xv) A few nouns form their plural by a vowel change.

Singular: man, woman, foot, tooth, goose, mouse, louse, etc.

Plural: men, women, feet, teeth, geese, mice, lice, etc.

Note: The plural of *ox* and *child* is *oxen* and *children*.

(xvi) In compound nouns, the last word is made plural.

Singular: boy-friend, woman-hater, in-law, break-down, etc.

Plural: boy-friends, women-haters, in-laws, break-downs, etc.

(xvii) In 'noun + preposition + noun' structure the first word is made plural.

Singular: brother-in-law, father-in-law, grant-in-aid, etc.

Plural: brothers-in-law, fathers-in-law, grants-in-aid, etc.

(xviii) When man or woman is the first word in a two-word construction, both the words are made plural.

Singular: man servant, woman teacher, man driver, etc.

Plural: men servants, women teachers, men drivers, etc.

But the plural form of *man eater* is *man eaters*.

Nouns of Foreign Origin

(i) A few nouns of foreign origin ending in 'um' change to 'a' in the plural.

Singular: bacterium, erratum, ovum, stratum, corrigendum. agendum, datum, etc.

Plural: bacteria, errata, ova, strata, corrigenda, agenda, data, etc.

Note: 'Agenda' and 'data' are now used in both singular and plural numbers. The use of agendum and datum is avoided.

The data is/are correct.

The agenda of the meeting has/have been finalized.

(ii) But other nouns ending in 'um' take an 's' in the plural.

Singular: asylum, harmonium, album, museum, premium, referendum, etc.

Plural: asylums, harmoniums, albums, museums, premiums, referendums, etc.

(iii) Some nouns ending in 'um' take either 'a' or 's' in the plural.

Singular: curriculum, forum, medium, memorandum, stadium, symposium, ultimatum, etc.

Plural: curricula/curriculums, fora/forums, media/mediums, memoranda/memorandums, stadia/stadiums, symposia/symposiums, ultimata/ultimatums, etc.

(iv) Nouns ending in 'is' change into 'es' in the plural.

Singular: analysis, hypothesis, basis, crisis, synopsis, diagnosis, oasis, etc.

Plural: analyses, hypotheses, bases, crises, synopses, diagnoses, oases, etc.

But *precis* has an unchanged plural form.

(v) Some nouns ending in 'us' take 'i' in the plural.

Singular: alumnus, bacillus, locus, stimulus, etc.

Plural: alumni, bacilli, loci, stimuli, etc.

The plural form of 'genus' is 'genera' (not generi)

(vi) Some nouns ending in 'us' take either 'i' or 'uses'.

Singular: cactus, focus, fungus, syllabus, etc.

Plural: cacti/cactuses, foci/focuses, fungi/funguses, syllabi/syllabuses, etc.

(vii) Some nouns ending in 'a' takes 'ae' or 'an' in the plural.

Singular: antenna, formula, vertebra, etc.

Plural: antennae/antennas, formulae/formulas, vertebrae/vertebras, etc.

(viii) Nouns ending in 'eau' form their plural by adding either 's' or 'x'.

Singular: plateau, bureau, etc.

Plural: plateaux/plateaus, bureaux/bureaus, etc.

Nouns and the Gender System

The classification of a noun based on sex is called gender.

They are of four kinds.

(i) Masculine—It denotes male.

man, horse, boy, etc.

(ii) Feminine—It denotes female.

woman, mare, girl, etc.

(iii) Common—It denotes both male and female.

teacher, animal, doctor, etc.

(iv) Neuter—It denotes neither male nor female. In other words, it denotes things that are lifeless.

book, pen, chair, room, etc.

But some lifeless nouns are usually personified and regarded as living beings.

Look at these.

(i) The nouns that are associated with *strength, valour* and *violence* are regarded as males:

sun, death, chivalry, thunder, winter, summer, etc.

Death doesn't spare anyone from *his* icy hands.

The sun gives *his* light and heat to all worldly things equally.

(ii) The nouns that are associated with *beauty, love, grace, sweetness, gentility* and *hope* are regarded as females.

moon, earth, nature, peace, hope, love, etc.

To know *Nature* is to love *her*.

(iii) The living beings such as small *children, babies, animals* and *insects* are normally regarded as neuter gender.

The baby is sleeping in *its* cradle.

Note: Sometimes '*a he*' or '*a she*' is also used to indicate sex.

Is your baby *a he* or *a she*?
My baby is *a he*, not *a she*.

Formation of Feminine Gender

The feminine of nouns is formed in three ways.

(i) By using an entirely different word

Masculine	Feminine	Masculine	Feminine
boy	girl	king	queen
man	woman	husband	wife
brother	sister	lord	lady
father	mother	son	daughter
dog	bitch	uncle	aunt
horse	mare	sir	madam
bachelor	spinster/maid	nephew	niece
bull	cow	papa	mummy
monk	nun	wizard	witch

(ii) By adding 'ess' and 'ine'

actor	actress	host	hostess
lion	lioness	poet	poetess
God	Goddess	Jew	Jewess
prince	princess	heir	heiress
master	mistress	author	authoress
tiger	tigress	hero	heroine
waiter	waitress	hunter	huntress

(iii) By adding she/girl/woman or placing a word before or after

he-goat	she-goat	businessman	businesswoman
he-beer	she-beer	bull-calf	cow-calf
boyfriend	girlfriend	cock sparrow	hen sparrow
salesman	saleswoman	peacock	peahen

Common Gender Nouns

(i) Most of the nouns related to profession or occupation are in the common gender.

doctor	minister	novelist	president
magician	neighbour	person	player
author	judge	scientist	secretary
principal	lawyer	fool	worker
person	friend	enemy	writer
politician	student	infant	lecturer

(ii) The structure '*noun + man/woman*' is replaced by '*noun + person*' to indicate common gender.

chairman /woman	chairperson
spokesman/woman	spokesperson
sportsman/woman	sportsperson

But the nouns that end with the suffix [-ship] take *man*, not *woman* or *person*.

Chairmanship, not chairwomanship or chairpersonship
Workmanship, not workwomanship or workpersonship

(iii) Nouns denoting degrees, qualifications and titles are always in the common gender.

BA, MA, B.Sc, M.Sc, MBBS, MD, MS, etc.

(iv) Nouns denoting caste, religion and nationality, are always in the common gender.

Suman is a Hindu. He is an Indian.
Mary is a Christian. She is a Britisher.

Nouns and Possessive Case

Possessive case nouns express ownership, authorship and relationship. It is formed either by the addition of *noun* + *'s* or by *of* + *noun phrase*. '*Noun* + *s*' is mainly used with the name of human beings, animals or birds while '*of* + *noun phrase*' is usually used with lifeless things.

This is *Ali's car.*
It is *a bird's nest.*
The window of the room is new. (not, *room's window*)
The wall of the school is old. (not *school's wall*)

Note: Living beings may take either *noun* +*'s* or *of* + *noun phrase* but lifeless things normally don't take *noun* + *'s.*

Formation of Possessive Case Nouns

It is formed:

(i) by adding ['s] to the singular nouns:

Akbar's car, a parrot's cage, Sohan's book, Keats's poem (keats' poem), a cat's tail, Ali's house, a baby's toys, etc.

Note: Personal names ending in [s] usually take only an apostrophe ['].

(ii) by adding only an ['] apostrophe to the plural nouns that end in [s]:

boys' hostel, girls 'common room, doctors' club

(iii) by adding ['s] to the plural nouns that don't end in [s]:

Men's club, children's park, women's polytechnic, etc.

(iv) by adding ['s] to nouns denoting measurement, time, space or quantity:

a week's vacation, two days' leave, a year's absence, today's post, a pound's worth, a hair's breadth, a stone's throw, etc.

(v) by adding ['s] to traditional idiomatic expressions:

at his wit's end, for God's sake, in my mind's eye, to your heart's content, at arm's length, etc.

(vi) by adding ('s) to lifeless things when they are personified:

nature's law, the sun's rays, at duty's call, heaven's will, earth's surface, at death's door, etc.

(vii) by adding ['s] to a noun denoting the name of a city, country, state, continent, etc.

Libya's petro-dollars, India's economic policy, Delhi's metro, Asia's cotton industry, etc.

(viii) by adding only ['] to the following expressions:

for Jesus' sake, for conscience' sake, for goodness' sake and for Justice's sake, etc.

(ix) by adding ['s] to the noun without a head noun:

I will go to butcher's today. (i.e. butcher's shop)

She visited her aunt's. (i.e. aunt's house)

(x) by adding ['s] to the noun to make a comparison:

Saroj's house is bigger than Sara's.

Dolly's hair is longer than Aisha's.

(xi) by adding ['s] to the last noun in a compound noun:

Is this your father-in-law's house?

(xii) by adding ['s] to both the nouns to show separate possession and to the last noun to show joint possession:

Omar bought Adel's and Ahmed's shirts. (separate possession)

This is Ali and Abdullah's house. (joint possession)

(xiii) by adding 'of + noun phrase' to lifeless things:

The legs of the table are broken.
The hands of the watch are moving.
The tyres of the car are old.

Usually, *of + noun phrase* is used to indicate a part of the whole.

Function of Nouns

A noun functions in a sentence occupying different places.

(i)	*A girl* opened the window.	subject
(ii)	I saw *the girl.*	object
(iii)	She was *a small girl.*	subjective complement
(iv)	I called *the girl* baby.	objective complement
(v)	Then I talked to *the girl.*	prepositional phrase
(vi)	I gave a chocolate *to that girl.*	prepositional object

Nouns Used as Singular

Abstract and material nouns are normally uncountable and have nothing to do with number system of nouns. Look at a few nouns.

advice	dust	sand	wood	bread
death	truth	oil	wine	silk
beauty	pride	silver	wool	jam
baggage	furniture	dirt	housework	machinery
information	scenery	cutlery	homework	imaginary
rubbish	weather	traffic	poetry	clothing
knowledge	wisdom	bravery	equipment	luggage

They are neither used in plural forms nor do they take *a* or *an* before them.

We like old poetry.	(not, an old poetry)
The scenery of Kashmir is very enchanting.	(not, sceneries)
We watched the scenery amazingly.	(not, a scenery)
Please do your homework.	(not, homeworks)
I have to do homework.	(not, a homework)

But they take *a lot of/plenty of/a piece of/pieces of*, etc. to denote amount or quantity.

I have to do a lot of homework.
Several pieces of furniture are new.
She gave me many pieces of advice.
Ali ate five loaves of bread.

Note: These nouns retain their uncountable identity in all cases.

Some material and abstract nouns take *s/es* at their end and become common nouns with a changed meaning.

kindnesses	-	acts of kindness	woods	-	forest
coffees	-	cups of coffee	works	-	creation
coppers	-	copper coins	pains	-	suffering
irons	-	fetters	returns	-	recurrence

Nouns Used as Plural having Inseparable Identity

These words indicate two parts of the same garments, tools and instruments.

jeans	shoes	scales	binoculars	bellows
pants	breeches	fetters	tongs	bowels
trousers	flannels	glasses	tweezers	sheers
shorts	bloomers	goggles	pliers	pincers
pajamas	suspenders	spectacles	scissors	knickers
pantaloons	tights	mirrors	braces	drawers

My shoes are torn.
Your glasses are new.

Note: Countability of these nouns can be expressed by means of *a pair of, two pair/pairs of/many pair/pairs of*.

I have bought a pair of shoes today.
Salma has many pair/pairs of jeans.

Note: With plural numbers, *pairs* should be preferred: *two pairs/three pairs*.

Some Plural Nouns having Special Expressions

congratulations (an expression of joy over one's success)
thanks (a grateful feeling for offer or favour)
curds (a milky thick substance)

riches (wealth)	funds	(money)
arrears (unpaid dues)	pains	(care, suffering)
clothes (dress)	eatables	(articles of food)
condolences (deep feeling of sympathy)	guts	(stamina)

greens (vegetables)	looks	(appearance)
earnings (income)	regards	(compliments)
annals (history)	savings	(balance)
wages (punishment)	arms	(weapon)
contents (chapters/topics)	teens	(nearly 13 to 19 years of age)
premises (campus/building)	effects	(results, property)
surroundings (environment)	quarters	(lodgings)
troops (soldiers)	lights	(lamps)
archives (record)	peoples	(nations)
stairs (staircase)	fruits	(rewards)
belongings (property)	odds	(probability)
airs (showy/affected manners)	advices	(information)
brains (talented/cleverest person)	outskirts	(outer part of a city)

She is the brains of this class. (cleverest girl)

The peoples of the world should live with love and brotherhood. (nations)

Nouns Singular in Form but Plural in Sense

Vermin, youth, people, cattle, folk, peasantry, infantry, police, clergy, gentry, cavalry, poultry, children, etc.

The police have arrested the thief.

The gentry of the town are meeting today.

The youth should have the sense of competitiveness.

Nouns Plural in Form but Singular in Sense

Crossroads, billiards, darts, gallows, innings, mumps, measles, rickets, shambles, shingles, summons, civics, semantics, mathematics, physics, statistics, athletics, gymnastics, acrobatics, tactics, etc.

No news is good news.

Parul is standing at a crossroads. (not, a crossroad)

I received a summons today. (not, a summon)

Note: The plural of summons is summonses.

But nouns related to subject or science are used in the plural to indicate quality.

His mathematics are good.

The classics of Hindi literature are superb.

Nouns having the Same Form in Singular and Plural

deer, sheep, public, salmon, stone, craft, aircraft, trout, carp, grouse, offspring, etc.

I have three deer and five sheep. (not, deers or sheeps)

The general public don't take interest in politics. (not, publics)

But the nationality words as nouns ending in [ese] don't take plural form.

He is a Chinese.

My servant is a Japanese.

They are Nepalese. (not Nepaleses)

Some Nouns of Confusing Nature

(i) issue/issues

I have no issue. (offspring)

We discussed several issues in the meeting. (topics/points)

(ii) fish/fishes

I eat rice and fish. (food)

Ali caught five big fishes yesterday. (animals)

(iii) hair/hairs

My hair is black. (uncountable collective noun)

I have a few grey hairs. (here, hair is considered separately)

(iv) word/words

He is a man of word. (promise)

Use these words in the blanks. (vocabulary)

(v) work/works

I have to do a lot of work. (doing or working something)

The works of Shakespeare are superb. (creations)
He works hard. (verb)

But homework and housework are always singular.

He has done his homework.

He has to do many housework.

Note: '*Ironworks*' takes both singular and plural verb but '*fireworks*' takes plural verb only.

The ironwork is/are going on in the factory.

The fireworks have damaged the building.

Nouns of Number, Weight and Amount

Brace, million, billion, hundred, thousand, dozen, score, etc.

These nouns are in singular form when they refer to a definite number.

five hundred students, ten thousand people

one million dollars, two dozen pens.

These nouns have plural form to refer to a large number or amount in 'of + plural noun' constructions.

hundreds of students	dozens of books.
thousands of people	millions of stars.
billions of dollars	scores of boxes.

Nouns with Different Meaning in Plural

Abuse	- wrong use	Abuses	- unjust practices
Compass	- range	Compasses	- an instrument
Iron	- a metal	Irons	- chains
Respect	- regard	Respects	- compliments
Sand	- small grains of rock	Sands	- desert
Water	- liquid	Waters	- ocean/sea

Plural Nouns having Two Meanings

colours	hues	flag of a regiment
parts	portions	abilities
morals	moral lessons	conduct

grounds	reasons	enclosed land
effects	results	property
spectacles	sights	glasses
manners	methods	correct behaviour
premises	propositions	buildings
numbers	quantities	verses

Plural Nouns having Two Different Forms

(i) brothers – boys of the same parents

brethren – members of the same religious community

(ii) cloths – pieces of cloth

clothes – dress

Note: *Series* and *species* have the same form in both the numbers.

He went on telling a series of stories.

Many birds are of the same species.

Nouns Used in Different Constructions

(i) *Noun + fraction*

Fractions can be used in two ways.

1. five and a half kilos

   five kilos and a half

2. four years and a half

   four and a half years

(ii) *Numeral + noun + noun*

Plural nouns used in numbers with hyphen (-) is always singular:

five-man committee, a ten-dinar note, a three-year plan, an eighteen-year old boy, a six-month old child, etc.

We can't say:

He is an eight-years old boy.

(iii) *One of + plural nouns*

'*One of*' always takes plural noun but singular verb.

One of my friends is a doctor.

One of the students of my college has got a scholarship.

(iv) *'Noun + preposition + noun' takes singular verb*

Tree after tree has been cut.

Boat after boat sank in the stormy sea.

(v) *Adjectives used as plural nouns*

1. Certain adjectives become plural nouns when they take 'the' before them and function as common nouns.

The rich hate the poor.

(the rich people) (the poor people)

The strong oppress the weak.

(the strong men) (the weak men)

2. Some adjectives are used as plural nouns because they express the sense of things and materials:

bitters, sweets, odds, goods, movables, particulars, essentials, breakables, explosives, dues, etc.

Explosives are dangerous.

Goods are available in the market.

Everyone has to experience the sweets and bitters of life.

(vi) *Nouns denoting material*

Material nouns used in making something is always singular.

The window is made of wood and glass.

My house is made of brick, iron, cement and stone.

The cartoon is made of paper and ink.

Correct Usage of Certain Italicized Nouns

Sentences	Correct words
Salma is my *cousin sister*.	cousin
The *hole* of a needle is small.	eye
Ali is a *copier*.	copyist
You are a *cooker*.	cook
My watch has three *needles*.	hands
You are a *cheater*.	cheat

Yuvraj is a good *batman*.	batsman
He has joined *doctory*.	medical profession
He has applied for *lecturership*.	lectureship
This is no *place* in this compartment.	room
She likes *teachery* as a profession.	teaching
Leaders work for the *upliftment* of the nation.	uplift
Man can't live without *fooding and drinking*.	food and drink
I pay five hundred dinars for *boarding and lodging*.	board and lodging
I got *two breads*.	two loaves of bread
It is a nice *poetry*.	poem
Good night, sir, you are welcome.	Good evening
He lost *a quantity of* books.	a number of
This is the *cause* why we don't like it.	reason
I saw a *daughter* on the sea-shore.	girl
I need some *cardboards* for this.	cardboard
Some new *equipments* have been purchased.	equipment
His *luggages* are at the station.	luggage
I have got full *mark* in mathematics.	marks
His *whereabout* is not known.	whereabouts
His *asset* was seized.	assets
I have no *scale* to weigh vegetables.	scales
She bought two *sheeps*.	sheep
Everyone should have some basic *educations*.	education
He travelled on *horsebacks*.	horseback
Quote the lines from *heart*.	memory
She got a *freeship*.	freestudentship
I applied for *teachery*.	teachership
The *weather* of Kashmir is very good.	climate
Ahmed is learning *alphabets*.	alphabet

EXERCISE-1

Classify these Nouns and Put them in the Given box.

Malta, pen, army, woman, crew, Najat, dog, country, India, health, class, forest, table, oil, mango, tree, freedom, Friday, day, life, illness, family, cattle, bravery, wood, computer, teacher, bench, cat, Delhi, luck, house, river, The Quran, man, girl and boy.

Proper	Common	Collective	Material	Abstract
....	....	....	....	....
....	....	....	....	....
....	....	....	....	....
....	....	....	....	....
....	....	....	....	....
....	....	....	....	....

EXERCISE-2

Write the plural forms of the following Nouns.

Appendix, analysis, criterion, datum, calf, piano, bamboo, foot, wife, chief, 2010, monkey, plateau, vertebra, demon, harmonium, curriculum, bacterium, father-in-law, four, six, t, f, radio, duty, potato, gas, kiss, copy, dynamo, bench, fox, wife, loaf and piece.

EXERCISE-3

Correct these sentences.

1. He has bought two dozens eggs.
2. Taj is a three-stars hotel in Lucknow.
3. Puja is still in her teen.
4. I have been here for three and a half year.
5. I dye my hairs every month.
6. I received a cheque for six thousands dollars.
7. These are new phenomenas.
8. This is my sister's-in-law's flat.
9. We saw a lot of sceneries in Kashmir.

10. It is bad manner to harass others.
11. Ahmed in an alumna of this school.
12. I purchased a lot of stationeries.
13. Congratulation! You have done well in the examination.
14. This well is twenty-feet deep.
15. I have to provide some good educations to our children.
16. Gandhi always thought for the upliftment of the nation.
17. He gave me many pieces of advices.
18. His informations are based on facts.

EXERCISE-4

Correct these sentences.

1. Soha is a sixteen-years old girl.
2. An all-parties meeting is going to be held in August.
3. The peoples of Libya are good at driving cars.
4. Summons have been served to the concerned man.
5. Thank a lot for your kind help.
6. Measle is not a fatal disease.
7. The thief was sent to jail in fetter.
8. Rich have wings.
9. The chair is made of woods.
10. He has two dozens pens.
11. There are many Abdullah in Kashmir.
12. Collect all the datas and finalise the agendas.
13. Most of the thesises are worthless.
14. What is the criteria of selection?
15. Ships after ships sank in the sea.
16. This book cost me two and a half dinar.
17. The weaks and the braves should live together.
18. Economic is not an easy subject.

19. You should learn Arabic alphabets to write Arabic.
20. Many teachers live in university quarter.

EXERCISE-5

Correct these sentences.

1. Sarita is my cousin sister.
2. Omar sent a letter of condolence to Ahmed.
3. It is against the will of the publics.
4. The poors are helpless.
5. Many polices were there.
6. The watch's hands are not moving.
7. My house is made of bricks and stones.
8. I have a lot of furnitures.
9. We are Chineses.
10. He takes pain in getting our work done.
11. One of my brother is a rich man.
12. *The Waste Land* is a great poetry.
13. He gave me some pieces of papers.
14. I read many paper daily.
15. Cattles are grazing.
16. A flock of sheeps is sitting in the fence.
17. Does she wear glass?
18. I bought a pair of shoe yesterday.
19. I want to eat a bread.
20. May she be granted two days leave?

2
Pronoun

What is a Pronoun?

A pronoun is used instead of a noun or a noun phrase to avoid the repetition of the same person or thing.

Example: Ram went to see Sita because Sita was Ram's wife.

Ram went to see Sita because she was his wife.

Kinds of Pronoun

1. Personal Pronouns

I, we, you, he, she, it and they

These pronouns are used in a speech act. They have three sub-classes:

(i) First person (*I/we*)
It refers to the speaker.

I am an Indian.
We are doctors.

(ii) Second person (*you*)
It refers to the listener.
You are my friend.

(iii) Third person (*he/she/it/they*)
It refers to the whole people and things of the world.

He is a boy.

She is a girl.

It is a pen.

They are farmers.

These pronouns have different forms according to *number, person, case* and *gender*. The following table illustrates these distinctions.

Person	Subjective pronoun	Objective pronoun	Possessive determiner	Possessive pronoun	Reflexive pronoun
1st person singular	I	me	my	mine	myself
2nd person singular	you	you	your	yours	yourself
3rd person singular, masculine gender	he	him	his	-	himself
3rd person singular, feminine gender	she	her	her	ours	herself
3rd person singular, neuter gender	it	it	its		itself
1st person plural	we	us	our	ours	ourselves
2nd person plural	you	you	your	yours	yourselves
3rd person plural	they	them	their	theirs	themselves

Position of Personal Pronouns

(i) When 1st, 2nd and 3rd person pronouns are used together as a subject, they take their position in the following order.

Subject	Order of persons
<u>*You, he and I*</u> are going.	(2nd + 3rd + 1st)
<u>*You and he*</u> are going.	(2nd + 3rd)
<u>*You or I*</u> am going.	(2nd + 1st)
<u>*He as well as I*</u> is going.	(3rd + 1st)

(ii) When 1st, 2nd and 3rd person pronouns are used together as a subject they take 1st person plural number possessive *determiner*.

You, he and I are doing *our* work.

(iii) When 2nd and 3rd person pronouns are used together as a subject, they take second person possessive *determiner*.

You and he didn't do *your* duty.

Note: An objective form of pronoun is always used after a verb or a preposition.

There is no friendship between *him* and *me*.

Let *him* and *me* do the work.

Gender System of Pronoun

Like nouns, personal pronouns follow the gender system. Except third person singular number pronouns (*he, she, it*), all kinds of pronouns are common gender pronouns, i.e. *I, we, our, them, your, one, each, ever*, etc.

Exceptions:

(i) Third person singular number neuter gender pronoun (*it, its*) is usually used for non-personal things. But in some cases, it is used for small *children, babies, insects* and *animals*.

The child is weeping because *it* is hungry now.

(ii) Sometimes masculine gender pronoun (*he, him, his*) is used for lifeless things such as *sun, love, death, time, war*, etc. to express strength or force.

Death will come when *he* is least expected.

(iii) Feminine gender pronoun (*she, her*) is used for inanimate objects such as *ship, country, nature, peace, mercy, fortune*, etc. to express affection or familiarity.

To know Nature is to love her.

Various Functions of 'it'

(i) *It* is used to identify somebody.

Who is *it*?

(ii) *It* is used with expressions of *time, date, distance* and *weather conditions.*

It is 8 o'clock/morning/evening/night.

It is raining/snowing/freezing.

It is winter/summer/cold/warm/dark.

It is three kilometers from my house to school.

(iii) '*It is*' or '*it was*' comes before the real subject to emphasize the statement.

It is I who can do it.

It was these students who made a noise in the class.

(iv) *It* is used to express impersonal statements.

It (*the letter*) says that the health of your mother is not good.

(v) It is used as a subject of the infinitive and an object of a clause.

It is not easy *to get* good marks. (subject of the infinitive)

To get good marks is not easy.
I think that it is necessary to go to bank.
I think it is necessary to go to bank.
I think *it* necessary to go to bank. (object of a clause)

Note: Empty *it* is usually used as a formal subject though it doesn't convey any meaning.

2. Possessive Pronouns

Possessive pronouns are used predicatively (after verbs) and are never followed by a noun. These are *mine, ours, yours, his, hers.*

These books are *mine*.
That bag is *yours*.

But possessive determiners (*adjectives*) are always followed by nouns. They can be used with subjects as well as objects. These are *my, our, your, his, her, its, their*.

This is *my book*.

His father is a teacher.

Note: '*Its*' is always used as a determiner, never as a possessive pronoun.

This is a pillow and that is *its cover*. (not, that cover is *its*.)

3. Demonstrative Pronouns

Demonstrative pronouns are used to point out or mention something or somebody. They are: *this, that, these* and *those*. *This* and *that* have singular reference; *these* and *those* have plural reference.

This and *these* refer to what is near in space, time or conception to the speaker.

This is my book.
These chocolates are for children.
That and *those* refer to what is away from the speaker.
That is his car.
Those are your books.

The function of demonstrative pronouns:

(i) When previous statement is referred.

That/this is what I said.

(ii) When instruction is implied.

Those who come late will not be allowed to enter the examination hall.

(iii) When something is indicated.

That is my new car.

(iv) When formal announcement or introduction is made.

This is Sukari, my friend.

This is CNN giving you the news.

4. Reciprocal Pronouns

Reciprocal pronouns *each other* and *one another* usually express a mutual relationship between two or more persons.

Sita and Gita love *each other*.
The three brothers hate *one another*.

The convention in English was to use *each other* in the case of two persons and *one another* in the case of more than two persons.

But now they are used interchangeably.

The three brothers love *each other.*

The two sisters love *one another.*

Each other and *one another* may also be used with the apostrophe ('s) construction.

My friend and I always use *one another's/each other's* car.

Note: *Each other* or *one another* is never used as a subject.

5. Reflexive Pronouns

Reflexive pronouns refer back to subject forms of personal pronouns. They take *self* in the singular form and *selves* in the plural.

Singular: *myself, yourself, himself, herself, itself*

Plural: *ourselves, yourselves, themselves*

Examples:

He hurt *himself.*

We really enjoyed *ourselves* in the party.

History repeats *itself.*

The following verbs always take reflexive pronouns as an object.

absent, avail, pride, acquit, adapt, address, enjoy, conduct, behave.

Ali absented *himself* from the class.

Salma prides *herself* on her beauty.

6. Emphatic Pronouns

Emphatic pronouns have the same reflexive forms but they are used to emphasize either subject, or object, or object of preposition or an expression of time and space.

(i) He *himself* wrote a letter. (subject emphasized)

He wrote a letter *himself.* (object emphasized)

Note: Reflexive pronoun may come after the subject or object to emphasize the subject itself. (see the above examples)

(ii) I met *Anil himself*. (object emphasized)

(iii) I talked *to Nasir himself*. (object of preposition emphasized)

(iv) This book can be finished *today itself*. (time emphasized)

Note: Sometimes, emphatic pronouns take *by* before them to express the sense of *'alone'* or *'without help'*.

I did this work *by myself*. (alone)

This machine works *by itself*. (automatically/without help)

7. Interrogative Pronouns

Interrogative pronouns are: *who, whom, whose, which* and *what*. They are used in forming questions and they always come before the verb.

What are you doing?
Who wrote this book?

The function of interrogative pronouns:

(i) *Who* is used in both subject and object forms. *Whom* is used only in object form and usually take a preposition. But both refer to a person only.

Who did this work? (as subject)

Who do you have faith in? (as object)

or

In *whom* do you have faith?

Note: *Whom* is rarely used as an object in current English.

(ii) *Whose* is used for both personal and non-personal nouns in interrogative expressions.

Whose are these books? (interrogative pronoun)

Whose books are these? (interrogative determiner)

(iii) *Which* is also used for personal and non-personal nouns.

Which is your brother's friend?

Which of the novels do you like most?

(iv) *What* is used in both subject and object forms to refer to non-personal nouns.

What happened yesterday? (as subject)

What does she want? (as object)

who versus what and *what versus which*:

Who is used to know a person's identity and *what* is used to seek information about his profession.

Who is that boy talking to your son? He is Ali.

What is he? He is a clerk.

What is used to make a choice from an unlimited number and *which* from a limited number of things.

What do you like? (some drink)

Which is your coat? (the red one)

Emphatic use of interrogative pronouns:

Sometimes *ever* or *else* is used after *who, what* and *which* to make the sentence emphatic.

Who ever heard of such a silly question?

Who else is going to respect you? (no one)

What else can we do today? (nothing)

(*Which else* is rare in use.)

Note: *Else* or *ever* is written as a separate word.

Who ever, *what else*, *who else*

8. Relative Pronouns

Relative pronouns join clauses. They are *who, whom, whose, which, what,* and *that.*

The relative pronoun *who* has an object form *whom* and a possessive form *whose*. But *who* is commonly used in both subject and object position.

Those *who* live in Libya use olive oil.

The girl *who(m)* I met last year is still unmarried.

Those are the cars *whose* windows are broken.

He *that* is down needs fear no fall.

Some people eat snakes, *which* is unusual.

9. Distributive Pronouns

Distributive pronouns are used to express separate identity of people or things. They are *each, every, either*, and *neither*. They are always singular.

Either of the two girls is tall.

Each of you should read this book.

But *every* as a pronoun always takes *one* or *thing* after it.

Everyone of them was present.

The function of distributive pronouns:

(i) *Each* is used for two or more people or things.

I bought two shirts yesterday, *each* of them is expensive.

(ii) *Every* is used for three and more people or things.

There are five bookshops in Khoms. *Every* shop is selling dictionary.

(iii) *Either* means *one or the other of the two.*

Either of the two shirts is new shirts.

(iv) *Neither* means *not one nor the other of the two.*

Neither of the two boys is clever.

Distributive pronouns usually take a singular gender pronoun.

Everyone must do *his* work.

Neither has done *his* work.

When they refer to feminine gender noun, they take feminine gender pronoun.

Each of the girls obey *her* parents.

But *his or her* construction is sometimes used to refer to both sexes.

Everyone was called to submit his or her documents.

10. Indefinite Pronouns

Indefinite pronouns show various degrees of indefiniteness. They have three main classes.

(i) Compound pronouns

Compound pronouns are: *some, every, any* and *no.*

	Some	Every	Any	No
+one	someone	everyone	anyone	no one
+body	somebody	everybody	anybody	nobody
+thing	something	everything	anything	nothing

All are compound words except *no one* that is used as none when put together.

No one can do it.

(ii) Quantifying pronouns

Quantifying pronouns are: *enough, few, many, most, such, other, another*, etc. But most of them take 'of' and a noun phrase after them.

Some, all, both, several, little, few, much, none, any, etc. + of + a noun phrase.

Some of the girls are intelligent.
Most of the people are dishonest.

(iii) The pronoun one

One has mainly two uses as a pronoun.
'One' is used as a substitute for a noun.
I have two shirts. I want to buy a new *one*.
These apples are sour. I like sweet *ones*.

Note: *Ones* replaces plural nouns.

One is used to refer to people in general.

It has a possessive form *one's* and a reflexive form *oneself*.

Example:

One should do *one's* duty.

One shouldn't absent *oneself* from the class.

Note: *One* used as a subject is always singular.

EXERCISE-1

Choose the right alternative and fill in the blanks:

1. She doesn't obey ...... parents. (his, her)
2. Are these glasses ....? (your, yours)

3. He ought to be ashamed of .... (himself, myself)
4. .... school is big. (our, ours)
5. It is ...... who has broken this chair. (he, him)
6. He and I believe in doing ...... work. (my, our)
7. One shouldn't betray .... friends. (one's, his)
8. He acquitted .... as a statesman. (him, himself)
9. ..... is the tallest girl in the class. (what, which)
10. They are looking at .... (he, him)
11. Who is he? He is .... (a teacher, Rakesh)
12. I don't know the man ...... is there. (which, who)
13. Let ..... do it. (he, him)
14. Tell .... your address. (we, us)
15. Nobody could answer except .... (I, me)

EXERCISE-2

Correct these sentences.

1. My father, which lives in India is an old man.
2. One should love his country.
3. This is mine new car.
4. You, he and I are doing their work.
5. I am the man who have won a prize.
6. This is a book and that is it's cover.
7. I think foolish to tease a snake.
8. He is one of those who does what he says.
9. It is BBC giving you the news.
10. This apple is small. I want big one.
11. It was Ahmed that helped me.
12. Neither of the five girls will win the race.
13. It is all between you and I.
14. This is mine own car.

EXERCISE-3

Match the group of words under A and B to make correct sentences.

A	B
Each of us	his wife.
Everyone	her husband.
She is	herself from school.
He is	wants to be happy.
The girl absented	has a problem.

3

Adjective and Determiner

What is an Adjective?

An adjective describes people, things and events, and so, it is traditionally defined as a describing word.

Examples: This is a *big* building.

They are *good* people.

It is a *serious* accident.

In these sentences, '*big*', '*good*' and '*serious*' are adjectives that describe the nouns '*building*', '*people*' and '*accident*' respectively.

Usually, a noun refers to its class in general but adjective limits its general application.

The nouns '*building*', '*people*' and '*accident*' refer to any such things that belong to their class, but the adjectives '*big*', '*good*' and '*serious*' limit their application. So, the more specific the noun is, the more limited is its application. Look at another example.

This is a *big new white* building.

Here, the three adjectives '*big*', '*new*' and '*white*' are used to tell more about the '*size*', '*condition*' and '*colour*' of the building. They almost give the fullest picture but at the same time they narrow its application. Thus, adjectives specify the description of nouns.

Kinds of Adjective

(i) Descriptive Adjectives or Adjectives of Quality

These adjectives express *quality, colour, size, feeling, taste, behaviour,* etc. of someone or something.

i. *Quality* -	easy, difficult, interesting, boring, true, false, etc.
ii. *Colour* -	red, white, green, black, etc.
iii. *Shape* -	round, circular, flat, rectangular, etc.
iv. *Size* -	long, small, tall, short, thick, thin, narrow, etc.
v. *Taste* -	bitter, sour, sweet, salty, etc.
vi. *Condition* -	good, bad, fresh, stale, happy, healthy, etc.
vii. *Feeling* -	soft, hard, dry, wet, hot, etc.
viii. *Behaviour* -	kind, cruel, gentle, clever, polite, rude, etc.
ix. *Impression* -	pleasant, smart, beautiful, nasty, nice, etc.

(ii) Quantitative Adjectives

These adjectives which are also called quantifiers express quantity. They are used with both countable and uncountable nouns.

Some, any, no, little, much, many, few, a little, all, enough, etc.

Countable nouns	Uncountable nouns
I have *some books.*	I want *some sugar.*
All men are mortal.	I spent *all the money.*

(iii) Numeral Adjectives

These adjectives express the *number* or *position* of an item in a collection of things.

It is of two kinds.

a. Definite Numeral Adjectives

b. Indefinite Numeral Adjectives

Definite numeral adjectives have two subdivisions (CLASSES).

Cardinal numbers and *Ordinal numbers*

Cardinal numbers are *one, two, five, eleven, twenty, hundred*, etc. whereas *first, second, fifth, tenth, hundredth*, etc. are ordinal numbers.

In current usage, *last, next, following, preceding, subsequent + noun* are also treated as ordinal numbers to show the position in a series or sequence.

Indefinite numeral adjectives are *many, several, all, any, some, both, few, a number of, lots of, a lot of, some of, most, most of*, etc., e.g.

Definite Number	Indefinite Number
I bought *two* books.	I have *many* friends.
He got the *second* prize.	*Most* students are laborious.
Last lesson I was taught about noun.	*A few* students are clever.

Note: Some adjectives of *number* function as adjectives of *quantity* such as *all, some, any, certain, enough, no, more, most*, etc.

Adjectives of number	Adjectives of quantity
All students want to pass.	They lost *all their wealth*.
I received *no letters* today.	There is *no sugar* in tea.
Some students are clever.	*Some milk* is left in the pot.

(iv) Demonstrative Adjective

These adjectives indicate the position and pointing gesture of nouns.

This, that, these, those such, same + noun.

They are also used as pronouns

Demonstrative adjectives	Demonstrative pronouns
This mobile is new.	*This* is a new mobile.
These books are costly.	*These* are costly books.
Such advice is rare.	*Such* is the case with him.

(v) Possessive Adjectives

These adjectives always come before nouns to show the sense of possession and relationship.

My, your, his, our, their, its, her + noun

But possessive pronouns *mine, ours, yours, his, theirs,* etc. never come before nouns, they normally come after verb.

Possessive adjectives	Possessive pronouns
This is *your pen.*	This pen is *yours.*
This is *my house.*	This house is *mine.*

'His' and *'its'* have the same form as adjectives and pronouns but there is a difference between the two.

'His' can be used before the noun as well as after the verb in a sentence.

That is *his pen.* (before the noun)
That pen is *his.* (after the verb)

But *'its'* can be used only before the noun and not after the verb.

This is my car.

This is *its key.* (not, this key is *its.*)

Sometimes, a possessive pronoun comes before verbs as a subject in place of possessive adjective and noun.

His book is new. *Yours* is old. (yours = *your book*)

Your house is small. *Mine* is big. (mine = *my house*)

'*Noun + of + possessive pronoun*' is used to show relation, e.g.

Ali is *a cousin of mine.*

He is *a friend of yours.*

But structures like these can't take possessive pronoun to show relationship.

This cousin is *mine.* (x)

This friend is *yours.* (x)

(vi) Interrogative Adjectives

These adjectives always take nouns to ask questions.

Which, what, whose + noun

They are also used as pronouns.

Interrogative adjectives	Interrogative pronouns.
Whose book is this?	*Whose* is this book?
What name did you say?	*What* is your name?
Which way will you go?	*Which* is the shortest way?

(vii) Distributive Adjectives

These adjectives express each one of a number.

Either, neither, each, every + noun

But distributive pronouns don't take a noun after them.

Distributive adjectives	Distributive pronouns
Each pen is costly.	*Each* got a pen.
Every student was present.	*Either* will work.
Neither statement is false.	*Neither* was present there.

(viii) Proper Adjectives

These adjectives are formed from proper nouns, particularly from names of countries, continents and states.

Kashmiri girl, Arabian horse, Indian school, etc.

Note: These adjectives begin with capital letter.

Proper nouns	Proper Adjectives
Ambika hails from *Britain*.	She has a *British* passport.
Omar lives in *Libya*.	He is a *Libyan*.
We belong to *India*.	We are *Indian* citizens.

(ix) Intensifying Adjectives or Intensifiers

These adjectives reduce or heighten the effect of the noun they qualify.

Sheer, mere, utter, own, the very, quite, etc.

Examples: It is a matter of *sheer chance*.
She is an *utter fool*.
This is my *own house*.

Note:

(i) *'Own'* or *'very own'* takes possessive adjective before it.

This is *my own* mobile.

That is *your own* book.

Don't use: This is *own pen*. That is *own book*.

(ii) *'Quite'* can take an article + noun:

quite a beauty, quite the fashion.

She is *quite a healthy girl.*

(x) Participle Adjectives

These adjectives are formed from verb by taking either present participle (*-ing*) or past/perfect participle (*-en/ed*) form.

Examples:

Look at the *flying* bird. ....

This is a *moving* camera. present participle

My father is a *retired* teacher. ....

It is a *written* statement. past participle

(xi) Nominal Adjectives or Classifiers

These adjectives, basically nouns, function to modify another noun describing material or quality.

Examples: This is a *Hindi* film.
She has a *gold* ring.
This is a *stone* wall.
I went to a *book* fair.

(xii) Exclamatory Adjective

'what' is used as an exclamatory adjective to show the sense of wonder or surprize.

What nonsense!
What a piece of work is a man!
What genius!

Note: Adjectives are invariable for *number, gender, person,* or *case*. The only exception is demonstrative adjectives *'this'* and *'that'* which change to *'these'* and *'those'* before plural nouns:

Singular	Plural
This pen	*these* pens
That book	*those* books

Position of Adjectives

Adjectives are of two kinds in terms of the position they occupy in a sentence.

A. *Attributive* B. *Predicative*

A. (i) An attributive adjective occurs before a noun.

He is a *good boy*.

His pen is red.

(ii) Adjectives like the following are used attributively.

Upper, atomic, elder, thankless, bridal, former, chief, main, utter, only, indoor, outdoor, eldest, remedial, lone, knotty, preconceived, eventual, etc.

Alok is my *eldest son*.

He is an *utter fool*.

Dr. C.P. Thakur is a member of the *Upper House*.

B. (i) Predicative adjectives occur after the verb or after the object.

The dog is *asleep*. (after the verb)

The car is *red*. (after the verb)

He painted *the door blue*. (after the object)

Geyser makes *the water hot*. (after the object)

She dyed *her hair black*. (after the object)

(OBJECT COMPLEMENT)

(ii) They usually occur after the linking verbs:

(*To be*), *has/have/had* + *been, will/shall* + *be* + adjective and some main verbs such as *appear, look, seem, feel, smell, taste, sound, become, get, grow, keep, make, turn*, etc.

He *has been* honest.
Sunil *is* clever.
She looks beautiful.
She *will be* happy.
I *got* angry.

It *sounds* harsh.

Note: *Linking verbs* are also called *copulas*.

(iii) Adjectives like the following occur after a linking verb.

asleep, awake, alive, alone, aware, afraid, alike, ashamed, ill, well, etc.

The baby is *asleep*.	(not, It is an asleep baby.)
Both the pens are *alike*.	(not, Both are alike pens.)
He is *ill*.	(Here *'ill'* stands for *'unwell.'*)

But *'ill'* in the sense of *bad* can be used attributively.

I don't have ill will against Mr. Ahmed.

(iv) Certain structures take adjectives only after a linking verb. The use of adverb is not possible in this context.

Honey tastes *sweet*.	(not, sweetly)
Arti looks *beautiful*.	(not, beautifully)
It sounds *harsh*.	(not, harshly)
I feel *happy*.	(not, happily)

(v) Certain adjectives take a prepositional phrase.

(a) at + phrase

frightened at, disgusted at, shocked at, surprised at, amazed at, annoyed at, (something), etc.

(b) of + phrase

fond of, proud of, aware of, capable of, devoid of, etc.

(c) to + phrase

injurious to, allergic to, devoted to, adjacent to, accustomed to, addicted to, etc.

(d) with + phrase

annoyed with (someone), content with, satisfied with, conversant with, compatible with, etc.

Examples: He is *fond of* music.
Cigarette smoking is *injurious to* health.
I am *shocked at* the news.
I am *satisfied with* my work.

(vi) Certain adjectives take a clause: that clause/ infinitival.

It is necessary *that you work hard.*

Salma is bound *to come first in the class.*

He is adamant *to fight with his elder brother.*

She is confident *that she will get the first prize.*

Except these special position of adjectives, most of them are used both attributively and predicatively, e.g.

Attributive	Predicative
This is a *big house.*	This house is *big.*
This is a *Punjabi dress.*	This dress is *Punjabi.*
He is a *smart boy.*	The boy is *smart.*

Sequence of Adjectives

Sometimes various adjectives are used to modify a noun phrase in a sentence. In such situations, adjectives are usually placed according to the order shown in the table, though there is no fixed rule.

article	*quality*	*shape and length*	*colour*	*noun or gerund*	*noun*
A	new	long	black	iron	rod
A	beautiful	small	green	flower	vase
An	attractive	round	red	rubber	toy

Examples: A new long black iron rod
A nice round red table cloth

Above table is taken from *A Guide to Patterns and Usage in English by* A.S. Hornby.

Function of Adjectives

The function of adjectives in English is variable. The same adjective may function as a different class of word that is fixed on the basis of its position in a sentence.

(a) Adjective functioning as nouns

(i) with the definite article *the rich, the poor, the deaf, the brave, the weak, the dead, the English, the French, the Irish*, etc.

These nouns refer to a class of people and take a plural verb.

The strong oppress *the weak*.

the strong = strong people

the weak = weak people

Note: But plural nouns are used in *the Germans, the Italians, the Indians, the Americans*, etc.

But when they refer to an abstract quality, they take a singular verb.

The good in her overpowers *the bad*.

(ii) with plural suffix

butters, totals, criminals, elders, blacks, nobles, seniors, juniors, superiors, inferiors, wrongs, secrets, solids, valuables, morals, majors, etc.

Example: Please convey my regards to *seniors* and blessings to *juniors*.

These words behave as plural nouns.

(iii) young, black, white, cold, cool, great, high, low, etc.

Examples:

Girls are dressed in *blue/red/white*. (clothes)

The baby has caught a *cold*. (exposure)

The mother bird feeds its *young*. (newly-born baby)

(b) Adjective functioning as pronouns

all, both, much, many, neither, one, some, such, that, etc.

Adjective	Pronoun
All men are mortal.	*All* agreed to go to Tripoli.
We work with *both hands*.	*Both* of them were present.
There is *much sugar* in tea.	*Much* of the news is false.

What is *that noise*?	*That* is what I said.

(c) Adjective functioning as verbs ready, black, dry, calm, grey, cool, empty, etc.

Adjective	Verb
Jayant has *grey* hair.	He has *greyed* his hair.
The bottle is *empty*.	He *emptied* the whole bottle of wine.
We eat dry fruits.	She *dried* her hair in the sun.

(d) Adjective functioning as adverbs

close, easy, fast, hard, high, live, loud, quick, late, sharp, sure, early, etc.

Adjective	Adverb
He is a *late riser*.	He always comes *late*.
He is a *fast runner*.	He runs *fast*.
It is a *live coal*.	The match will be telecast *live*.

(e) Adjective functioning as prepositions

above, down, near, next, round, up, etc.

Adjective	Preposition
Look at the *above examples*.	He is *above* suspicion.
He came by the *down train*.	Tears ran *down* her face.
Alok is my *near relation*.	He is standing *near* the taxi station.
It is a *round table*.	The earth moves *round* the sun.

(f) Adjective functioning as conjunctions

both, either, else, neither, only, that, etc.

Adjective	Conjunction
Who is *that man*?	He reads *that* he may pass.
Adel is my *only son*.	Take all that I have, *only* let me go.
One can't be gainer *both ways*.	*Both* Ali and Ahmed are clever.

Comparison of Adjective

Most attributive adjectives are gradable adjectives. They are used to express a quality of an equal or unequal degree. This is known as degrees of comparison.

There are three degrees of comparison.

(i) positive, (ii) comparative, and (iii) superlative

(i) positive degree: It is used to modify a noun phrase.

He is clever.

(ii) comparative degree: It is used to compare two persons or things.

He is cleverer than me.

This room is bigger than kitchen.

Note: '*Than*' is normally used after a comparative form of adjective.

(a) *Than + noun/pronoun* (objective form)

Ahmed is richer than *me*.

He is older than *her*.

Since '*than*' is a preposition in this structure, it takes a pronoun in the objective form.

(b) *Than + noun/pronoun* (subjective form)

He behaves better than *you* do (behave).

She loves her more than *I* do (love her).

In this structure, '*than*' is a conjunction used after a comparative adjective/adverb to introduce an adverb clause of comparison, so it takes a pronoun in the subjective form.

Some other constructions of comparative form take '*of*' or '*to*' in place of '*than*.'

(i) The + comparative form + of the two.

He is the wiser of the two brothers.

This is the better of the two.

(ii) Only seven Latin comparatives junior, senior, inferior, superior, prior, anterior and posterior take 'to' after them.

He is senior to me.

Alok is inferior to Shyam in intelligence.

Other Latin comparatives have lost their meaning and are used as positive adjectives. They are: *major, minor, exterior, ulterior, interior*, etc.

It is a *major issue.*

He is *an interior decorator.*

(iii) '*To*' is used with preferable without '*more*' *or* '*less*'.

Fish is preferable *to* meat.

Bread is preferable *to* rice.

(iii) *Superlative degree*

(a) It is used when more than two persons or things are compared.

He is *the cleverest* boy in the class.

Alok is *the tallest* boy in the village.

She is *the worst* of the candidates.

Note:

(i) We use '*in*' or '*on*' with place and '*of*' with people and things in a superlative structure.

(ii) '*The*' is always used before the superlative degree of adjective.

(iii) We never use '*all other*', '*any other*' *anything else, anybody else,* etc. in this construction, Don't make a sentence like

Salini is the best of all other girls. (x)

(b) When '*most*' is used in the sense of '*very*', it doesn't take '*the*' before it.

You are *most* welcome. (very)

But it takes '*a*' or '*an*' before it when there is a noun after adjective.

Dr. Damodar Thakur is *a most* renowned scholar of Linguistics. (very)

(c) Some other constructions of superlative form take *one of + superlative + plural noun*, e.g.

Shakespeare is *one of the greatest dramatists* of the Elizabethan age.

Intensifiers like *'the very'*, *'by far'*, *'far and away'*, *'much 'the'*, etc. express the sense of emphatic superlatives.

Tendulkar is *by far* the best cricketer.

I want *the very* best quality of cloth.

Some adverbs like *undoubtedly, obviously, easily, certainly, definitely, decidedly*, etc. are used before the superlative degree of adjective.

He is *certainly* the best teacher.

Ali is *undoubtedly* the greatest player.

Note: The use of double superlatives in a sentence or the use of superlative form to compare two people or things is not possible.

Example: Don't make a sentence like

This is *the most happiest* occasion. (x)

(Double superlatives)

Who is *the tallest*—Salma or Najat? (x)

(comparing two people by using the superlative form)

Non-gradable (Degreeless) Adjectives

Non-gradable adjectives are those that can never be used in comparative or superlative form. They express an extreme degree, so they are called degreeless adjectives.

> absolute, whole, wrong, universal, ideal, full, extreme, unique, excellent, entire, dead, chief, blind, dumb, deaf, complete, round, right, etc.

This is a *wrong* decision.

It is an *excellent* meal.

Note: Non-gradable adjectives *'full'* and *'perfect'* in the comparative and superlative forms are sometimes used to express a nearer approach to the absolute.

A *fuller* view of the earth can't be observed roughly.

Formation of Comparatives and Superlatives

(A) One-syllable adjectives

(i) Add *'er'* and *'est'* to the comparative and superlative form respectively.

Positive	*Comparative*	*Superlative*
Tall	taller	tallest
Smart	smarter	smartest
High	higher	highest
Sweet	sweeter	sweetest

(ii) Add *'r'* and 'st', to one syllable adjectives ending in *'e'* in the comparative and superlative form.

fine	finer	finest
wise	wiser	wisest
brave	braver	bravest

(iii) Add *'er'* and *'est'* after doubling the last consonant that has taken a vowel before it.

big	bigger	biggest
thin	thinner	thinnest
hot	hotter	hottest

(iv) Add *'er'* and *'est'* after changing *consonant* + *y* adjectives into *'i'*.

easy	easier	easiest
dry	drier	driest

But *vowel* + *y* is not changed into *'i'*.

gay	gayer	gayest

(B) Two-syllable adjectives

Add *'er'* and *'est'* after changing *consonant* + *y* adjectives into *'i'*.

pretty	prettier	prettiest
happy	happier	happiest
lucky	luckier	luckiest
tasty	tastier	tastiest

Add *'er'* and *'est'* to these adjectives ending in *'le'*, dropping the final *'e'*.

Humble	humbler	humblest
Noble	nobler	noblest
Simple	simpler	simplest
Ample	ampler	amplest

Add *'more'* and *'most'* or *'er'* and *'est'* to form comparative and superlative degrees of these words.

Pleasant	pleasanter	pleasantest
Pleasant	more pleasant	most pleasant
Common	commoner	commonest
Common	more common	most common
Friendly	friendlier	friendliest
Friendly	more friendly	most friendly

Other adjectives of the group are:

sincere, stupid, tender, narrow, polite, bitter, clever, etc.

(C) Three-syllable adjectives

Add *'more'* and *'most'* or *'less'* and *'least'* to form the comparative and the superlative degrees of adjectives.

Interested	more interested	most interested
Beautiful	more beautiful	most beautiful
Important	more important	most important
Excited	less excited	least excited
Frightening	less frightening	least frightening

Irregular comparisons

Bad	worse	worst
Good	better	best
Well	better	best
Little	less	least
Much/many	more	most
Far	farther	farthest (of distance only)
Far	farther	further (used more widely)

Old	older	oldest (of people and things)
Old	elder	eldest (of people only)

Uses of Comparison

(A) *Positive degree*

(i) A comparison is made between two things or people of equal degree by using *as* + *adjective* + *as* in the affirmative.

Ali is *as* brave *as* a lion.

Food is *as* important *as* water.

(ii) *As* + *adjective* + *as* can be replaced by *adjective* + *like* in some contexts.

Saloni is *as* gentle *as* a lamb.

Saloni is gentle *like* a lamb.

Note: '*As....as*' is omitted in such contexts.

Some idiomatic comparisons:

as white *as* snow	*as* black *as* coal
as sharp *as* a neddle	*as* busy *as* a bee
as hot *as* fire	*as* clear *as* crystal
as sure *as* death	*as* cunning *as* a fox
as fresh *as* a daisy	*as* dry *as* bone

Note: *Objective case* + *noun/pronoun* is used after preposition and *subjective case* + *noun/pronoun* is used after conjunction *in 'as....as'* construction to show equality.

He is as tall *as me.* (preposition).

He ia as tall *as I (am)*. (conjunction)

(iii) '*Not so/as....as*' is frequently used to show inequality in the negative structure instead of *'less* + *positive degree* + *than'*.

Your pen is not so expensive as that.

You are not so wise as her.

'*Less* + *positive degree* + *than*' structure is rarely used in such structures, though it is not wrong.

He is *less* wise *than* her.

(iv) *Not* all *that* + *adjective* can also be used instead of *'not so/as……as'* construction.

It is *not all that* big.

It is *not so big as* that.

(v) '*Numeral* + *times* + *as* + *positive degree adjective* + *as*' is also used comparatively to express weights and measures.

This room is two times as big as that.

Those books are three times as heavy as these ones.

Note: A comparative form is also acceptable here.

This room is *two times bigger than* that.

Those books are *three times heavier than* these ones.

(i) '*As many* + *countable nouns* + *as*' is used comparatively to show numbers.

He has *as many books as she (has).*

You have *as many friends as I (have).*

(ii) 'As much + uncountable noun + as' is used to show quantity.

She doesn't have as much honey as I (have).

(iii) '*Fewer/less/more* + *noun* + *than*' is also used comparatively.

I have fewer books than pens.

I have less coffee than tea.

I have more chairs than he (has).

I have more hair than you (have).

Note: *'More'* is used with both number and quantity.

'Fewer' is used with number only.

'Less' is used with quantity only.

(iv) *'As…….as'* and *'not so/as'* are used to express the gerundial or infinitival comparison of actions.

Speaking is *as difficult as writing.* (affirmative)

Speaking is *not so difficult as writing.* (negative)

It is *as easy to run as swim.* (affirmative)

It is *not as easy to run as swim.* (negative)

Note: *'As'* takes an infinitive without *'to'*

(B) *Comparative degree*

(i) *Comparative adjective + than* is also used to express gerundial or infinitival actions.

Walking is *easier than running.*

It is easier *to walk than run.*

Note: *'Than'* takes an infinitive without *'to'*.

(ii) Comparison of actions (verb) is expressed on the basis of the given structures.

(a) *Sub + prefer + gerund + to + gerund*: (verb + ing)

We prefer *writing* to *reading.*

(b) (i) *Sub + prefer/would prefer + infinitive + rather than* + infinitive (without 'to'):

I *prefer/would prefer to run rather than walk.*

I *prefer/would prefer to walk rather than sit idle.*

In this construction, gerund can also be used instead of infinitive.

I *would prefer/prefer walking rather sitting idle.*

(ii) *'Prefer/would prefer .... rather than'* can also take a noun or adjective.

I *prefer/would prefer* to be *a social worker* rather than *a politician.*

I *prefer/would prefer* to be *rich* rather than *poor.*

(iii) But *would rather/would sooner/had better/had sooner/had rather* take infinitive without *'to'*.

He would rather/sooner *die* than beg.

I had better/rather/sooner *die* than beg.

(iv) These structures can take a noun or adjective.

I would rather be *gentle* than *cruel.*

I would rather be *a master* than *a slave.*

(C) *Comparison of qualities (adjectives)*

(i) *'More + positive form + than + positive form'* is used to compare two qualities of the same person or thing.

Here, comparative forms ending in *'er'* are never used.

He is more *polite* than *dull.*

She is more *wise* than *old.*

You are more *strong* than *tall.*

(ii) *'The + comparative form + and + comparative form'* is used to express gradual increase or decrease.

The condition of the patient is getting *worse and worse.*

Tea is getting *colder and colder.*

(iii) *'More + and + more'* or *'less + and + less'* is used with two or three-syllabic adjectives.

Her lecture is getting *less and less intelligible.*

He is getting *more and more sophisticated.*

(iv) *'Comparative + than + all other/any other + noun'* is used to compare more than two people or things. So it is comparative in form but superlative in sense.

Alok is taller than *all other students.*

Alok is taller than *any other student.*

Note: *'All other'* takes a plural noun but *'any other'* takes a singular noun.

The use of *'other'* is necessary in such sentences.

(v) *'Comparative + than + anybody/anyone/anything + else'* is also used to show superlative sense.

Anil is wiser than *anybody* else.

A good wife is better than *anything* else.

Bill Gates is richer than *anyone* else.

(D) *Wrong use of comparisons*

(i) The comparative form of adjective is used to compare two people or things.

Arabic is easier than *English.*

Iron is heavier than *cotton.*

It is wrong to compare more than two people or things in constructions like these.

Arabic is easier than *French, Latin* and *English.*

(ii) A comparison is always wrong between two entirely different items, e.g.

Alok's flat is bigger than *Anil.* (*a flat* compared with a person *'Anil'*)

My pen is cheaper than *you.* (*a pen* compared with a person *'you'*)

The climate of Patna is better than *Gaya.*

(*climate* compared with a place '*Gaya*')

The roads of New Delhi are wider than *Patna.*

(*roads* compared with a place *'Patna'*)

These comparisons of different items are quite wrong in expression. The correct expressions are:

Alok's flat is bigger than *Anil's.*

My pen is cheaper than *yours.* (your pen)

The climate of Patna is better than *that of Gaya.*

The roads of New Delhi are wider than *those of Patna.*

Note: (i) Singular noun before *'of'* (genitive case) takes *'than that of + noun'* and plural *'than those of + noun'*.

(ii) Apostrophe *'s'* is used with noun after *'than'*.

Saloni's hair is longer than *Raushni's.*

(E) (i) Double comparative structures like *'more' or less + comparative form* (er) are quite wrong.

Alok is *more richer* than Anil. (incorrect)

She is *less smarter* than Saloni. (incorrect)

Alok is *richer than* Anil. (correct)

She is *smarter than* Sabita. (correct).

Note: Intensifiers like *'much', 'very much', 'far', 'by far', still, yet,* etc. can be used to make the comparative emphatic.

Alok is *much richer* than Anil. (correct)

She is very *much smarter* than Sabita. (correct)

(ii) Sometimes intensifiers are repeated to emphasize the adjectives, e.g. *'much much', 'far far.'*

This place is *much much* better.

This gift is *far far* better.

(iii) Some adverbs and phrases are also used to intensify comparative.

> rather, somewhat, a little, a bit, a tiny bit, a lot, a shade, etc.

He is *rather/a little/a bit/a shade* better today.

But '*fairly*' can't be used before comparatives. e.g.

She is *fairly better* today. (incorrect)

She is *rather better* today. (correct)

(iv) '*Comparatively + positive form*' is used to express the sense of '*in comparison with*'. It does not mean '*rather*' or '*fairly*'.

He is *comparatively* good today.

She is *comparatively* tall.

(v) *Comparative form of adjective* is used to compare two things only.

Which is *cheaper*	-	apple or banana?	(not apple, banana or mango)
Which is *bigger*	-	rubber or book?	(not, rubber, pen or book)
Who is *taller*	-	Sabita or Saloni?	(not, Sabita, Saloni or Salu)

(F) Superlative degree

(i) Superlative degree of adjective takes the intensifiers like '*much the*', '*the very*', '*by far the*', '*out and out the*' to make the sentence emphatic.

> This is *out and out the* best book.
>
> This is *by far the* best book.
>
> This is *the very* best book.
>
> This is *much the* best book.

(ii) Double superlative structures like *'the most'* or *'the least'* + *superlative form* (est) are quite wrong.

This is *the most biggest* building in Chapra. (incorrect).

Babita is *the most richest* of all girls. (incorrect)

This is *the biggest* building in Gaya. (correct)

Usha is *the richest* of all girls. (correct)

(iii) Superlative form of adjective is used to compare three or more people or things only.

Who is *the tallest* – Tanya, Jolly or Jully?

Which is *the cheapest* – mango, apple, or banana?

Which is *the cheapest* – mango or banana? (incorrect)

This is the best of all the books.

Note: *'Other'* is not used with *'all'* in superlative sentences.

(iv) When possessives (my, his, Ali's, our, etc.)

'The' is always omitted.

He is *my best* friend.

It is *Omar's best* book.

(v) Two or more adjectives combined by *'and'* take the same degree of comparison.

He is a brave and wise man. (positive form)

He is braver and wiser than me. (comparative form)

He is the bravest and wisest man. (superlative form)

Note: No *'article'* is used before the second adjective.

Some confusing comparative and superlative adjectives

(1) *Elder/eldest*

It is used to compare the members of the same family relation like *brother, sister, son, daughter*, etc. It indicates seniority rather than age.

My *eldest daughter* is still a student. (not, oldest daughter)

His *eldest brother* is a teacher. (not, oldest brother)

Note: *Elder/eldest* is not used to refer to things or animals.

(i) *Elder* doesn't take *'than'* or *'to.'*

He is *older than* his brother (not, *elder than* his brother)

(ii) *Elder/eldest* takes '*the*' before it when it is used predicatively.

He is *the elder* of the two brothers.

He is *the eldest* of the five sons.

(2) *Older/oldest*

It is used of both people and things to express age. It is used for comparison within the same class of people or things.

Sonu is *older than* Alok. (not, elder)

My house is *the oldest* building in Hajipur. (not, eldest)

(3) *Farther/further*

' *Farther*' means greater distance.

Chapra is *farther* from Patna than Hajipur.

Note: '*Further*' is also used of distance.

Sarai is *further* than Bhagwanpur.

'*Further*' means something extra/additional.

Further information will be given later on.

Let us go for a walk without *further* delay.

(4) *Fewer/less/lesser*

'*Fewer*' is used of number.

There are *fewer* than ten students in the class.

Fewer people are honest.

'*Less*' is used of quantity.

I have *less* money today.

We have *less* time for our examination.

Note: '*Less*' is also used after *a cardinal number + plural noun* that denotes a definite amount/quantity.

There are twenty students *less* for class today.

You can give me two rupees *less*.

(iii) '*Lesser*' means '*less* important'/'*less* serious'.

The *lesser* novelists of *the Victorian age* were Anthony Trollope, Charles Reade and Walter Besant.

(5) *Former/latter*

'*Former*' means the first of the two and '*latter*' means the second of the two people or things mentioned earlier.

I met an American and a Russian in Tripoli.

The *former* (the American) was tall and the *latter* (the Russian) was short.

(6) *First/last*

'*First*' or '*last*' is used to refer to more than two people or things.

'*First*' comes before *all others in order* and '*last*' comes after *all others in order*.

Saturday in the *first* and Thursday is the *last* day of the week in Arab countries.

January is the *first* and December is the *last* month of the year.

(7) *Nearest/next*

'*Nearest*' denotes distance.

Which is the *nearest* post office?

'*Next*' denotes position.

He is sitting *next* to his wife.

(8) *Later/latter; latest/last*

'*Later*' and '*latest*' denote time.

He came five minutes *later* than me.

I don't have the *latest* information.

'*Latter*' and '*last*' refer to position or place.

The *last* letter of English alphabet is z.

Marlowe and Shakespeare were great dramatists. *The former* died in his thirties but *the latter* died in his fifties.

Determiners

What is a determiner?

A determiner signals the coming of a noun in a noun phrase. In other words, it establishes the identity of a noun in course of modifying it.

Kinds of Determiners

(i) Articles (a/an, the)

He met *a* teacher.

The teacher was sitting on a chair.

(ii) *Demonstrative determiners* (*this/that/these/those*)

I want *this* computer not *that* one.

These books are cheaper than *those* books.

(iii) *Possessive determiners* (*my, our, your, his, her, its, their*)

This is *my* pen.

That is *your* book.

(iv) *Distributive determiners* (*each, every, either, neither*)

Each book is costly.

Every student was present.

Either side of the road is dirty.

(v) *Nouns as possessive determiners* (*Ali's, Bill's, Dolly's,* etc.)

Dolly's hair is longer than *Honey's* hair.

(vi) *Quantifiers* (*all, any, few, many, much, some, no, enough, little,* etc.)

Many students were present.

Some books are expensive.

There is *little* sugar in tea.

(vii) *Partitives* (*slice of, glass of, ounce of, litre of, loaf of, bit of, acre of,* etc.)

I bought an *acre of* land.

This is a *glass of* water.

(viii) *Cardinal numbers* (*one, two, three, four, ten,* etc.)

I have *two* red shirts.

She has *five* pens.

(ix) O*rdinal numbers* (*first, second, fourth, next, last,* etc.)

He got the *second* prize.

He stood *fourth* in his class.

(x) *Multipliers* (*double, triple, twice, thrice, five times,* etc.)

Raj got an offer that was *double* the amount that he was getting.

(xi) *Fractions* (*three-fourths, two-thirds, one-half, one-fifth,* etc.)

One-fifth of my homework is over.

(xii) *Interrogative determiners* (*what, which, whose,* etc.)

Which novel do you like most?

What colour is your car?

Whose mobile is this?

Determiners and their Order of Appearance

Determiners fall into three groups that describe the relative order of appearance before head nouns.

(i) *Predeterminers*

(ii) *Central determiners*

(iii) *Postdeterminers.*

ORDER OF DETERMINERS IN NOUN PHRASE

Predeterminers	*Central determiners*	*Postdeterminers*
Quantifiers — all, both, half, just, only, some, etc. *Multipliers* — double, twice, three times, etc. *Fractions* — three-fourths, one-fifth, two-thirds, etc.	*Articles* — a, an, the *Possessive* — my, our, her, etc. *Nouns as possessives determiners* — Alok's, Anil's, Aziz's, etc. *Demonstrative determiners* — these, those, this, that *Quantifiers* — any, every, some, either, neither	*Cardinal numbers* — one, two, five, ten, etc. *Ordinal numbers* — first, second, another, next, etc. *Partitives* — a jar/glass/cup/bottle/loaf/pair/acre, etc. + of. *Quantifiers* — many, much, few, little, less, more.

(i) *Predeterminers*

Predeterminers, as the name suggests, always come before *central determiners*.

(a) *Quantifiers*—All, both, half, only, just, some, etc.

(b) *Multipliers*—once, twice, thrice, double, triple, four times, etc.

(c) *Fractions*—one-half, three-fourths, two-thirds, etc.

Examples:

All my books are new. (not, my all books)

Some of the mangoes are ripe. (not, the some of mangoes)

Half of the sugar is left in the bag. (not, the half of sugar)

Both the teachers are hardworking. (not, the both teachers)

The expressions of number and quantity like *a lot of, some of, half of, plenty of,* etc. are *predeterminers*, as they can be followed by *articles, demonstratives* or *possessives.*

As regards *determiners*, only one *predeterminer* can occur in a noun phrase.

Both these books are cheap.

All these books are cheap.

We can use either *'all'* or *'both'* in this construction.

(ii) *Central Determiners*

Articles, possessives, and *demonstratives* are *central determiners.* They don't co-occur. If one of them is present, the others can't be used. They are mutually exclusive.

We can say *a pen, the pen, his pen, this pen, Ali's pen,* etc.

But we can't say:
A this pen
That a pen
A Dolly's pen
The India's economic policy.

These *determiners* are called *central* because they usually come before the noun.

This is *her* book.
She is *Dolly's* sister.
I want *a* pen.

If distributives like *each, every, either, neither* and some of the number expressions quantifiers like *any, some, no*, occur alone, they share the properties of *determiners.*

Neither girl is tall.

She helps *every* student.

I don't have *any* problem.

(iii) *Postdeterminers*

Postdeterminers always come after *central determiners*:

(a) *Cardinal numbers* - one, four, ten, etc.

(b) *Ordinal numbers* - first, second, last, etc.

(c) *Partitives* - a pair/glass/jug/bottle + of, etc.

The first two articles were published in India.

(not, first two the article)

Unlike *predeterminers* and *central determiners*, *one* or more than *one postdeterminer* can occur in a noun phrase.

The *first four* books, the *last ten* items.

Where more than one *determiner* can be used together, there is almost a fixed order in which they occur.

quantifiers	*article* or *possessive* or *demonstrative*	*numeral*	*head noun*
All	His	three	sons
All	The	five	bags
Half	a	------	dozen
-----	My	first	book
Both	his	-------	sons

All, both and *half* can come before *articles, possessives* and *demonstratives* but *quantifiers* such as *any, few, many, more, some*, etc. and *numerals* cannot.

When *quantifiers* and *numerals* occur first. They take *'of'*, e.g.

Four of my articles are published.

I have solved *some of* my problems.

Differences between Adjectives and Determiners

Determiners	*Adjectives*
1. It has no variable forms *a* boy, *this* book, *your* pens.	1. It has variable forms *tall, taller, tallest.*
2. Two determiners of the same kind can't be used in an NP. This is *my his* (x) book.	2. Two adjectives of the same kind can be used. He is a *strong* and *brave* man.
3. It always comes before a noun that means as attributive. This is *my* pen.	3. It comes before as well as after a noun that means both as attributive and predicative. I have a *red* pen. The pen is *red.*
4. A determiner always comes before an adjective if both occur in an NP. This is *my* new book.	4. An adjective always comes after a determiner if both occur in an NP. This is a *new* book.
5. A determiner can't be used without a noun. This is *a* pen.	5. An adjective can be used without a noun. He is crazy.

Use of Determiners

(A) *Each, every, either, neither*

These *determiners* are always used with a singular noun.

Each pen is red. *Every pen* is red.
Either pen is red. *Neither pen* is red.

Note: *Every* takes a plural noun when the plural numeral adjective is used after it.

He takes medicine at an interval of *every three hours.*

She visits the zoo *every four months.*

(i) *Each* is used for two or more people or things.

I bought *two books* last week. *Each of them* was expensive.

(ii) *Every* is used for more than two people or things.

There are *ten book-shops* in Hajipur. *Every book-shop* sells dictionaries.

(iii) *Each* and *every* take a singular countable noun to make the sentence emphatic.

(iv) 'Each of' can function as a predeterminer, but '*every of*' can't.

Each of the girls is tall. (not, *every of*)

(v) '*Either*' means '*one of the two*'.

You can eat *either an apple* or *a banana* in breakfast.

(vi) '*Neither*' means '*not one nor the other of the two*'.

There are two girls standing there. *Neither girl* is married.

(vii) '*Either*' and '*both*'

Either means *both/each of the two.*

When one part is complementary to the other.

either side of a road (*both sides*)

either bank of a river (*both banks*)

There are boats on *either bank* of the river.

Her either sons failed in the examination. (incorrect)

'*Both her sons*' should be used here because *both her sons* are not complementary to each other.

(B) '*Much* 'and '*Many*'

(i) '*Much*' is used before singular uncountable nouns to denote quality.

She has got *much patience.*

(ii) '*Many*' is used before plural countable nouns to denote number.

I have bought *many books* this year.

(iii) '*Much*' and '*Many*' are used with how to ask questions.

How *many children* have you got?

How *much money* is needed?

(iv) '*Much*' and '*Many*' are normally used in interrogative and negative sentences.

Are *many teachers* coming here?

Is *much milk* left in the bottle?

There is not *much space* between the two lines.

There aren't *many girls* in this class.

(v) '*Many*' *a/an* takes a singular countable noun.

Many a man comes and goes to market daily.

Note: '*Many*' *a/an* is rarely used.

(C) *Few, a few, the few* and *little, a little, the little*

Few denotes numbers and *little* denotes quantity.

Plural countable nouns are used with *few, a few,* and *the few.*

Singular countable nouns are used with *little, a little,* and *the little.*

(i) Number	Quantity
He has *few* friends.	I have *little* sugar.
He has *a few* new books.	He has *a little* milk.
The few friends I have are rich.	*The little* money I have will be spent soon.

(ii) But '*few*' and '*little*' have semi-negative expressions. They mean '*not any*'.

He has *few* friends. (no friends)

He has *little* money. (no money)

(iii) '*A few*' and '*a little*' are positive in meaning. They mean '*some*'.

I have *a few* books. (some books)

I have *a little* money. (some money)

(iv) The few means '*all that are there*' and '*the little*' means '*all that is there*'

I ate *the few apples* that I had.

I spent *the little money* that I had.

The few + *noun* and *the little* + *noun* are normally followed by a relative clause.

The few books that I have are old.

The little money that she had was spent.

(D) *'Other' and 'another'*

(i) When *'other'* is used to express the second of the two it takes singular verb.

The *other side* of the road is dirty.

(ii) But *'other'* and *'the other'* may take either singular or plural nouns.

I will visit you some *other day*.

Ali passed but *the other boys* failed.

(iii) *'Another'* is always used with a singular noun.

Give me *another* book.

Note: *'Another'* doesn't take article (*an* or *the*) because it is a determiner.

I want to drink *another glass* of juice. (not, an another)

Give me *another book*. (not, the another book)

(E) *'All'* and *'both'*

These are *predeterminers*. They are followed by *central determiners*.

All the students are intelligent.

Both his sons are smart.

(F) *'No'* and *'None'*

(i) *'No'* behaves like a determiner but *'none'* doesn't. So *'no + noun'* is used but *'none + noun'* is not used.

I have *no money*. (not, none money)

(ii) *'No + noun'* is used to express contrast.

She is *no scholar*. (she is not a scholar)

Saloni is *no beauty*. (Saloni is not a beautiful girl)

(iii) 'No + *good*'

Here' *'good'* means *advantage* and it functions as a noun. That's why *'no'* is used before it as a determiner.

It is *no good* crying over bad result.

(G) *'Some'* and *'Any'*

(i) Usually *'some'* takes affirmative verbs and *'any'* takes negative verbs.

I *have got some* good friends. (affirmative)

I *haven't got any* book. (negative)

But *'any'* is used with affirmative verbs to express the sense of *'every'*.

Any student can solve this sum. (every)

(ii) *'Any'* takes negative adverbs, too.

Hardly, scarcely, nor, never, neither, seldom, etc.

She has *hardly any* book.

I have *never seen any* English film.

(iii) *'Any'* is used to express doubt.

She asked me *if I had any dictionary* with me.

(iv) *Any* is used after *'if'* or *'whether'*

Send me an email *if you need any* book.

(v) Either *'some'* or *'any'* can be used in questions:

Has she got *any money*?

Has she got *some money*?

(vi) *'Some'* is used with a singular countable noun whose identity is unknown.

Some Sharma is calling you.

(vii) *Some* is also used in the sense of *'approximately'*.

There are *some fifty students* in the class. (approximately)

(viii) *'Some'* is also used to express a request in ordinary questions.

Could you lend me *some money*, please? (not, any money)

(ix) *'Some'* is sometimes used before a noun to mean considerable number or extent.

That is a matter of *some relief/satisfaction.*

This amount will be of *some help*.

(H) *Not any/no any*

(i) *'No any'* can never be used in place of *'not any'*.

Saloni *hasn't got any* pens. (not, no any pens)

'No' or *'not any'* is used after *'have'*, but *'have got'* usually takes *'not any'*, not *'no'*.

She *hasn't got any* pens. (not, she has got no pens.)
I have *no* books. (not, I haven't some *books.*)
I *haven't got any* books. (not, I haven't got no books)

(iii) *Some/any/no + noun* is used with both countable and uncountable nouns.

With countable nouns, it is plural.

I have *some books.* She has *no pens.* Ali hasn't got *any letters.* (countable)

I have *some milk.* She has *no money.* Ali hasn't got *any chance.* (uncountable)

But *Not any/no + singular noun* is used when *not any/no* means *'not even one'* or *'not a single.'*

I have *no book.* (not even one book)
She hasn't got *any house.* (not even one house)

EXERCISE-1

Fill up (IN) the Blanks with Suitable Adjectives.

1. You are a .... student.
2. I am ..... to see you.
3. Your shoes are ....
4. This is an .... car.
5. The wall is seven feet ....
6. She looks ....
7. Patna is a .... city.
8. There are .... months in a year.
9. That is a .... pot.
10. You are a .... man.
11. .... wood doesn't burn well.
12. I don't take .... tea.
13. Do you buy .... food?
14. She eats .... chicken.
15. Have you got .... friends?

16. Please give me .... rupees.
17. Has he .... money?
18. .... plants need water.
19. .... student is clever.
20. Have you .... further questions?
21. Give me .... more.
22. All .... sons are students.
23. .... sugar is left.
24. ...... of the mangoes are unripe.
25. She is .... to me.
26. We are .... teachers.
27. I have ...... pen.
28. Such .... amount will be of some help.
29. .... shore of the sea is full of sand.
30. The........ novel of Emily Bronte made her popular.

EXERCISE-2

Choose the right alternative.

1. You are sitting .... to her. (nearest/next)
2. .... man knows what to do. (all/each/every)
3. There is .... of milk in the bottle. (a number/ plenty)
4. I have never seen .... a place. (such a/such)
5. .... book is perfect. (no/none)
6. You can get down at the .... stop. (next/nearest)
7. Alok drank .... the milk. (all/whole)
8. He earns ...... than me. (little/less)
9. The president is .... (ill/sickly)
10. I haven't seen .... twin. (neither/either)
11. .... people speak like this. (much/many)
12. There are .... books. (any/some)
13. I wrote .... books. (a little/a few)

14. He looks .... than you. (smart/smarter)
15. The doctor says that Alok's health is .... than it was yesterday. (bad/worse)
16. Alok's car is ....than mine. (old/older)
17. .... children like chocolates. (each/all)
18. He has .... pens. (lots of/much)
19. .... boy has a bag. (each/none)
20. They are getting ...... (rich and rich/richer and richer)
21. I will see you ...... (latter/later)
22. He is my .... door neighbour. (nearest/next)
23. My .... son is intelligent. (older/elder)
24. He is the .... member of the congress. (eldest/oldest)
25. Ajay was the .... student to receive a prize. (last/latest)
26. Saloni is ...... than my daughter. (elder/older)
27. I don't have .... problem. (some/any)
28. It is they .... house is near the sea. (which/whom/whose)
29. My wife is .... of the two sisters. (wise/wiser/wisest)
30. There are .... twenty girls in this class. (less than/fewer than)

EXERCISE-3

Choose the right alternative.

1. She is the taller .... the two. (than/of)
2. You are junior .... me. (than/to)
3. She is .... good than clever. (much/more/most)
4. I am feeling .... pains. (much/many)
5. The climate of Ranchi is better than .... (Gaya/that of Gaya)
6. She is taller than .... girls. (all/all other)

7. Ali is wiser than .... boy. (all other/any other)
8. He is the best of .... students. (all/all other)
9. He prefers reading .... writing. (than/to)
10. I had better die .... beg. (to/than)
11. The towns of Bihar are smaller than .... (that of Delhi/those of Delhi)
12. I have five shirts .... of them is costly. (each/every)
13. Which is the .... apple, orange, banana? (cheaper/cheapest)
14. I have ...... money. (no/not any)
15. He has finished .... chapters of his novel. (the first four/the four first)
16. .... sons are wise. (all his/his all)
17. We are writing .... books. (any/some)
18. He has .... money. (any/a little)
19. This book is .... than that. (costlier/costliest)
20. Meat is preferable .... chicken. (than/to)
21. My .... brother is a school teacher. (older/elder)
22. Which of the two boys are the ....? (smart/smarter)
23. He is more wise than .... (dull/more dull)
24. Puloma is .... than her sister by four years. (elder/older)
25. He is .... all the men of his village. (stronger than/the strongest)
26. Of the two teachers I think him to be the .... (best/better)
27. I saw two women, the one was lame and .... was blind. (another/the other)
28. It is .... cold. (extreme/most extreme)
29. There are ..... than twenty girls. (no less/not fewer)
30. Bring me .... tea to take. (any/some)

EXERCISE-4

Correct the following sentences if necessary.

1. I have spent a little money I had.
2. The both sons are intelligent.
3. I saw a most unique sight.
4. It is better of the two books.
5. The most busiest hour is 10 o'clock.
6. The weather is warmer as last year.
7. He hasn't some pens.
8. I can't eat something.
9. This book is best than that one.
10. I found that cat more dead.
11. Salim is better than clever.
12. Alok has got no any brother.
13. My flat is much more cheaper than your flat.
14. Saloni is the dullest of all other girls.
15. I would better die than to beg.
16. Sumit has hardly some money.
17. Ask me any question if you have some doubt.
18. He is older than anybody here.
19. You are the most superior of all.
20. He is stronger and more wiser than my friend.
21. There is no any man there.
22. Ravi is elder than his friend, Hari.
23. India is ready to give us farther help.
24. She has no a book.
25. He is one of the taller boys in the class.
26. I am very fond of these kind of fish.
27. I am two years smaller than you.
28. You are five years bigger than your wife.
29. More you need, more you learn.
30. He acted well in comedies than in tragedies.

4

Verb

Introduction

A verb is that part of a sentence which talks of the state of action performed by or associated with the subject. It is an essential part of a sentence without which a formal sentence is not possible. It can be said that action is the centre of human existence. Each moment of our existence can be associated with some actions. All the actions like eating, sleeping, resting, dancing, breathing, etc. are actions whether static or dynamic.

For example, in the sentence, he sleeps, 'sleep' is a verb indicating the state of action. All the actions are described in terms of time—present, past and future. Hence, a verb gives the idea of time when the action is performed.

Look at these sentences.

Ankit *is* going. (Present)

Ankit *was* going. (Past)

Ankit *will be* going. (Future)

The difference in meaning of these sentences is realized through *verbs* only that indicate different times of action—present, past and future. Broadly speaking, language is basically used to express actions associated with human and non-human existence, and verbs indicate the state of these actions.

The Constituents of a Verb

A verb occurs in a sentence in the form of one word or a group of words. Look at these sentences in which *italicized* part indicates verb.

(a) I *go*. (one-word verb)

(b) She *has gone*. (two-word verb)

(c) They might *have gone*. (three-word verb)

(d) He *would have been going*. (four-word verb)

Here, we will look at the role that each part of a verb plays in a sentence. Actually, the attributes of an action may be multi-faceted, i.e. an action may have different kinds of features. For example, in the sentence (b) perfective aspect (has gone) is there, while in (c) modal (might) as well as perfective aspect is given. So the verb of sentence (c) has two features modal (possibility) and perfective, whereas the verb of sentence (b) has one feature 'perfective'. Likewise, we see that each part of a verb adds to its feature in one way or the other. All the features that can be attached to a verb may be shown through this diagram.

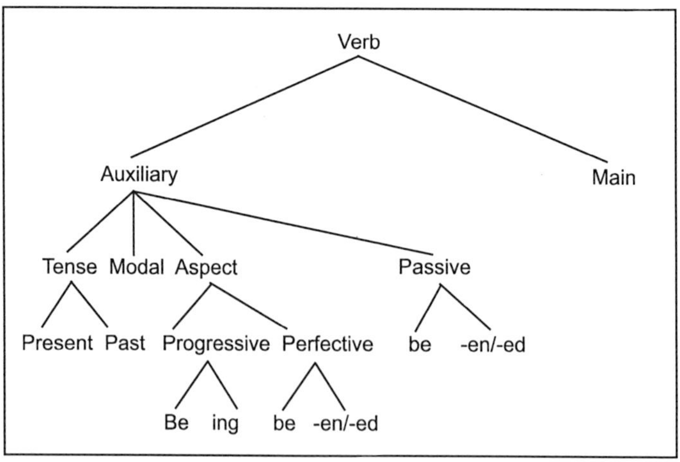

Here, we have assumed that a verb is always a combination of an auxiliary and main. An auxiliary verb talks about all the features shown in the diagram. A main verb basically presents the meaning feature which is modified by the attributes of auxiliary. It is meaning feature through which we differentiate between 'eat' and 'walk' as two separate verbs. Further, a verb has tense as an inseparable part, i.e. there can be no verb without tense and this tense as a feature is expressed through auxiliary only. Look at these sentences.

He is playing. (Present)

He was playing. (Past)

He has eaten. (Present)

He had eaten. (Past)

We know about the tense through auxiliary only in these sentences. Hence, it is reasonable to say that 'tense' feature is realized in a verb through auxiliary only. This auxiliary may remain hidden in some cases but it always exists. **Modal** as a feature expresses possibility or obligation as an auxiliary. The verbs like can, may, shall, will, might, could, etc. are modals. It will be talked about under the heading modal auxiliary verbs. **Aspect** refers to two features—whether a work is going on (progressive) or it has been completed (perfective). **Passive** refers to that feature of an action through which an object takes the central position compared to a subject. Let us analyse some verbs in the light of features given in the diagram.

(a)

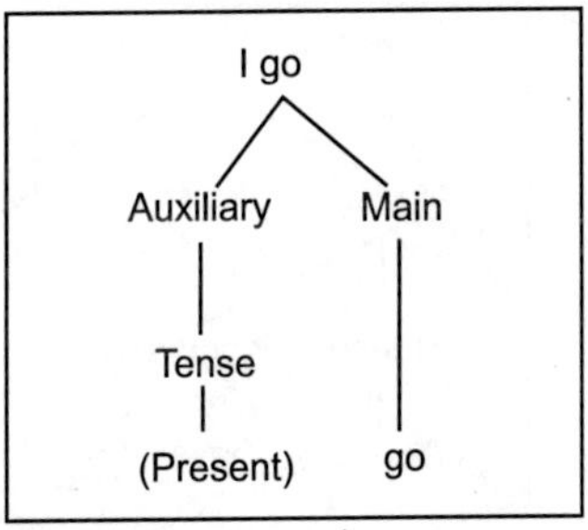

(b)

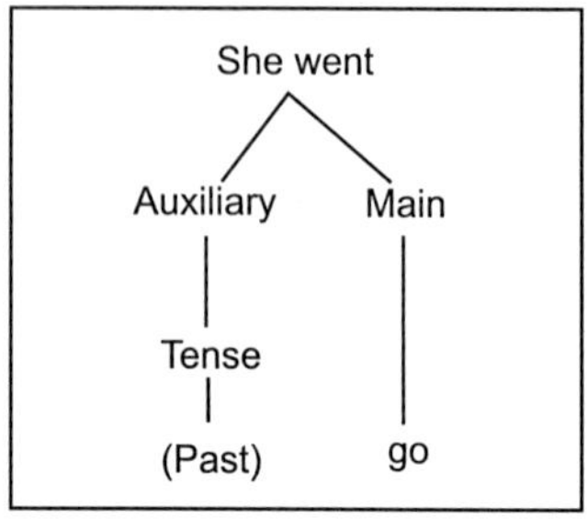
She went
Auxiliary
Main
Tense
(Past)
go

(c)

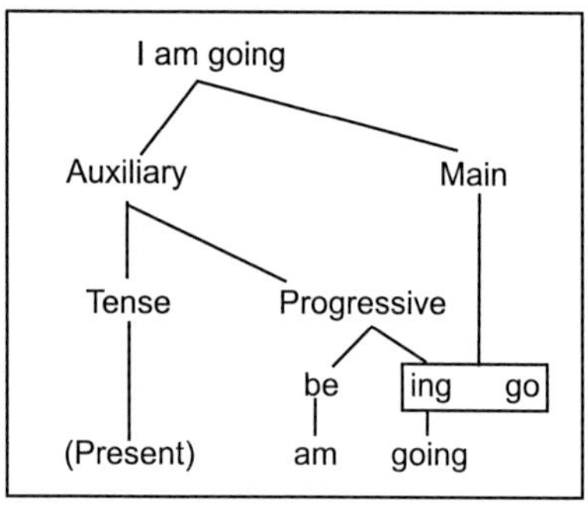
I am going
Auxiliary
Main
Tense
Progressive
be
ing
go
(Present)
am
going

(d)

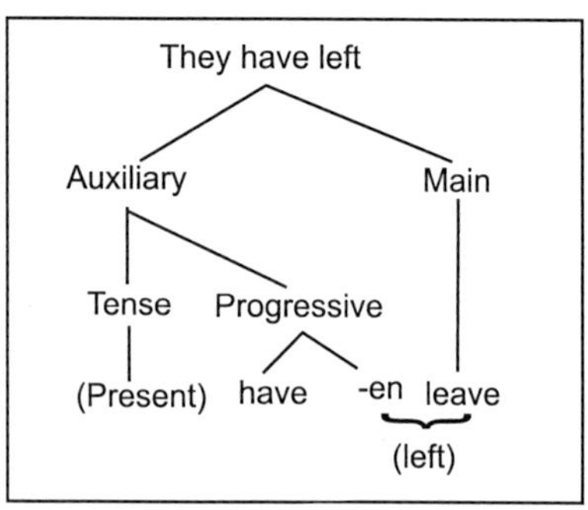
They have left
Auxiliary
Main
Tense
Progressive
(Present)
have
-en
leave
(left)

(e)

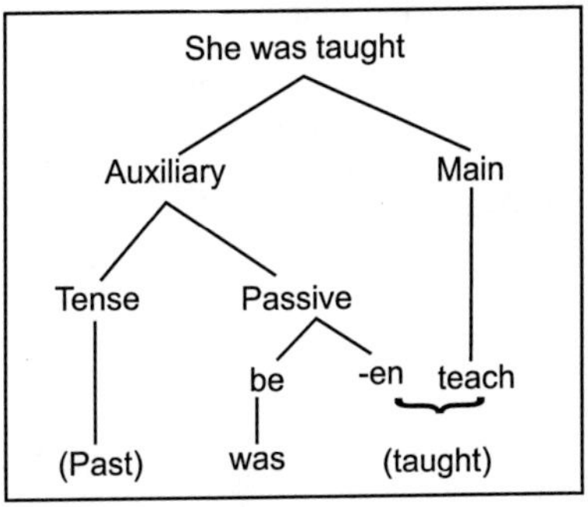

(f)

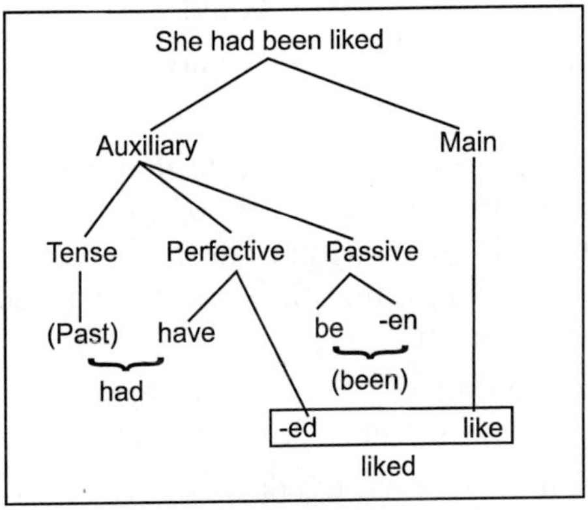

(g)

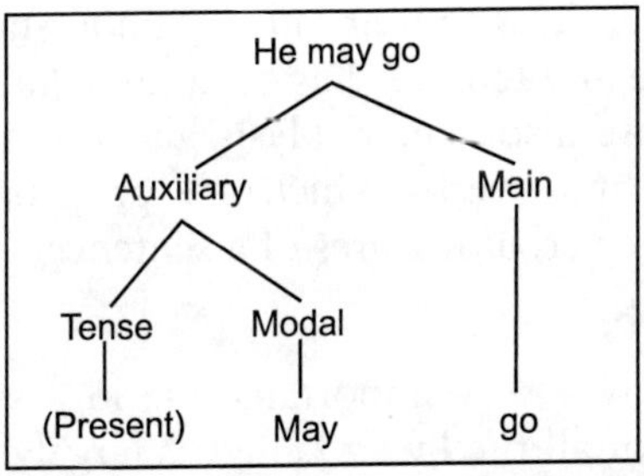

Thus, we see that a verb has got many constituents and each constituent adds to its feature. It is important to clarify further that there are only two forms of tense—Present and Past in English. Look at these.

Present		Past
is	be	was
am		were
are		
have		
has		had
do		
does		did
may		might
can		could
will		would
shall		should

These examples clearly indicate that verbs have two tenses only. Time may be present, past or future. But tense has got two kinds only that is present and past. There may be sentences indicating future time and present tense or past time and present tense, etc.

He is going to England tomorrow.
(time future, tense present)

He may have left ten days back.
(time past, tense present)

Therefore, it is important to understand the difference between time and tense. It has been talked about in the chapter time and tense also. The analysis given above is applicable in the case of finite verbs which are principally accounted for describing the verbal features of a sentence.

Types of Verbs

Verbs play a very important role in a sentence. We know that the life of all the living beings is largely described in terms of the actions. The identity of any living form is established in this universe in accordance with the action that it performs. It would not be an overemphasis to say that life is action and vice-versa. Since any action is described with the help of verb, a wide range of features is attached to it. Because of this multi-faceted dimension of verbs in general, we have many classifications based on different parameters. Here we will talk about these classifications.

Auxiliary and Main

This classification of verbs is based on meaning feature primarily. A main verb is usually a content word that gives the main idea of an action, whereas an auxiliary verb gives additional information about the main verb. An auxiliary verb contains attributes that add to the meaning of a main verb. Look at these sentences.

Ahmed is sleeping.

Abdul is crying.

She is laughing.

Here we see that auxiliary verb 'is' is the same in all the sentences but main verbs 'sleeping', 'crying', and 'laughing' are different from one another, and this difference in the meanings of the main verbs causes the difference among these verbs. Thus, the identity of a verb is established by the main verbs. The features like tense, aspect, passive and modal are attached to main verbs by auxiliaries that we have seen under the heading 'constituents of a verb'.

Now let us talk about the forms of auxiliary and main verbs.

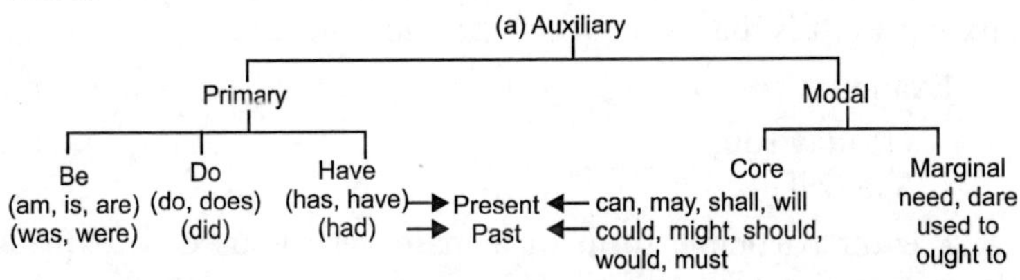

Primary auxiliary verbs are those which are used to express emphasis, aspect, passivity, etc. They are called primary because they are used in majority of the contexts both as main verbs and auxiliary verbs in English language.

Examples:

He does play. (emphasis)
He is playing. (aspect)
He is taught. (passive)

Modal auxiliary expresses possibility, obligation, permission, ability, etc.

He may go. (possibility)
He must go. (obligation)
He can go. (permission)
He can lift this box. (ability)

Some modals are called marginal modals because they have some characteristics other than that of modals. For example, 'used' and 'ought' are used with 'to' as a particle unlike other core modals which are used without a particle. Likewise, 'need' and 'dare' show the features of modal only in negative and interrogative sentences. Moreover, 'need' and 'dare' are used as main verbs also unlike core modals.

He need not go there. (modal auxiliary)
He may need a pen. (main verb)
I dare not do so. (modal auxiliary)
I may dare for it. (main verb)

(b) Main Verb

non-finite form | present participle form | past participle form

Non-finite form of a main verb usually comes after modal auxiliaries. It is that form which has no inflection.

Examples:

He may run.
She will go.

Present participle form of a main verb is used to express the progressive aspect of an action.

Examples:

He is going.
I am teaching.

Past participle form of a main verb is used to express the perfective aspect and passivity of an action.

Examples:

He is beaten. (passive)
She has gone. (perfective aspect)

Finite and Non-finite Verbs

This classification of verbs is based on the relationship between subjects and verbs in sentences.

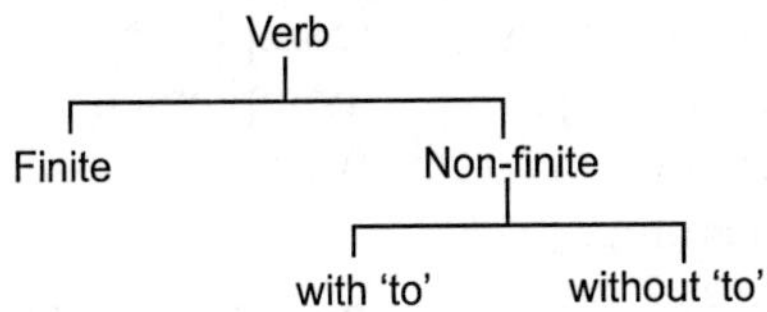

Finite verbs are those which are controlled by the subjects in a sentence.

He writes a book.
They are reading.
I am tired.

In all these sentences, the verbs 'write', 'are' and 'am' have come to indicate the agreement with the subjects. These verbs have been conditioned by the subjects and so, they are called finite verbs.

Non-finite verbs, on the other hand, are not controlled by the subject of the sentence. They are of two kinds. Some of them are used with 'to' in which 'to' is a part of this verb, not a preposition, while some are used without 'to' also. Look at these sentences.

He wants to go now. (with 'to')
They have decided to visit Tripoli. (with 'to')
I saw him leave the house. (without 'to')
I made him laugh loudly. (without 'to')

Because of the lack of control of subjects over the non-finite verbs, they are used as non-verbal forms (subject, object, complement, etc.) also in different sentences.

To study is not easy. (subject)
He is to leave. (complement)

Linking, Transitive, Intransitive

This classification is based on structural pattern of English sentences. Depending on the grammatical nature of words that follow a verb, we have these three kinds of verbs.

A **linking verb** is that which is followed by a complement. That means a linking verb requires something after it to complete the meaning of a sentence. All the underlined verbs are linking verbs in these sentences.

He is a teacher.	(complement)
She became nervous.	(complement)
They remain busy.	(complement)

We see that such verb always need a complement for the realization of meaning.

A **transitive verb** is that which is followed by an object. This verb shows the transfer of action from the subject to the object. Look at these underlined verbs which are transitive.

She plays chess.	(object)
They drink milk.	(object)
She beats her sister.	(object)

In all these sentences, we find that the transfer of action takes place from the subject to the object. Depending on the nature of words that come after a transitive verb, we have three kinds of it.

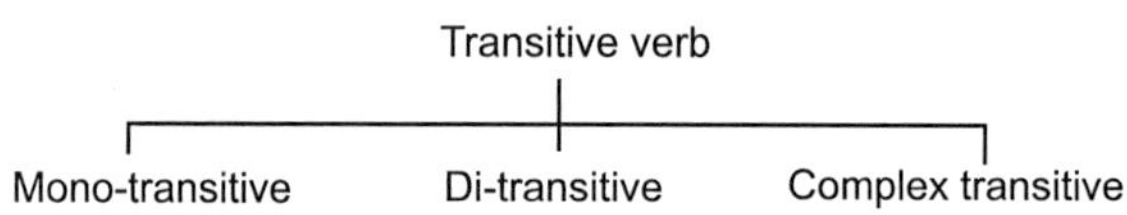

A mono-transitive verb is that which takes one object after it. A di-transitive verb is that which takes two objects after it. A complex transitive verb is that which takes an object followed by a complement. Look at these sentences.

Ali bought a pen.

(mono-transitive)

She	gave	a pen	to me.
	(di-transitive)	(object direct)	(object indirect)

They made him captain.
(complex transitive) (object) (complement)

An **intransitive verb** is that verb which neither takes an object nor a complement after it. No transfer of action takes place in the case of intransitive verbs. An action remains confined to the subject only. Look at these transitive verbs which are underlined.

She laughs.

Ali sleeps.

In these verbs, only subject is affected by the action.

Here, it is important to note that the same verb may be treated as linking or transitive or intransitive, depending on the structure and meaning of a sentence.

He	turned (linking)	red. (complement)
He	turned (transitive)	the table. (object)
He	turned (intransitive)	himself.

In these sentences, the verb 'turn' has been shown as belonging to all the three classes depending on the structure and meaning of the given sentences. But it does not mean that all the verbal words have got this characteristic.

Phrasal, Prepositional and Phrasal-Prepositional Verb

This classification of verbs is based on the nature of particle attached to a verb. A verb may have an adverb or a preposition or an adverb as well as preposition attached to it. Hence, we have three kinds of verbs according to this parameter.

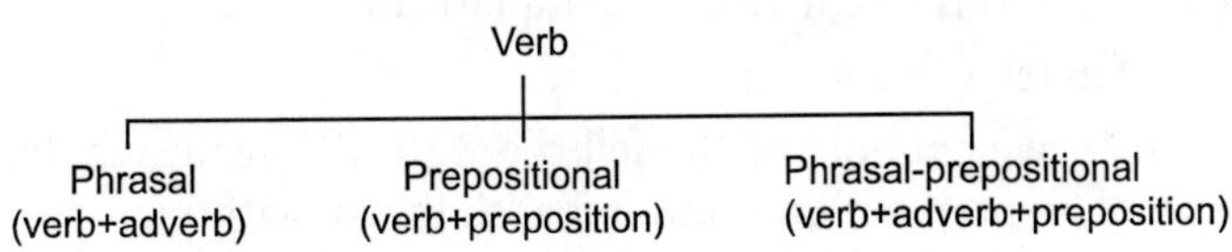

A **phrasal verb** is that which has got an adverb attached to it.

He switched off the fan.
They went up.
I moved on.

Here, all the underlined particles are adverbs and so, the verbs are phrasal verbs.

A **prepositional verb** is that which has got a preposition attached to it.

He fell off the wall.
They looked into the matter.
Everyone runs after money.

All the underlined particles are prepositions and verbs are prepositional.

A **phrasal-prepositional** verb is that which has got an adverb and preposition attached to it.

They looked down upon him.
Ahmed went up to the college.
Sana came out of her house.

All the underlined particles are a combination of 'adverb + preposition' and the verbs are phrasal-prepositional.

Now it is important to know how to differentiate between an adverb and a preposition. It must be kept in mind that an adverb may be removed from its place without changing the meaning, whereas it is not possible in the case of preposition. Look at these sentences.

I switched off the fan.
I switched it off.

Here, the replacement of adverb doesn't change the meaning, and the sentence is grammatically correct.

He fell off the wall.

Here, we cannot say 'he fell the wall off'. It means that the place of a preposition cannot be changed without damaging the grammaticality and meaning of a sentence.

Uses of Some Modal Auxiliaries:

(a) *Can, Could, May, Might*

Though 'can' and 'may' are used interchangeably to express possibility, permission, ability, etc., there is a difference between the two. Look at these sentences.

I can do that work.
I may do that work.

The first sentence shows a high degree of confidence of the doer. In the case of seeking permission 'may' is used.

May I go out?

'May' is used to show something about which you are not sure to a great extent. In seeking permission, you don't know whether you will be given permission or not. We use—'It may rain' as we can't speak with a very high degree of confidence about the occurrence of *rain*.

'May' and 'can' are the present forms and 'might' and 'could' are their past forms. 'Might' is used to express much politeness or in formal context, even for describing present situations.

Might I come in, sir?
Might I know what will happen next?

'Could' is usually used to express past form of 'can'.

He could do that work last year.
I could go there after he permitted me.

'Might' is also used as past form of 'may'.
He said that he might see the exhibition.

In modern English, the difference between 'may' and 'can', 'might' and 'could' has largely been bridged, but we should be careful in their uses.

(b) *Should, Must, Ought*

'Should' and 'ought' have almost the same implication of their use. But 'must' expresses something of obligatory nature, that can't be avoided.

He should go to college in time.
He ought to go to college in time.

He must go to college in time.
She should take medicine regularly.
She ought to take medicine regularly.
She must take medicine regularly.

The difference between should and must lies in the degree of emphasis. 'Must' is an emphasized form of 'should'. The second sentence given above gives much emphasis on going to college in time compared to the first sentence, and so is the case between third and forth sentence. Moreover, 'should' is generally used in casual contexts, while 'must' indicates of formal contexts.

As regards 'ought', it is used in the cases where moral obligation is realized.

For example,

We ought to respect our elders.
They ought to serve their ailing mother.
I ought not to do that sinful work.

Uses of Non-finite Forms of Verb

Non-finite forms of verb function in different ways also in sentences. It means '*verb + ing*' '*to + verb*' and '*verb + ed/en*' function as other grammatical categories also, like subject, noun, adjective, etc.

Look at these examples.

Laughing is a good exercise.	(noun)
To study is to gain knowledge.	(subject)
Flying birds look beautiful.	(adjective)
Broken chairs are useless.	(adjective)
Fractured bones are usually weak.	(adjective)

In all these sentences, the underlined words are not verbs but they have been derived from verbal forms, that is to say, the source of their words has been verbs like laugh, study, fly, break and fracture. These non-finite forms participate in sentences in different forms and hence they are called participles. These participles are realized in three forms.

Participle

- Present participle (verb + ing)
- Past participle (verb + -ed/-en)
- Perfective participle (having + verb + -ed/-en)

When a present participle is used as a noun, it is called gerund. These participles function as clauses also.

Looking at the picture, he fell down.
(subordinate clause)

Having played chess, I left for college.
(subordinate clause)

Taken the things for granted, he invited trouble for himself.
(sub-ordinate clause)

Present and past participles are frequently used as adjectives.

Look at these noun phrases.

(present participle)	(past participle)
rising star	born idle
shining glass	defeated team
rolling stone	tortured soul
running dog	pampered boy

Thus, we see that there are diverse uses of non-finite forms of verbs. It is reasonable to say that because of wide range of uses, the name non-finite gets its justification as a grammatical concept.

EXERCISE-1

Identify whether the following verbs are linking, transitive or intransitive.

1. He plays tennis.
2. He became mad.
3. They got annoyed.
4. It weighs five kilograms.
5. Alok weighed that iron bar.
6. He sleeps late at night.

7. She became mad.
8. We are running in the field.
9. Boys are naughty.
10. Ankit wrote two books.
11. Niraj likes games.
12. My father lives in India.
13. Samir has left for England.
14. We sing a song.
15. They like swimming.
16. I got angry.

EXERCISE-2

Identify finite and non-finite verbs in these sentences.

1. They like to live in Delhi.
2. I want to go to Varanasi.
3. She has decided to get married.
4. Considering the problem challenging, Amit decided to leave it.
5. Though he is young, he gets tired soon.
6. The way she does her work, is not justified at all.
7. They decided to leave the country on the first of August.
8. Walking on the road, he saw a snake.
9. Suraj likes to eat sweets.
10. She came to meet me.
11. Having done this work, I left home.

EXERCISE–3

Identify phrasal verb, prepositional verb and phrasal-prepositional verb in the following sentences.

1. They got off the bus.
2. She has been brought up by him.
3. Aniket blew up the horn suddenly.

4. She went up the stairs.
5. Abhishek looked for a cup of tea.
6. Salma came in her car.
7. They ran out of fear.
8. His car broke down there.
9. I took off my hat.
10. They pushed up their neighbour.
11. The criminals blew up the bridge.

EXERCISE-4

Fill up the blanks with the most suitable modal auxiliary verb given in the bracket.

(ought, can, need, may, could, will, would, shall, should, must)

1. ---------------- I go to Kanpur?
2. ---------------- I come in, sir?
3. It ----------------rain heavily today.
4. You ------------ love your country.
5. She ------------- succeed only last year.
6. They ------------- to serve the poor and helpless.
7. He -------------- not go there soon.
8. Arjun ---------------- not do that sinful act.
9. You ------------ respect your elders.
10. When I was young I ------------ run a mile at a stretch.
11. ---------------- you speak English?
12. You ------------- go know?
13. If I were you, I -------------- give him a good retort.
14. She -------------- go to market tomorrow.
15. We --------------- not to insult others.

EXERCISE-5

Draw the tree diagrams showing the constituents of these underlined verbs.

1. She may have gone.
2. His father is running for help.
3. Mr. James has troubled foreign teachers.
4. They would have returned.
5. I would have been staying there.
6. She will be taken to hospital.
7. A cow eats grass.
8. Naseer must have helped him.
9. He did his best.
10. We should have decided for it.

EXERCISE 6

1. What do you mean by a verb?
2. Show the difference between these terms.
   (i) Finite and non-finite verbs
   (ii) Auxiliary and main verb
   (iii) Prepositional and phrasal verb
   (iv) Transitive and intransitive verb.
3. What do you mean by marginal modal auxiliaries? Why are they called so?
4. What do you mean by participles? What are its kinds? Give examples of each.
5. What do you mean by the constituents of a verb? What are these constituents?

5

Adverb

What in an Adverb?

An adverb modifies a verb, an adjective, a phrase, a clause, a sentence and another adverb as well.

Examples

Read attentively.	modifying a *verb*
It is very cold.	modifying an *adjective*
She speaks English fairly well.	modifying an *adverb*
Almost all the students are present.	modifying a *noun phrase*
You are just in time.	modifying a *prepositional phrase*
I found the mobile *where* I had left it.	modifying a *clause*
Actually, I don't want to smoke.	modifying a *sentence*

Words or phrases used as adverbs usually answer the questions *when, where, how, how often,* etc. in relation to time, place, manner, reason, frequency, degree, etc. They are used to give various kinds of meaning.

Examples	Types
She walks *slowly*.	Manner
I shall go *tomorrow*.	Time
Your pen is *here*.	Place
We *always* watch TV.	Frequency
Ali is *very* intelligent.	Degree
Surely, I will do it.	Certainty
She has left this place *temporarily*.	Duration
He didn't help me. *On the contrary*,	

he opposed me.	Contrast
Move fast *otherwise* you will be late for school.	Condition
This girl is just sixteen and *therefore* her marriage is not legal.	Reason

Kinds of Adverb

(1) Adverbs of Manner

Well, badly, quickly, slowly, carefully, clearly, foolishly, quietly, fast, etc.

These adverbs refer to *how* something happens.

How is he speaking?	He is speaking clearly.
How does she behave?	She behaves rudely.

(2) Adverbs of Place/Position/Direction

Here, there, somewhere, upstairs, away, out, under, up, above, below, left, right, near, behind, etc.

These adverbs refer to *where* something happens.

Where is my mobile?	It is here.
Where is your mother?	She is upstairs.

(3) Adverbs of Time

Now, ago, yesterday, today, tomorrow, early, late, after, before, since, yet, still, soon, etc.

These adverbs express *when* something happens.

When do you get up?	I get up early.
When did you buy a car?	I bought it yesterday.

(4) Adverbs of Frequency (Number)

Once, twice, occasionally, daily, often, always, never, usually, frequently, monthly, yearly, etc.

These adverbs refer to *how often* something happens.

How often do you go to market?	I go to market daily.
How many times does she pray?	She prays twice a day.

(5) Adverbs of Degree (Intensifiers)

Very, too, quite, almost, nearly, entirely, fairly, enough, just, much, of course, utterly, etc.

These adverbs refer to *how much* or *to what extent* something happens.

How much clever is he?	He is very clever.
To what extent is it true?	It is quite true.

(6) Relative Adverbs

When, where, why, whenever, wherever, etc.

These adverbs refer to a noun (antecedent) in the main clause like relative pronoun and join clauses. They function as adverbs as well as conjunctions.

That is the place *where* I live.

Do you know the exact time *when* the match will start?

Give me one reason *why* you did that.

Here, *"where"*, *"when"* and *"why"* refer back to their antecedent *place, time* and *reason* just like relative pronouns.

But they function as relative adverbs because they modify the verb *live, start* and *did* in the relative clause. Here, modification is quite adverbial related to *place, time* and *reason.*

(7) Interrogative Adverbs

Where, when, why , how, how many, how often, etc.

These adverbs are used to ask questions.

Where are you going?

Why are students making a noise in the class?

When will you come?

(8) Adverbs of Affirmation and Negation

Yes, no, yeah, etc.

These adverbs express one's affirmative or negative response to a question.

Do you know English? *Yes*, I do.

No, I don't.

Is he a teacher? *Yes*, he is.

No, he isn't.

Note: '*yes*' or '*yeah*' (colloquial) is always used with positive statement and '*No*' with negative statement.

Though '*Not*' is a negative adverb, it can't replace '*No*' as an adverb of negation.

Is he smart? *No,* he isn't.

"*Not*, he isn't" is always a wrong expression.

(9) Exclamatory Adverbs

How, What, etc.

These adverbs express the degree or extent of exclamation.

How ugly she is!

What an idiot you are!

'*What*' also expresses the sense of exclamation in the form of a question.

Ali's dog is so strong that it can kill a sheep. *What?*

(10) Sentence Adverbs

Obviously, frankly, fortunately, certainly, etc.

These adverbs modify the whole sentence.

Luckily, I had a narrow escape.

Fortunately, I could get a good job.

Sentence adverbs convey the speaker's comment or attitude, viewpoint or opinion. They are placed at the beginning of a sentence.

(11) Linking Adverbs/Connectives

Moreover, consequently, on the contrary, therefore, besides, on the other hand, otherwise, etc.

These adverbs link and relate clauses and sentences to one another and express the ideas of similarity, contrast, cause, condition, etc.

Salma is quite competent; *moreover*, she speaks better English.

He didn't support me, *on the contrary*, he opposed me.

Note: Connective adverbs are both adverbs and conjunctions at the same time. As adverbs they modify the clauses that come after them or the verbs in those clauses.

Formation of Adverbs

1. Most of the adverbs of manner and some adverbs of degree and frequency are formed by adding 'ly' to adjectives.

Adjective	Adverb	Adjective	Adverb
active	actively	fair	fairly
easy	easily	frequent	frequently
extreme	extremely	happy	happily
immediate	immediately	slow	slowly
immense	immensely	usual	usually

2. Some adverbs ending in '-ly' are formed with nouns and they are used both as adjectives and adverbs.

hour	hourly	body	bodily
month	monthly	day	daily
year	yearly	leisure	leisurely
coward	cowardly		

What is your <u>monthly</u> income? (Adjective)

I go to Egypt <u>monthly</u>. (Adverb)

3. Certain adverbs ending in -ly have no adverb forms such as lovely, brotherly, friendly, motherly, sisterly, fatherly, gentlemanly, manly, womanly, likely, godly, lowly, partly, elderly, seemly, etc.

4. Some words function both as adjectives and adverbs in the same form.

High, far, tight, early, late, much, little, direct, fast, near, wrong, kindly, enough, pretty, right, etc.

Adjective	Adverb
He is a *late* riser.	He gets up *late*.
She is a *hard* worker.	She works *hard*.
It is a *straight* road.	It goes *straight* to the bank.

It is a *high* wall.	Birds are flying *high*.
She gave a *kindly* look.	*Kindly* leave me alone.

5. Some adverbs are formed by adding (prefix) 'a' with nouns and adjectives.

ashore	aboard	anew	afoot
aloft	ahead	along	away
aflame	aloud	afloat	asleep

6. Some adverbs are formed by adding (prefix) 'be' or prepositions with nouns, adjectives and adverbs as well.

Below, betimes, today, tomorrow, behind, without, before, within, overboard, wherein, hereafter, etc.

Note: '*Be*' is the old form of preposition '*By*'.

7. Some adverb phrases are joined by conjunction 'and'.

now and again	by and by
again and again	far and away
out and out	far and wide
now and then	far and near
over and over	

8. Some adverb phrases are formed by placing a preposition before a noun.

at length, of course, in fact, at random.

9. Some compound adverbs are formed by joining an adjective and a noun.

Sometimes, meanwhile, yesterday, otherwise, midway, etc.

10. Some adverbs are formed by adding the following 'Suffixes'.

-wise	-ways	-ward	-fashion	-style
Clockwise	sideways	backward	schoolboy-fashion	Indian style

Position of Adverbs

Adverbs don't have fixed position like subject and verb. They may take initial, medial or final position in a sentence.

(i) *Initial Position Adverbs*

(a) Interrogative adverbs take the initial position.

Where are they going?

Why did she do that?

(b) Adverbs of affirmation or negation take the initial position.

Yes, you are right.

No, it is not correct.

(c) Sentence adverbs come in the initial position.

Obviously, his remarks didn't have proof.

(d) The adverbs used in the exclamatory sentences always have initial position.

Away they went!

Here comes the bus!

There goes Salma!

(e) Adverbs or adverb phrases take initial position to emphasize a statement. In such cases, the subject comes after the verb.

hardly, scarcely, not only, nowhere, only, nor, rarely, seldom, before, never, neither, etc.

Never is he late.

Hardly had he reached the airport when the plane took off.

(f) The following adverbs and adverb phrases may take initial position.

evidently, certainly, however, first, originally, now, fortunately, surely, how far/much/long/often, at first/last/present/least, later on, sooner or later, perhaps, etc.

(ii) *Medial Position Adverbs*

(a) Adverbs of frequency usually take medial position before the main verb.

Always, never, often, almost, hardly, just, already, still, frequently, etc.

I *always* get up early.
I *almost* forgot to inform you.

These adverbs are placed after the auxiliary verb but before the main verb.

He will *always* come in time.

You should *never* tell a lie.

(b) An adverb can be placed before the preposition in a sentence.

I looked *angrily* at him.

(c) An adverb may also be placed before the main verb for the sake of emphasis.

He *briefly* narrated the whole story.

(d) Adverbial particles such as up, down, out, off, away, back, in, on, etc. are placed before an object that functions as a noun phrase.

Sub	verb	adverbial particle	noun phrase
He	threw	*away*	all the old books.
She	took	*off*	the new shoes.

(e) Adverbs of degree are placed before the adverb, adjective and verb also.

She is *almost* crazy.
He drives very *fast*.
I have *already* done it.

(f) We often place an adverb before a negative auxiliary verb.

She *certainly* wasn't very good today.

(iii) *Final Position Adverbs*

(a) Adverbs of manner, place and time usually come at the end of a sentence.

It is raining *heavily*.

Put the book *here*.

I met him *yesterday*.

But we can place the adverb of time at the beginning of a sentence for the sake of emphasis.

Last night I visited a film.

Yesterday we came here.

(b) If there are two or more adverbs of time, the more detailed expression goes before the more general.

I will meet you at 2 o'clock tomorrow.

I was born at 4 o'clock in the morning on Tuesday in 1960.

(c) If there are several kinds of adverbs, the preferential order is generally adverbs of manner + place + time.

Salma worked well here yesterday.

(d) An adverbial particle always takes final position if the object is a pronoun.

Lift it up.

She let me in.

Note: An adverbial particle may take medial or final position in a noun phrase.

Take the shoes off.

Take off the shoes.

(e) In a "*Sub + verb + obj*" structure the adverb is placed in the final position.

She is eating bread slowly.

He explained the case clearly.

Adverbs as Adverbials

What is an adverbial?

An adverbial may be a single word adverb, a noun phrase, a prepositional phrase or a clause.

Salma works *hard.*	adverb
We visited Bengal *last year.*	noun phrase
Students sit *at the desk*.	prepositional phrase
We walk *before we take tea*.	clause

Kinds of Adverbial

There are three kinds of Adverbial.

(i) Adjunct – An adjunct is integrated within the structure of the sentence. It usually takes medial or final position in a sentence.

I can *now* understand the point.

She is waiting *inside*.

(ii) Disjunct – A disjunct is used to express one's comment or viewpoint. It usually takes initial position.

Fortunately, he won the election by a narrow margin of votes.

(iii) Conjunct – A conjunct functions as a connective. It usually takes medial position.

My father gave me money, *otherwise* I couldn't have gone abroad.

Note: Adverbial is always an optional constituent in a sentence. It is used to give some additional information.

Comparison of Adverbs

Adverbs have three degrees of comparison like adjectives.

(i) Positive Degree Adverb

They compare two persons or things to an equal degree.

Structure— (a) as + adverb + as (Positive statement)

(b) negative + as + adverb + as

Ali runs as fast as Ahmed.

A bird can't fly as high as a plane.

(ii) Comparative Degree Adverb

They compare two persons or things of an unequal degree.

Structure: (a) comparative form + than

(b) of the two + comparative form

(c) the + comparative ..... the + comparative

Examples: Ali runs faster than Ahmed.

Of the two teachers Samir behaves more politely.

The more you read; the more you learn.

Structure (c) is used to express parallel increase or decrease.

(iii) Superlative Degree Adverb

They compare three or more persons or things to an unequal degree.

Structure: (a) Superlative form + of all.

(b) most + adverb

Examples: Ali runs faster of all.

Salma behaves most rudely.

Here, 'most' is used in the sense of 'very'. Omission of 'the' before superlative degree has become the current trend. But 'the' before it is also a correct expression.

Formation of comparative and superlative.

(i) Generally, one syllabic adverb adds '-er' in comparative and '-est' in superlative degree of adverbs.

Positive	Comparative	Superlative
Adverbs of manner		
Fast	faster	fastest
Hard	harder	hardest
Adverbs of Time		
early	earlier	earliest
late	later	latest
often	oftener	oftenest
soon	sooner	soonest
Adverbs of distance or direction		
high	higher	highest
near	nearer	nearest

Note: 'Early' and 'often' are two syllabic words but they take *'-er'* and *'-est'* in comparative and superlative degree.

(ii) Adverbs ending in '-ly' form the comparative by adding *'more'* or *'less'* and the superlative by adding *'most'* or *'least'*.

Brightly	more/less brightly	most/least brightly
Effectively	more/less effectively	most/least effectively

(iii) Some irregular comparisons of adverbs

good/well	better	best
little	less	least
much	more	most
badly	worse	worst
far	farther	farthest (distance)
far	farther	farthest (time/distance)

(iv) Most adverbs don't have degrees of comparison.

Very, once, here, yes, where, ago, now, there, too, almost, etc.

(v) Adverbs ('in', 'out' and 'up') are used only as adjectives in comparative and superlative degrees.

in	inner	innermost
out	outer	outermost
up	upper	uppermost

Notes on some commonly used adverbs

(a) *ago/long ago/back/far back*

These adverbs are always used with past simple tense.

He came here one year *ago/back*.

Ali met me *long ago/far back*.

(b) *before*

It is used with past simple as well as present perfect tense.

I never met the president *before*.

I have visited Leptis Magna *before*.

(c) (i) *Just/so far/already/yet/uptil now/since/till now/even now* usually take present perfect tense.

I haven't met him *since then*.

I have written one book *so far*.

He has *just* gone out.

I have *already* finished my lunch.

I haven't received the cheque *till now/even now*.

Has the plane landed *yet*?

He hasn't finished the work *yet.*

Note: '*yet*' is mainly used in negative statement and question.

(ii) '*Just/yet/already*' refers to present time as well.

I am *just* to go.

It is *just* 8 o'clock.

It is 4 o'clock *already.*

She has *yet* to go a long way.

(iii) *Just* is also used in the sense of *only/barely/exactly*

She *just* approached me to get a job.

I was there *just* to meet Shahban.

This is *just* what I wanted to say.

(d) *Firstly (first), secondly, thirdly, fourthly, lastly, finally.*

These adverbs are used to express a list of reasons or arguments.

They can also be replaced by *one, two, three* and *four* especially in technical references.

Examples:

The cabinet took three major decisions in its meeting.

First, it enhanced the salary of teachers.

Secondly, it passed a bill to clear the arrears.

Thirdly, it decided to appoint new teachers.

Note: '*First*' is both an adjective and an adverb.

But as an adverb, firstly is preferred.

(e) *Too*

(i) It is used in the sense of '*in addition to*', '*as well*' and '*also*' in affirmative sentences.

He ate chicken and fish, too.

He ate chicken and fish also.

He ate chicken and fish as well.

(ii) It is used to express excess of a quality (more than enough) in a negative sense.

Structure: too + adj + adv + infinitive.

He is too weak to walk.

(He is so weak that he can't walk).

The weather is too cold.

(The weather is colder than *it should be/it is proper*)

(f) *Much/very*

Much and *very* are always used before adjectives and adverbs.

But the difference between the two lies in their use.

(i) '*Much*' qualifies comparative degree adj/adv.

Ali is *much* taller than Ahmed.

'*Very*' qualifies positive degree adj/adv.

She is *very* beautiful.

It is *very* hard.

But *very* is used before *much* in comparative degree adj/adv. He is *very much* taller than his wife.

(ii) '*Much*' is used as an adverb to qualify a past participial adjective and '*very*' a present participial adjective.

I am *much* worried today.

This book is *very* interesting.

But '*very*' is used before some past participial adjectives like *tired, pleased, surprised satisfied, bored, shocked, interested, disappointed, contented, excited, dejected,* etc.

(iii) Article '*the*' is placed before '*very*' and after '*much*' when it is used to qualify superlative degree adjective or adverb.

Ali is *the very* best boy in his class.

Salma is *much the* best girl in her class.

(iv) '*Much*' meaning 'a lot' modifies a verb, e.g.

She talks *much*.

She doesn't eat *much*.

He reads *much* but understands a little.

(g) *Enough*

Enough follows its adjective or adverb.

He walks fast *enough* to catch the taxi.

Ali is strong *enough* to lift this box.

Note: It is used in a positive sense.

(h) *Only/even/merely/simply/just*

These adverbs are placed immediately before the word they modify.

1. He can *only* dance (He can't do anything else).
2. It is *purely* imaginary.
3. I *merely* answered his question.
4. He didn't *even* talk to me.
5. I am *just* coming.

(i) *Fairly/Rather*

Fairly is mainly used with favourable adjectives or adverbs to express one's liking or approval.

Henna is *fairly* tall. (tall for her age)

'*Rather*' is used to express one's dislike or disapproval.

Sana is *rather* tall. (taller than her age)

(j) *Little/A little*

Little has a negative meaning. (not at all)

Little did I doubt that he would fail. (I didn't doubt)

A little has a positive meaning.

I feel *a little* disturbed today.

Note: '*the little*' is used only as an adjective.

I spent *the little* money that I had.

(k) *Quite*

It has basically two meanings.

(i) It means '*completely*' when it is used with non-gradable adjectives or with a very strong adjective or adverb like *fall, right, wrong, sure, empty, dead, perfect, amazing, horrible, surprising*, etc.

The cup is *quite* empty.

I am *quite* right.

(ii) It means '*moderately*' when it is used to modify an adjective in the sense of "*less than very but more than a little*".

She is *quite* famous. (less than very famous)

Note: '*quite*' always takes *a/an* (article) after it.

It is *quite a* funny story.

(l) *Not/No/None*

'*Not*' is always placed after auxiliary verb.

He is *not* here.

She is *not* learning English.

She ca*n't* speak English.

'*No*' in used before adjectives or adverbs to mean '*not*' after the main verb.

I am feeling *no* better today.

'*None*' is used with '*the*' before comparative adjectives to mean '*not at all*' after the main verb.

I am *none the* worse for the experience.

(m) *Never/Ever*

'*Never*' is mainly used before the affirmative main verbs or after the auxiliary verb to mean "*at no time.*"

I have *never* studied French (not, haven't ever)

'*Ever*' is used after a verb in a negative statement.

He hasn't *ever* seen the sea. (not, ever hasn't seen)

'*Ever*' means '*at any time*' when it is used in questions.

Have you *ever* seen the Taj Mahal?

'*Ever*' like '*never*' means '*at no time*' when it is used with a negative verb.

I haven't *ever* been to England.

(n) *Double Negative*

Hardly/scarcely/rarely/seldom/barely

These adverbs express almost negative meaning and always take *'any'* or *'ever'* in place of *'no'*, *'not'* and *'never'* to avoid double negative expressions.

I have *hardly* any book on Linguistics.

She *rarely* goes to school.

There was *barely* any smell.

We *scarcely* ever meet.

(o) *Double form adverbs*

A few words have two adverb forms. One form is like an adjective and the other form ends in '-ly'. But they have different meaning. Look at the difference.

(i) *Hard/Hardly*

'Hard' means 'with all force'

I have to work *hard*.

'Hardly' means 'almost not'

I hardly know him.

(ii) *Late/Lately*

'Late' means 'after the expected time.

I got up late today.

'Lately' means 'recently'

My new book will appear lately.

(iii) *Direct/Directly*

'Direct' means 'straight'

I went direct from the station to the wedding.

'Directly' means 'immediately after' or 'in a direct way.'

I'll phone you directly if I hear anything.

You are directly responsible for my termination.

(iv) *Short/Shortly*

'Short' means 'reduced' or 'not enough of anything.'

I cut short my holidays to see my ailing mother.

I am running short of money.

'Shortly' means 'soon' or 'in a little time.'

She came shortly after me.

(v) *Sharp/Sharply*

'Sharp' means 'exactly.'

Please come here at 9 o'clock sharp.

'Sharply' means 'quickly', 'suddenly' and 'loudly' also.

She moved sharply to close the window.

(vi) *Last/Lastly*

'Last' means 'at the end.'

He came last.

'Lastly' means 'finally'

Lastly, I would like to ask you a question.

(vii) *Free/Freely*

'Free' means 'without paying'.

Airline staff can fly free.

'Freely' means 'independently' or 'without control'.

Stray dogs move freely.

(viii) *Near/Nearly*

'Near' means 'close'.

The taxi station is quite near now.

'Nearly' means 'almost'.

I have nearly run out of bread.

(ix) *High/Highly*

'High' means 'above.'

Some birds fly high.

'Highly' means 'very'.

A cobra is a highly poisonous snake.

EXERCISE-1

Underline the given adverbs and name their class.

Ex: The little boy behaved badly. (Adverb of manner).

1. Omar speaks English well.

2. He travelled abroad.
3. Sign your name below.
4. He will be back soon.
5. I often have a cup of tea after dinner.
6. This lesson is very difficult.
7. How do you go to school?
8. I am not quite sure.
9. Yes, I do my homework daily.
10. That is the building where Ali lives.
11. Can you tell me the time when the president will come?
12. I have already done it.
13. She has gone out.
14. We rarely meet.
15. He is rich enough to maintain a car.
16. I am not going to market.
17. How sweetly she sings!
18. What a beautiful girl she is!
19. Fortunately, I got a good job.
20. He is intelligent; moreover, he works hard.

EXERCISE-2

Change the following sentences into one sentence using the structure (too + adj/adv + infinitive)

Example: My grandfather is very old. He can't travel.

My grandfather is too old to travel.

(i) I am very hungry. I can't work.
(ii) The box is very heavy. I can't lift it.
(iii) This paper is very dirty. I can't read it.
(iv) The milk is very sour. I can't drink it.
(v) The bulb is very high. I can't change it.
(vi) He is very poor. He can't buy a car.
(vii) The car was very expensive. I can't buy it.

(viii) Tea is very hot. I can't take it.

(ix) Ahmed is very short. He can't reach the shelf.

(x) I am very sleepy. I can't drive.

EXERCISE-3

Use the correct form of adverb given in brackets.

Example: She came (late) than we expected.

She came later than we expected.

1. He is coming (close) to me.
2. He works (hard) than anyone else.
3. Ali writes (correctly) than he used to.
4. I live (far) from the centre than you.
5. Could you please speak (slowly)?
6. Ali is (clever) of all.
7. Of all my sisters, Amal lives (close) to me.
8. She arrived (early) than I expected.
9. She danced (much) gracefully of all.
10. The higher you go. The (cold) it is.
11. Of the two boys, Ahmed behaves (much) politely.
12. The (early) we start; the sooner we will arrive.

EXERCISE-4

Put these sentences into the right order.

Example: Never he late for school is.

He is never late for school.

1. Before lunch the letter quickly read he.
2. The school missed bus Ali today.
3. Yesterday, a book I from the library borrowed.
4. My teacher listen to I carefully.
5. Blood is in colour always red.
6. Difficult too is this exercise to answer.
7. Water you will the orange trees tomorrow.
8. He go will tomorrow evening to London at 7 o'clock.

9. Built they in our city last year a new hospital.
10. The little boy an apple this morning ate quickly in the kitchen.
11. Saw I Ali yesterday morning at school.
12. At seven came he this morning.

EXERCISE-5

Correct these Sentences.

1. Send out him.
2. He didn't write to me since.
3. They come back in this morning.
4. She was not seen nowhere.
5. I go last never to college.
6. You have to back up him.
7. He let in me.
8. He has left this place far back.
9. Never he is late.
10. She hasn't hardly any gold.

EXERCISE-6

Use the right word given in brackets.

1. He ______ the truth. (always speaks/speaks always)
2. Has the plane landed _____? (yet/already)
3. When _______ coming? (are they/they are)
4. He is ______ to lift this box. (enough strong/strong enough)
5. She runs _______ of all. (faster/fastest)
6. ______ tell a lie. (seldom he does/seldom does he)
7. Why _____ happy today. (are you/you are)
8. I haven't _____ seen the sea. (ever/never)
9. She is _____ dancer. (a quite good/quite a good)
10. He passed the examination ____ (last year/next year)
11. This book is ____ interesting. (much/very)

12. Who came _____ in the race. (second/secondly)
13. I hit the ball _____. (hard/hardly)
14. Tendulkar was ____ bowled. (cleanly/clean)
15. She has _____ done the work. (just/yet/already)
16. When ____ go there? (will you/you will)
17. _____, I like fish. (yes/no)
18. The hall is ______ empty. (quite/very)
19. ______ it is my first mistake. (second/secondly)
20. He worked hard _____. (all night/on all night)

6

Preposition

What is a Preposition?

A preposition is a word usually placed before a noun (noun phrase) or a pronoun to show its relation with other words in a sentence.

Look at the sentences.

The peon is *at* the gate.

The bag is *on* the table.

The teacher is *in* the office.

Here prepositions *'at'*, *'on'* and *'in'* establish a relationship between *'the peon'* and *'the gate'*, *'the bag'* and *'the table'* and *'the teacher'* and *'the office'*. Thus, prepositions generally link two nouns or noun phrases.

The noun phrases (*the gate, the table* and *the office*) that have come after the prepositions *'at'*, *'on'* and *'in'* are called object of the prepositions or prepositional objects.

The whole phrase structure including the preposition (*at the gate, on the table* and *in the office*) is called a prepositional phrase.

Note: Prepositional phrases function mainly as a prepositional modifier, adverbial (modifying a verb) or as the complement of an adjective.

Examples:

(i) The dramas <u>of Shakespeare</u> are very popular. (post nominal modifier)

(ii) She played chess <u>during the leisure</u>. (Adverbial) (modifying the verb)

(iii) Omar is very fond <u>of macaroni.</u> (complement of an adjective)

Classification of Prepositions

Prepositions can be classified on the basis of form and function (meaning).

(A) *Formal Classification*

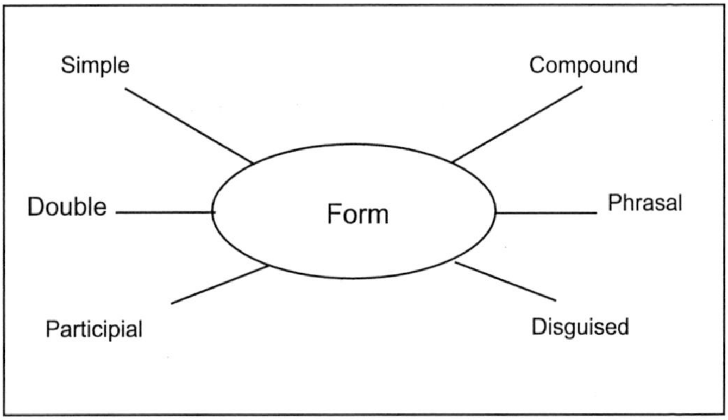

(i) *Simple prepositions* – at, in, to, on, up, with, out, over, under, through, down, off, opposite, till, since, for, from, etc.

He is sitting *under* a tree.

I have not seen him *since* Monday.

(ii) *Compound prepositions* – Prefixes are generally used to form compound prepositions.

inside, outside, below, beneath, beside, within, without, underneath, about, above, among, along, across, amidst, etc.

He is sitting *beside* me.

The bird is *inside* the cage.

(iii) *Double prepositions (preposition + preposition combinations)* from behind, down beside, down around, from within, from under, from inside, from beside, out of, from among, etc.

The snake crawled *from under* the table.

She walked *down around* the pond.

From behind the hut, a snake suddenly emerged.

(iv) *Phrasal prepositions*

on account of, with reference to, in the back of, in the light of, with the exception of, in favour of, in front of, in spite of, in place of, etc.

He didn't speak even a single sentence *in favour of* me.

There is a pond *in front of* my house.

(v) *Participial prepositions*

concerning	(about)
notwithstanding	(in spite of)
considering	(taking into account)
touching	(with regard to)
respecting	(concerning)
regarding	(concerning)
barring	(apart from)
pending	(while awaiting, until)

There is no news *regarding* our salary payment.

There are many rumours *concerning* her love-affairs.

Pending further orders, Omar will act as the Dean of Language Centre.

(vi) *Disguised prepositions*

It is the weakened form of the preposition *'on'* and *'of'*.

Examples:

It is just ten *o'clock*. (of the clock)

He has gone *a-fishing*. (on fishing)

Note: Some prepositions like *'sans'*, *'save'* and *'atop'* are rarely used.

He put some cream *atop* the slice bread. (at the top of)

I know nothing about Amiri *save* his name. (except)

We ate rice and chicken *sans* curry. (without)

But *'times'*, *'plus'*, *'minus'*, *'Into'*, *'by'* (in calculations) and *'versus'* (against) and *'via'* (through) are frequently used.

Examples:

Six *times* four is twenty-four.

Five *minus* two is three.

Two *plus* two is four.

Five *into* twenty is four.

Four multiplied *by* two is eight.

Ten divided *by* two equals five.

Tendulkar scored two hundred runs in South Africa *versus* India one day match.

We went to Delhi *via* Dubai.

Note: *'Versus'* and *'via'* are prepositions of Latin origin.

B. *Functional classification*

Under functional category, the same prepositions are used in different contexts to express various kinds of meaning in relation to time, place, means, movement, manner, etc.

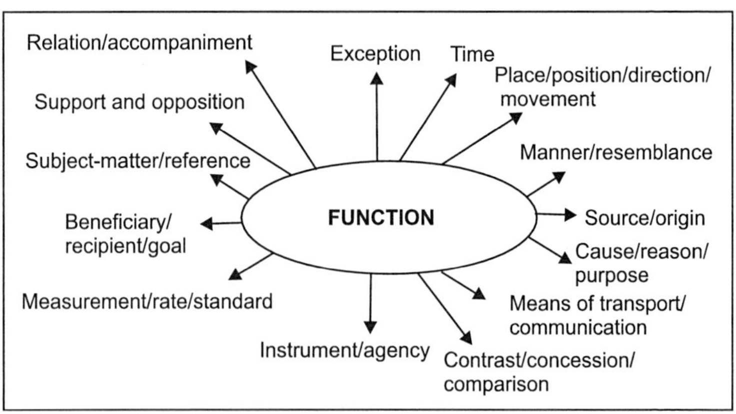

(i) Preposition of Time

These prepositions refer to an action or event related to time.

About (Approximate time)- It is about 8 o'clock.

Around (Approximate time)- It is around 7 o'clock.

After (later than)- I reached there after 6 o'clock.

At (exact point of time/meal time/festival)

I get up at 5 o'clock daily. (exact time)

We will discuss this issue at dinner/lunch. (at meal time)

He will be at home at Xmas/Diwali. (festival)

Before (earlier than)- I came here before 9 o'clock.

Between (refers to any time between the two points mentioned).

You can meet me between 4 pm and 6 pm.

Behind (late) The train is running behind time.

By (before/not later than)

I shall finish writing this book by July.

During (known period of time).

I was in India during summer vacation.

For (duration/a period of time)

I shall go with you for two hours only.

She stayed in Shimla for two nights. (past terminated action)

I have lived here for two years.

I have been living here for three years. (continued time)

From (starting point of time)

Patel lived in Kolkata from 2007 to 2009.

The football match will start from Monday.

I am on leave from 10 March.

There is a great demand for taxi from seven in the morning.

From ... to/till/until/up to (complete duration)

People work from Saturday up to/until Thursday in Libya.

We work from 8 am to/till 2 pm.

In – It is used with months/years/seasons/centuries and part of the day.

Computer revolutionized the world in the late 20th century.

I will see you tomorrow in the morning/afternoon/evening.

Shakespeare died in 1616.

He will work on computer in a few minutes.

We go to India in summer.

I will complete this exercise in a month.

Past – (after) It is half past ten. (British English)

It is half *after* ten. (American English)

On – It is used with a more general point of time like days of the week, dates and days.

She will come on Friday.

My wife will come on Sunday evening.

My birthday falls on 10 May.

Of – (refers to certain time)

She is to come on the seventh of March.

My first child was born within two years of marriage.

Over – (during/a period of time)

We can discuss this matter over a cup of tea.

Note – Now 'over' is used with longer period of time also.

We taught English here over two years.

To – (before the fixed/exact time) It is ten minutes to two. (British English)

It is ten of nine. (American English)

The train is running to time.

Till/until (up to the specified time)

Saroj works in the office until 2 o'clock.

My college was not open till 8 o'clock.

Towards – (closer to a point of time)

I shall finish this work towards the end of April.

Through (for a longer period of time)

He will not live through the night.

Throughout (during the whole period of time)

Leptis Magna is open daily throughout the year.

Since (point of time with reference to past time)

I have been teaching since 2007.

Within (before the referred time)

I shall reach there within two hours.

(ii) Prepositions of place/position/movement/direction

These prepositions indicate the place/position/movement and direction of a noun phrase.

Above (refers to a higher place or position)

The plane is flying above the clouds.

He is above you in rank.

About/Around (moving in several directions)

We were travelling about/around Delhi last week (here and there)

Across (moving from one side to the other side)

He is swimming across the river.

He ran across the road.

After (next to someone/something in position)

His name comes after my name in the list.

Against (touching somebody/something)

Put the ladder against the wall.

Along (direction: from one and towards the other)

He is walking along the road.

Among (relates to the position of a person/thing to more than two or indefinite numbers)

He is standing among his friends.

Ali's flat is the smallest among all the flats in the building.

Around/round (refers to circular motion or position)

It takes ten minutes in walking around the park.

Boys were playing hide and seek around my house.

The earth moves round the sun.

At – (refers to a position at a point/place of group activities and direction)

I live at Kankarbag in Patna. (place)

He is looking at the whiteboard. (direction)

She is standing at the door/bus stop. (position)

Omar lives at 20 street, Kashmir. (place)

He is at home/college/school. (place)

Before (in front of)

The thief knelt before the queen.

Behind (at the back of)

There is a garden behind my school.

She is standing behind the curtain.

Beside (position – by the side of, by, near)

Go and sit beside/by/near him.

Below (refers to a lower position or level than somebody/something).

I live below her.

She lives on the second floor and I live on the first floor.

He dived below the surface of water. (level)

A constable is below an inspector. (position)

Between (refers to a position of two or more than two persons or things of a definite number)

B comes between *A* and *C* in English alphabet.

Salma is standing between Najat, Rabia and Sana.

Switzerland lies between France, Germany and Italy.

There is friendship between five great nations.

"Between" can be used for more than two things or persons to denote some reciprocal action or relation.

Beyond (refers to far off places)

The bridge is beyond that big building.

By (near/beside) - Come and sit by me.

My flat is by the sea.

Down (movement from a higher point/place to a lower one)

Tears rolled down her cheek.

Go down the road till you reach the taxi station.

From (destination)

Boys are coming from college.

From (shows separation as well as distance of two places or positions)

You can see the sea from here.

I was hardly ten yards away from the scene of accident.

Dead leaves fall from the trees.

For (refers to distance)

For miles and miles there is not a house in the Sahara desert.

In (indicates to an area within boundaries/enclosures. It is also used with village, city, country, continent, etc.)

Abdul Latti lives in Harati street.

He is in the room/office/cinema hall/house/car.

I was born in India.

We live in our village.

The bird flies in the sky.

Dr. Thakur is in Yemen.

Inside (within a certain area)

My wallot is inside the shelf.

Into (movement towards)

He dived into the sea.

He ran into the office.

We poured juice into a glass.

Of (direction)

Leptis Manga is to the north of the faculty of Economics.

Off (away at a small distance/movement)

Ali's cafe is just off the main road.

He jumped off the horse.

Near (indicates a shorter distance)

She came near me.

Do you live near here?

Past (on or to the other side of somebody or something)

Ahmed lives in the house just past the mosque.

A tall man walked past me.

On (touching the surface)

He pasted the routine on the notice board.

The book is on the table.

There is a golden ring on her finger.

Onto (indicates movement onto the top of a building/vehicle, etc.)

I got onto the bus.

He climbed onto the roof.

Over (indicates resting position or a bit higher position or from one side to the other)

The bridge is over the river. (from one side to the other side)

Spread the blanket over the sleeping child. (resting position)

I put my hand over her mouth to stop her from screaming.

The bulb is hanging over our head. (higher position)

The bird is flying over the tree.

Opposite (direction or position)

The bank is opposite the town hall.

Through (indicates direction)

The police is marching through the town.

To (direction movement towards some place/direction and touching position)

He drove to the airport with his wife.

He is going to school/market/hospital.

The Mediterranean sea is to the north of Libya.

Put pen to paper.

Place the cursor to the left of the first word.

Towards (direction)

He is going towards the sea/shop.

Under (position: It indicates either contact or a space between two surfaces)

The dog is sitting under the table.

I put my purse under the pillow.

Up (indicates upward movement towards a place/position)

He climbed up the hill.

She ran up the stairs.

Upon (touching position)

The watch is lying upon the table.

With (indicates position/direction)

Don't stand with your hands in your pockets.

Wood floats with the current.

Within (indicates inside position/place)

The cupboard is within the kitchen.

My house is within a mile of the taxi station.

(iii) Prepositions of manner and resemblance

These prepositions show the manner in which an action is performed.

As (manner) - He delivers lectures as a scholar. (in the capacity of)

By (manner) - I will contact you by letter.

I took him by the hand.

In - He greeted me in a friendly way.

You are like your brother.

Like - She behaves like a friend. (after the manner of)

With - Omar looks upon this work with pride.

He wrote about this cause with great passion.

(iv) Preposition of source and origin

These prepositions indicate the source and origin of an action or event.

From - I borrowed the book from Samir. (source)

This road goes from Tripoli to Benghazi.

Omar hails from Zliten. (place of origin)

'Truth is beauty' is a quotation from Keats. (source)

Dead leaves fall from the tree. (source)

It is a novel of Dickens.

Of - He is a child of a rich father. (origin)

Off - Salma fell off the ladder. (source)

(v) Prepositions of cause, reason and purpose

These prepositions indicate the reason, cause and purpose for any action.

At (cause) - He did it at my request.

Behind (cause) - What is the reason behind his resignation?

For (purpose) - A few people work for the good of mankind.

(cause) - Ali will suffer for his bad habits.

(reason) - Mumbai is famous for its film industry.

From - Light comes from the sun during day.

Skill comes from constant practice.

Of (cause) - He died of cholera.

(reason) - She is proud of her noble birth.

On (reason) - The thief was acquitted on the verdict of the jury.

To (purpose) - I invited him to breakfast.

Through (reason) - You can get good marks through correct answer.

Over (reason) - Many people always quarrel over their paternal property.

With (cause) - He is sick with fever.

The leaves are wet with dew.

(vi) Prepositions of means of transport and communication

These prepositions express means of travel and communication.

By (It is used before a singular noun without an article or an adjective to express means of transport and communication.)

He came here by car/taxi/air/sea. (means of transport)

Omar went to London by air.

I got a letter by fax/post/email. (means of communication)

I informed him by phone.

In (It is used before a singular or plural means of transport with an article, adjective and adjective clause)

He came here in a red car.

We went to Tripoli in many cars.

They travelled to Malta in their own boats.

The taxi Ali was travelling in, fell into a ditch.

On (It is used without an article and adjective in place of *in* with bicycle/horseback/camel/motorcycle, foot, etc.)

He goes to market on foot/bicycle/pony/camel/horseback.

Note: (i) *'By'* can be used with bicycle and motorcycle instead of *'on'*.

He went to market by motorcycle.

(ii) 'On' is also used with article to refer to a big public vehicle as a means of transport.

We are now on the plane to Dubai.

He took his lunch on the Delhi – Mumbai Train.

Without (it is used to express the absence of means of transport)

We can't travel fast without a car/bus.

We can't fly to Dubai without a plane.

Via (it is a preposition of Latin origin used to express the 'route' by way of which some vehicle passes through).

I flew from Tripoli to New Delhi via Dubai.

(vii) Prepositions of material and ingredient

These prepositions indicate the material with which something is made.

From - Bread is made from flour. (material changed)

Some medicines are made from natural plants. (material changed)

Of - This is an apartment of stone. (material is intact)

The chair is made of plastic/wood. (material is intact)

With - She makes cake with coconut powder.

We can make a house with mud and clay. (material)

Without - We can't make an omellete without eggs.

Note: '*of*' expresses the same material in existence.

'*From*' loses its existence.

'*With*' or '*Without*' refers to ingredients.

(viii) Prepositions of instrument and agency

These prepositions express means, instrument, doer and agency with which an action is performed.

At - He sells clothes at auction. (agency)

By - Ali sent the parcel by mail/post. (means)

Please send this message to me by email. (means)

She earns a lot by teaching small children. (means)

'Macbeth' is a drama by Shakespeare. (agent)

My house was destroyed by fire. (means)

In - He speaks in English. She writes in Arabic. (means)

In - *in + pen/pencil/ink* (without an article)

He writes in ink/pen/pencil. (instrument)

Through - I heard this news through a friend. (agency)

With - *with + a pen/pencil* (with an article)

He writes a letter with a pen/pencil. (instrument)

Ali cut the apple with a knife. (instrument)

We walk with our legs. (means)

On - She rebuked me on the telephone. (instrument)

He is playing on the drum. (instrument)

We listen to the news on the radio. (means)

We watch the serial on television (instrument)

Without (absence of instrument/means)

We can't row a boat without oars.

We can't walk without legs.

A tree can't be cut without an axe.

(ix) Prepositions of measurement, rate, value and standard

These prepositions indicate measurement, rate, value and standard with which something is done.

At - Moneylenders charge interest rate at ten percent. (rate)

He is good/bad at painting. (standard)

He is clever at chess. (standard)

Rice sells at two dinars a kilo. (rate)

He drives his car at hundred kilometers an hour. (standard)

By - We get our salary by cheque. (standard)

Omar is taller than Raj by two inches. (measurement)

Taxi driver is paid wages by the hour. (measurement)

It is 7 o'clock by my watch. (standard)

Eggs are sold by the dozen. (rate)

For - She bought this scarf for ten dinars. (value price)

She is rather tall for her age. (measurement)

Of - I bought two kilos of chicken. (measurement)

To - My scooter does fifty kilometres to the litre. (measurement)

Bananas sell two to a dinar. (measurement)

(x) Prepositions of beneficiary, recipient, goal and target

These prepositions refer to the person who is recipient or beneficiary or who aims at a target.

Against - He is tossing the ball against the wall. (target)

At - I shot at the bird. (aim)

He ran at me. (target)

For - I purchased a flat for my son. (recipient)

This is a ring for you. (beneficiary)

To - I gave a pen to her. (recipient)

(xi) Prepositions of contrast, concession and comparison

These Prepositions show contrast or comparison.

After - (in spite of) After all his efforts, he couldn't succeed. (concession)

Against - There are three hundred students in medical college this year against two hundred last year. (comparison)

Apart from - (in spite of) Apart from getting high marks in test examination, he couldn't get top position in the final. (concession)

As - She is as good as me. (comparison)

Behind - Japan is not far behind developed nations in trade and commerce. (comparison)

Beside - My writing looks childish beside yours. (comparison)

Beside your earlier lecture, this is very influential. (comparison)

In spite of - In spite of ill-health, he could walk a mile.

Despite - Despite all his wealth, he is not happy.

For - For all his knowledge, he didn't do well in the final examination.

Like - She looks pleased like a cat to see a big fish.

To - He is senior to me.

I prefer walking to running.

Libya won the football match by 4 goals to 2.

Than - I am older than her.

With - With all her domestic engagements, she must spare time to study.

(xii) Prepositions of subject-matter and reference

These Prepositions refer to formal communication in speech and writing.

About/on/regarding. (subject-matter)

The teacher delivered a lecture on Linguistics.

This is a book about grammar.

That is a book regarding socialism.

As to - (about) As to my qualifications, I beg to submit that I am a graduate.

As for - (concerning) As for me, I would spend my summer vacation in India.

As regards - (regarding) As regards my experience as a technician, I worked for five years in Toshiba company.

Note: As regards, with regard to, with respect to, in connection with, regarding and concerning have almost the same meaning.

In pursuance of (in order to do something)

He needs money in pursuance of his studies.

In compliance with (the practice of obeying rules or requests made by people in authority)

Your application for ten years leave and lien is not in compliance with the university act.

On the matter of (related to an issue)

The government has given its consent on the matter of teacher's appointment.

(xiii) Prepositions of support and opposition

These prepositions express the viewpoint of individuals.

Against - Are you for or against the present education system? (opposition)

He is against me. (opposing)

Behind - (support) The whole nation was behind the team.

For - I stand for my brother. (in support of)

Is he for or against the Purdah system?

With - (agree/accept) we should go with the social system.

The coach was completely with the team. (supported)

(xiv) Prepositions of relation, accompaniment and possession

These prepositions show relation, possession and accompaniment.

Of - This is the car of my teacher.

Ali is the son of my uncle.

This is the house of Omar.

With - She dances with me.

She goes to market with her mother.

Without - I live here without my wife.

(xv) Preposition of exception

These prepositions refer to a person or thing about which a statement is not true.

Apart from (except) - I answered all questions apart from the last one.

But - (except) Nobody but Ali speaks English in the class.

Everyone was present but you.

'But for' (without or except) has a negative meaning.

But for you, we should have lost the match. (If you hadn't played well, we should have lost the match)

Except (apart from)

All except Anwar have passed.

We work everyday except Friday.

Position of preposition

'Pre' - means before and position means place, so the position of prepositions normally comes before nouns or noun phrases.

My son is at school.

Birds fly in the sky.

But prepositions may take initial, medial or final position in a sentence. Look at the following structure.

(i) Prepositions take initial position in Wh - questions (Whom/Which/What/Whose/Where) in formal construction and final position in informal construction that is almost acceptable.

In which subject are you interested?

Which subject are you interested in?

With what did he break the lock?

What did he break the lock with?

In whose house do you live?

Whose house do you live in?

To whom is she talking?

Who is she talking to?

Note- "who" never takes preposition before it.

(ii) If wh- question takes "be" (am, is, are, was, were) as a main verb, the preposition comes at the end.

What was it about?

Who is it for?

What is he like?

(iii) Relative pronouns take preposition but they may take it at the end (except "that" or "who") when they are not mentioned.

He is the man with whom she lives.

He is the man she lives with.

This is the house in which I live.

This is the house which I live in.

He is the man who is always talked about.

This is the play (that) I am fond of.

(iv) Prepositions usually come at the end in passive construction.

Who was this chair broken by?

The baby is being looked after.

She has already been operated on.

(v) Prepositions are also used at the end of an exclamatory sentence.

What a country we live in!

What a trouble he is in!

(vi) Prepositions are also used at the end of infinitive phrases.

There is no chair to sit on.

I have a pen to write with.

It is a lovely place to live in.

Note: "To + verb" is always infinitive and not a prepositional phrase.

I hope to see you soon.

(vii) Prepositions are also used after the object for the sake of emphasis, e.g.

He has travelled all the world over. (all over the world)

Omar is busy all the year round. (all round the year)

Correct usage of prepositions.

It is always important to bear in mind where to use a preposition and where to omit it in a sentence. Look at some important usage of prepositions.

(i) No preposition is used between a transitive verb and its object.

He accompanied me.

He has signed the treaty.

Following verbs don't take preposition in active voice.

Recommend, remind, ask, advise, beg, command, tell, encourage, implore, invite, order, warn, urge, refute, allow, prevent, let, etc.

I asked him a question.

I'll let you know later on.

He prevented me from making a noise.

(ii) No preposition is used before a noun when it functions as an adverb of place and time.

I shall go tomorrow.

Wait a second.

She goes home.

(iii) No preposition is used before adverbs of time and frequency.

(last, next, this, that, some, every, any, one each, all)

She will go next year.

You can see me any Friday.

I came last week.

He stood there all day long.

He is going for a swim this morning.

I was busy that day.

Note: We don't omit preposition before the name of the day or month, when "next" or "last" is placed after it.

He came on Monday last.

(iv) No preposition is used with expressions such as "twice a week", "two dinars a kilo", "four times a day", "hundred miles an hour". A or an is used instead of a preposition.

My wife observes fast twice a month.

He sells apples three dinars a kilo.

Take cough syrup four times a day.

Omar drives his car hundred kilometers an hour.

(v) No preposition is used before 'home' when it is used as an adverb and preceded by come, go, arrive, get, bring, send and take.

He comes home at 2 o'clock.

We brought the dead home.

When do you get home?

Let's us go home.

When 'home' is preceded by a genitive or a possessive adjective, it takes preposition because it functions as a noun.

I shall go to my uncle's home.

We shall get to your home at 4 o'clock.

Note: 'Leave' and 'reach' don't take preposition before 'home'.

He reached home safely.

I left home at 8 o'clock.

(vi) When two or more words require the same preposition, only one preposition is used with the last word.

He has a taste (for) and a passion for music.

He is desirous and confident of success.

But when different words take different prepositions, no omission is possible in that condition.

I am interested in and capable of buying a car.

He is thinking of going to Tripoli and living in a hotel.

(vii) Prepositions always take a gerund, not an infinitive.

I am thinking of leaving this country.

Read the letter before signing it.

He prevented me from going home.

Ali insisted on buying a dictionary.

I am in favour of giving you a party.

Note: Prepositions 'but' and 'except' take bare-infinitive only.

She did nothing but gossip.

My daughter does nothing except watch the movies.

(viii) Some verbs such as- go, come, write, listen, speak, talk, reply, complain, explain and say, take 'to' to address a person.

We go to Ali everyday.

You must reply to me.

They complained to me about the food.

Please explain to me what this means.

Prepositions with Other Classes.

It is difficult to decide the class of a word in isolation. It is its use that decides its grammatical class.

(i) Preposition and Conjunctions

Some prepositions such as after, before, since, than, as, until, but, except, etc. function both as preposition and conjunction. When they come before a noun phrase they function as preposition and when they come before a clause they function as conjunction.

After the lecture, I left my class. (preposition)

He made a call to me after I left my class. (conjunction)

She came here before 4 o'clock. (preposition)

The patient had died before the doctor came. (conjunction)

She is as tall as me. (preposition)

She is as tall as I. (as I am tall) (conjunction)

I would rather send a letter than phone. (preposition)

He is smarter than I. (conjunction)

I have been writing a novel since morning. (preposition)

I have not seen him since he left Libya. (conjunction)

She does nothing but complain. (preposition)

He is poor but happy. (but he is happy) (conjunction)

Sahban works until 2 o'clock (preposition)

I willn't go until she comes. (conjunction)

Everyone was present except you. (preposition)

He didn't tell me anything <u>except</u> that he needed money. (Conjunction).

(ii) Prepositions and adverbial phrases

Some prepositions function as adverbs and are called adverbial particles. Some of them are.

Below, above, besides, by, across, but, till, under, about, in, before, behind, on over, round, up, down, near, since, past, off.

Tears ran down her face.	(preposition)
Please sit down.	(adverb)
He put the bag on the table.	(preposition)
Put your coat on.	(adverb)
She came before 2 o'clock.	(preposition)
I have explained it before.	(adverb)
Salma is in the field.	(preposition)
When I opened the door, the dog came in.	(adverb)
The dog is behind me.	(preposition)
My dog ran behind in the race.	(adverb)
His expense is above his income.	(preposition)
He flew above very fast.	(adverb)
He ran up the stairs.	(preposition)
He went up in the line.	(adverb)
Don't go below this line.	(preposition)
See below for reference.	(adverb)
It is half past ten.	(preposition)
I called out to him as he ran past.	(adverb)
The beggar knelt before the king.	(preposition)
I haven't seen him before.	(adverb)
He climbed over the wall.	(preposition)
The time is running over.	(adverb)
The earth moves round the sun.	(preposition)

The wheels are going round.	(adverb)
Do you live near my house?	(preposition)
The examination is drawing near.	(adverb)

(iii) Prepositions used with adjectives and participles.

Adjective/participle + preposition + object (noun/pronoun)

Absent from class	Ashamed of a person
Absorbed in work	Associated with a person
Acceptable to a person	Associated in some business
Accomplished in an art	Attending to a lesson
Accountable to a person	Aware of his intentions
Accountable for a thing	Based on facts
Accused of a crime	Bent on doing something
According to a person	Blessed with a child
Accustomed to a thing	Blind to his own fault
Afraid of someone	Blind of one eye
Acquainted with a person	Born of rich parents
Acquitted of a charge	Born in Libya
Addicted to a habit	Careful of his money
Adjacent to a place	Careful about his dress
Alarmed at a noise	Close to or by a place
Amazed at anything	Composed of a menial
Angry with a person	Confined to a house
Annoyed at a thing	Contrary to rule
Annoyed with a person	Convicted of a crime
Answerable to a person	Deprived of a thing
Anxious about the result	Devoid of intelligence
Applicable about the result	Different from something
Appropriable to an occasion	Dispensed with a person
Disqualified for a post	Lame of one leg
Doubtful of success	Liable to error

Eager in the pursuit of knowledge
Easy to access
Engaged to someone
Envious of another
Exempted from s task
Exposed to danger
Faithful to a master
Familiar with a language
Familiar to a person
Famous for something
Fatal to health
Fit for a position
Fond of music
Free from blame
Gifted with abilities
Honest in his dealings
Hopeful of success
Horrified at the sight
Hungry after or for wealth
Inspired with hope
Intimate with a person
Introduced to a person
Involved in difficulties
Jealous of one's reputation
Transported with joy
Vexed at a thing
Worthy of praise

Liable to payment
Limited to a certain area
Loyal to the country
Move with pity
Negligent of duty
Noted for good work
Obliged to a person
Obliged for his kindness
Polite with a person
Polite to a person
Popular with everyone
Proud of one's work
Regardless of consequences
Related to a person
Relevant to the point
Responsible to a person
Responsible for his actions
Satisfied with one's work
Slow of hearing
Slow in making up his mind
Slow at accounts
Stained with blood
Suitable to the occasion
Tired of work
True to his word
Vexed with a person

(iv) Nouns with preposition

Noun + preposition + objects (noun/pronoun)

Ability for or in some work
Complaint about a thing

Abundance of food
Access to a person or place
Acquaintance with a person
Affection for a person
Desire for wealth
Apology for some fault
Arrival at a place in a country
Attention to study
Attraction to or towards a thing
Authority over a person
Bargain with a person
Care for his safety
Care for his book
Care for anxiety

Connection with a person
Control over a person
Anxiety for anyone's safety
Exception to a rule
Faith in a person
Fondness for anything
Freedom of action
Authority on a subject
Interest in a subject
Invitation to a dinner
Key to a problem
Lecture on a subject

Liking for a person/thing
Comparison with somebody
Comparison between two things
Comment on something
Objection to a proposal
Protest against a decision
Reference to a person or a thing
Reflection on a man's honesty
Remedy for something
Repentance for sin

Lust for money
Match for a person
Heed for assistance
Reply to a letter
Resemblance to a person
Victim of tyranny
Victory over his passion
Wonder at his rudeness

(iii) Verbs with preposition

verb + preposition + object (noun/pronoun)

Abide by a promise
Abound in something
Abstain from wine
Accuse of a crime
Acquit of blame

Believe in a person/creed
Beware of something
Boast of action
Break into a house
Burst into flame

Admit to an excuse
Agree to a proposal
Aim at an object
Allot to somebody
Appeal to a person
Confine to a place
Approve of an action
Argue with a person
Attend to business
Attend on a person
Get over illness
Avail of an opportunity
Get on with a person
Get through an examination
Glance at book
Glance over a letter
Hint at a fact
Hope for the best
Impress an idea on someone
Increase in number
Inquire into a matter
Play on a musical instrument
Insist on doing something
Introduce a man to someone
Jump at conclusion
Lament for the dead
Laugh at a person

Come across a person/thing
Compare with (for similar thing)
Compare to (for dissimilar thing)
Complain to a person
Appeal for redress or help
Consult with a person
Fall in love with a person
Fight with or against a person
Gaze at or on a thing/person
Get at facts (fond out)
Look upon someone as a friend
Make out the meaning
Make up for one's loss
Hanker after wealth
Meet with success
Object to some proposal
Part from a person
Part with a person
Play tricks with a person
Plunge into a river/ship
Ponder on or over a subject
Prefer to another
Prepare for work
Preside over a meeting
Prevent from doing something
Proceed with a work
Proceed against a person

Listen to a complaint
Live on simple food
Live by work
Live on an income
Live within means
Live beyond means
Look at something/someone
Look after one's good
Look into a matter
Rebel against authority
Recover from an illness
Refer to a matter
Reflect on a person or Subject
Talk in a language
Rely on a person
Remind of a thing
Result in a consequence
Rob of something

Run into debt
Search for a thing
Share in another's troubles

Shoot at a target
Speak about or on a subject
Speak to a man
Stand by a friend
Stare a person in the face
Struggle for the right
Struggle against a wrong
Submit to an authority
Suffer from a disease

Protest against injustice
Qualify for a post
Quarrel with someone
Talk of or about an event
Talk over a matter
Talk to or with a person
Think about/of something
Take off something
Resign from an organization
Trust in a person
Run after a person or thing
Tremble with fear/cold
Taste of salt

Tell about an event
Turn to somebody
Turn verse into prose
Vote for somebody
Warn somebody of something
Wish for something
Work of mathematics
Yearn for something/somebody
Yield to something/somebody
Zip up a chain

EXERCISE-1

Complete these sentences using a suitable preposition.

(i) I'll see you ___ Friday. (on/at/in)

(ii) We can't live ___ air. (with/without/by)

(iii) I can't see Ahmed became he is sitting ___ me. (by/behind/besides)

(iv) The sky is ___ our heads. (on/above/over)

(v) Is there water ___ this well? (in/at/to)

(vi) My grandmother stays ___ home. (in/at/to)

(vii) Did you come here ___ bus or ___ foot? (on/to/by)

(viii) We travelled to Malta ___ sea. (by/to/on)

(ix) He left ___ London ___ 9 o'clock ___ Tuesday. (on/at/for)

(x) What do you think ___ satellites? (at/of/for)

(xi) I heard this news ___ radio. (by/from/on)

(xii) We held a meeting ___ July 15th. (on/at/in)

(xiii) What are you laughing ___? (at/on/to)

(xiv) I prefer coffee ___ tea. (in/to/for)

(xv) We are interested ___ learning English. (in/at/for)

(xvi) The teacher talked ___ us ___ the live ___ bees. (of/as out/to)

(xvii) It is usually hot ___ summer. (at/in/to)

(xviii) One should smile ___ live. (at/in/on)

(xix) Aisha is clever ___ cooking. (in/at/for)

(xx) Excuse me I hit you ___ mistake. (by/with/for)

(xxi) She is angry ___ Ahmad. (at/with/form)

(xxii) Ali is friendly ___ her friends. (to/with/by)

(xxiii) This street is very quiet ___ night. (in/to/at)

(xxiv) Shakespeare died ___ 1616. (in/of/from)

(xxv) I work from 8 o'clock ___ 2 o'clock. (from/to/of)

EXERCISE-2

Fill up the blanks with suitable prepositions.

1. We depend ___ you.
2. His behavior resulted ___ a conflict.
3. He prevented me ___ doing it.
4. We arrived ___ Tunis very early.
5. Beware ___ mad dogs.
6. The doctor is sitting ___ the chair.
7. He is delivering a lecture ___ Shakespeare.
8. I get up ___ 6 o'clock.
9. I take tea ___ the morning.
10. I congratulated him ___ his grand success.
11. He plays ___ violin.
12. My brother has gone ___ my friend's home.
13. I always swear ___ Allah.
14. I am a teacher ___ English.
15. Could I please speak ___ the Dean?
16. You should apply ___ the post.
17. Always be prepared ___ the worst.
18. Can you cure him ___ this disease?
19. She is related ___ me.
20. This is the answer ___ that question.
21. There are four exception ___ this rule.
22. ___ whose home do you live?
23. I must consult ___ you ___ that matter.
24. The teacher was popular ___ his students.
25. He is good ___ English.
26. He died ___ cholera.

EXERCISE-3

Choose the correct preposition.

1. He cut a tree ___ an axe. (with/by/from)
2. She lives ___ the first floor. (on/at/in)
3. We go to school ___ bicycle. (in/by/on)
4. He has a taste ___ music. (of/in/for)
5. This is a cheque ___ 1000 dinars. (for/of/by)
6. Would you like to take your salary ___ cash? (in/by/for)
7. I write a letter ___ ink. (with/in/from)
8. I have no access ___ the desk. (for/to/of)
9. I shall meet you ___ the bus stop. (on/at/to)
10. Put your signature ___ the bottom of the application. (at/on/in)
11. The train stops ___ every station. (at/on/to)
12. We pray ___ God. (for/to/by)
13. Nobody is acquainted ___ him. (to/with/for)
14. The book is written ___ me. (by/to/for)
15. He invited me ___ lunch. (for/to/on)
16. He has no house to live ___. (in/on/by)
17. I came ___ his request. (to/at/for)
18. He shot a bird ___ a gun. (by/with)
19. I don't believe ___ God. (in/by/on)
20. He is ashamed ___ his conduct. (at/of/for)
21. I object ___ your statement. (of/to/for)
22. We can't do ___ money. (without/with/by)
23. He is trembling ___ fear. (from/of/with)
24. She compared her face ___ the moon. (to/with)
25. There is a treaty ___ five great nations, (between/with/in).

EXERCISE-4

Correct these sentences.

1. You are always angry at me.
2. She is sitting over a chair.
3. She is clever in English.
4. The window is made from glass.
5. We make butter of milk.
6. We can't go with bus.
7. Where are you coming to?
8. What are you driving on?
9. One should avail oneself from this chance.
10. He is repairing his car with a view to sell it.
11. It is between he and I.
12. The team has arrived Tripoli.
13. He is fond for fish.
14. He has been ill since a month.
15. She wrote me.
16. I spoke the chancellor about my problem.
17. She went to home early.
18. Ahmed Memon entered into my class.
19. I resigned from my post.
20. He resigned the party.
21. Translate this passage from English.
22. This town is the north of Mislata.
23. I slept at the floor.
24. He is eligible to the post for lecturer.
25. Many aspire of greatness.

7

Conjunction

What is a Conjunction?

A conjunction is that part of speech which joins two or more than two words, phrases and clauses.

Examples:

He is tall and smart. (two words combined)

An old man and a boy are standing on the road. (two noun phrases combined)

Ahmed Baba runs an institute and his wife teaches English. (two clauses combined)

Kinds of Conjunction

1. Correlative Conjunctions (Paired Conjunctions)

Correlative conjunctions always go in pairs and combine the same class of words (noun, verb, adjective, pronoun, etc.) after each correlative. The chief among them are either-or, neither-nor, not only-but also, both-and, etc.

a. I met neither Fathi nor Sahban in the office.
(noun + noun)

b. This book is both cheap and useful.
(adjective + adjective)

c. Girls are not only dancing but also singing.
(verb + verb)

d. Either you or I am responsible for it.
(pronoun + pronoun)

2. Coordinating Conjunctions (Coordinators)

Coordinating conjunctions connect at least two grammatical units of equal rank or pattern. They are of four kinds.

(i) *Cumulative or copulative conjunctions*

as well as, besides, likewise, moreover, and, both-and, not only-but also, etc.

These conjunctions merely add one idea or statement to another.

He likes to sing and dance.

Both Ahmed and Ali are intelligent.

The shirt is new; moreover, it is cheap.

(ii) *Alternative conjunctions*

or, else, otherwise, either-or, neither-nor, etc.

These conjunctions suggest choice between two alternatives.

Take this or that pen.

Do it or (otherwise) you will get into trouble.

(iii) *Adversative conjunctions*

but, yet, still, though, although, whereas, while, etc.

These conjunctions show contrast.

He is poor but honest.

He is rich, still he is not satisfied.

It is very good, although it is cheap.

I love the poor whereas he hates them.

(iv) *Illative conjunctions*

so, consequently, hence, accordingly, therefore, for, etc.

These conjunctions express an inference.

The rain started, so we didn't go out for a walk.

We shall die one day, for man is mortal.

He misbehaved with the teacher, therefore/consequently/ accordingly he had to leave the college.

3. Subordinating Conjunctions (subordinators)

The conjunctions in this group are used to introduce main clause and add information to it. They are of three kinds.

(i) *Simple subordinating conjunctions*

after, before, as, when, since, that, because, when, whether, unless, until, etc.

The patient had died before the doctor came.

She answered the phone when it rang.

Unless you read this book, you can't learn English.

He couldn't go to college because he was ill.

(ii) *Compound subordinating conjunctions*

so far as, as soon as, so long as, as long as, so that, provided (that) as if, as though, in case, on condition that, etc.

So far as I know, she is still unmarried.

As long as I am here, you need not worry.

Take as umbrella in case it rains.

He talks as if he were my boss.

(iii) *Correlative subordinators*

Such-that, so-that, as-as, if-then, the-the, no sooner-than, hardly/scarcely-when, etc.

He is as good as she is.

He is not so gentle as you think.

If I don't come today then inform the police.

Hardly had I reached there when the match started.

But relative pronouns (who, which, whom, that, etc.) and relative adverbs (when, where, etc.) also function as conjunctions.

The book which is lying there is very old.

Whenever he is in trouble I help him.

Had/were/should is used as a subordinating conjunction in conditional clauses in place of 'if'.

Examples:

Were I a bird, I would fly in the sky.

Had I been in your place, I wouldn't have done it.

Should the president not concede our demand, we would resign.

Note: All the above sentences may also begin with "if".

Use of Some Important Conjunctions

(i) *no sooner-than*

No sooner had I reached the hospital than it began to rain.

(ii) *hardly/scarcely-when/before*

Hardly had he finished his speech when a bomb exploded.

Scarcely had we reached there before it started raining.

(iii) *not only-but also*

Not only is Salma beautiful but also intelligent.

Note: When a sentence begins with neither, nor, only when, so, no sooner-than, not only-but also, hardly/scarcely-when, etc. the verb comes before the subject.

(iv) *whether-or (not)*

I don't know whether he is intelligent or dull.

I don't know whether he is intelligent or not.

(dull left out)

Note: "*Or not*" is used when the alternative is left out.

(v) *no, not, never ..., or (not nor)*

I have no book or pen.

She has not received a letter or a parcel.

I have never written a novel or a drama.

(vi) *either-or/neither-nor*

Either-or and neither-nor express a choice of two alternatives when they are used as *pronouns/adjectives*.

Neither of the two girls is married.

Either he or she has done it.

But they are not restricted to two alternatives when they are used as *conjunctions*.

She is neither intelligent, nor smart, nor refined.

Ali goes to market either by car or by scooter or on foot.

(vii) *nor/neither*

Nor or neither is used separately as a coordinator.

Ali doesn't go to college neither does Ahmed.

He doesn't read a novel nor do I.

(viii) *if/whether*

If/whether is used in indirect speech as a conjunction to connect direct question. (yes/no questions)

He said: "Do you know English?"

He asked me if/whether I knew English.

"*Whether*" is used before infinitive and after preposition. '*If*' is never used in such constructions.

I couldn't decide whether to buy chicken or fish.

It entirely depends on him whether he likes it or not.

(ix) *unless/until (if-not)*

Unless and until have a negative meaning. (*if-not*)

Unless you work hard, you will not pass the examination.

or

If you don't work hard, you will not pass the examination.

I can't go until you come.

(x) *'If' and conditional sentences*

If + present simple is used to express timeless possible condition.

If we heat water to 100°C, it boils.

If we don't water plants, they die.

If + present simple + future simple is used to express future possible condition.

If it rains tomorrow, we will not play football.

(xi) *If + past simple + future simple (past)* is used to express unreal, imaginary or impossible condition.

If I knew his phone number, I would talk to him.

If camels could fly, we wouldn't need planes.

(xii) *If + past perfect + future perfect (past = would) + have* + V_3) is used to express past impossible condition.

If he had met them, he would have helped them.

If you have watered the flowers, they wouldn't have withered away.

(xiii) *Sentence connectors* (*linking words*)

Sentence connectors connect sentences to establish a logical link between one idea and the other. They are not a separate class of words. They may be adverbs or adverbial phrases, prepositions or prepositional phrases and coordinating conjunctions.

Examples:

He is smart and intelligent. Also he is gentle. (Adverb)

I don't like expensive shirt. Besides I don't have much money. (preposition/adverb)

He doesn't go to hospital nor do I (coordinating conjunction)

Note: '*Nor do I*' is the short form of '*I don't go either*'.

Use of Sentence Connectors (Linking Words)

Sentence connectors are used to express different shades of meaning.

They are used:

(i) *to express addition*

too, also, moreover, nor, as well, similarly, likewisc, either, neither, etc.

Omar is kind and gentle. He is helpful, too.

He has a big house. He has a new car as well.

I don't like this suit. Besides it is expensive.

(ii) *to show contrast*

instead, on the contrary, rather, on the one hand, etc.

He didn't help me, on the contrary/rather he harmed me.

On the one hand, there is poverty, on the other, there is vast wealth.

(iii) *to express inference*

or, or else, otherwise, in other words, etc.

Bribery is a common practice. In other words, it has become the custom of the day.

Take a taxi, or else you will be late for your class.

(iv) *to express apposition*

namely, for example, that is, via, etc.

There are many books to read in leisure, you can, for example, read a novel or a story.

(v) *to express attitude/viewpoint*

in fact, indeed, actually, etc.

Shakespeare was a famous dramatist. In fact, he was a genius.

(vi) *to express concession*

still, however, nevertheless, yet, etc.

The car is quite old; still/however/nevertheless/yet it is in good condition.

(vii) *to express result*

as a result, thus, so, hence, then, etc.

He beat his classmate, as a result/consequently he was punished.

(viii) *to express transition*

meanwhile, by the way, in the meantime, etc.

I was in the market, meanwhile my ailing mother expired.

(ix) *to express enumeration/summation*

In conclusion, to conclude, overall, first of all, next, etc.

I am going to talk about English language today. First of all, I would like to tell you about its history.

EXERCISE-1

Correct these sentences.

1. Both Ali as well as Ahmed are clever.
2. He will either read a novel or a drama.
3. He can never write nor speak English.
4. Not only he gave me money but also book.
5. Hardly I had reached the station than the train left.
6. No sooner we saw a snake than we fled away.
7. I have no book nor pen.
8. Unless you don't read seriously, you will not pass.
9. I don't know if to accept or reject the offer.
10. Neither he can't sit nor stand nor sleep.
11. Hurry up and you will miss the plane.
12. She phoned neither me nor wrote to me.
13. He neither reads or writes well.
14. Do and die.
15. Make haste and you will miss the taxi.

EXERCISE-2

Choose the correct alternative from the given brackets.

1. I have not got a banana ..... an apple. (or, nor)
2. Hardly had I gone to school ..... it started raining. (than, when)
3. Both Ali ..... Ahmed can do it. (as well as, or, and)
4. No sooner did I get a letter ..... I left for home. (then, when)
5. The king ..... the queen are sitting. (and, or)
6. He will go neither to Dubai ..... to Mumbai. (or, nor).
7. ..... I stop here, I will find no time for work. (unless, as long as)
8. He went to school ..... the bell had rung. (before, after).

9. He had read the letter when a telegram arrived. (scarcely, sooner)
10. Work ..... you live. (until, as long as)
11. He will meet you ..... you leave for London. (before, after)
12. He can't pass ..... he works hard. (if, unless)
13. You ..... I am guilty. (and, or)
14. The teacher ..... the students is waiting for the chief guest. (and, as well as)

    Sana is tall ..... smart. (or, and)

    You are rich ..... cruel. (but, as well as)

EXERCISE-3

Fill up the blanks with a suitable conjunction.

1. He couldn't go to college ..... he was ill.
2. Polygamy is common in Islamic culture ..... a man can marry more than one woman.
3. He is rich ..... he is dishonest.
4. I couldn't decide ..... to join politics or bar.
5. Both Sarah ..... Najat are sisters.
6. We were playing football ..... a bomb exploded.
7. We worked till evening, ... we went home.
8. Do ..... die.
9. ..... I were she, I would give him a good retort.
10. ..... I would like to teach you grammar.
11. ..... I would start teaching language.
12. He as well as I ..... confident of our success.
13. I shall phone you ..... I reach there.
14. Both you ..... your brother are responsible for it.
15. She behaves ..... she were my wife.

8

Interjection

What is an Interjection?

An interjection is that grammatical category which is used to express an outburst of emotion or excitement. It is not grammatically linked with the other words of the sentence.

Usually, it comes in the beginning to show the feeling of happiness, hatred, hesitation, anger, sorrow, joy, applause, surprise, etc. and takes an exclamation mark or comma. Look at these examples.

Ah! I lost the game.

Alas! She is dead.

Bravo! We have won the match.

But all the words or phrases that are punctuated by exclamation marks are not interjections. Those words or phrases that show a sudden jerk of emotion and feeling of the heart are only interjections. It is not proper to think that all introductory words followed by an exclamation mark or comma are interjections. If the word in question does not show emotion, it is probably not an interjection.

Look at the following examples.

Rohit! Come and see the python.

Gunjan! See the hovering aeroplane.

Names like these are not interjections. They are nouns. These nouns are called direct address and not interjections. If the tone of voice that you say doesn't show emotion, it is not an interjection.

Stop! You will fall in a well.

Run! The snake will bite you.

The words '*stop*' and '*run*' show action and actions are verbs not interjections. Though these sentences themselves show the sense of urgency by their expression (who wants to fall in a well and who wants to get bitten by a snake.), yet they don't show emotion.

Interjections are rarely used in formal or academic writing. We use them quite often, more in speaking than in writing.

There are a few words and phrases to express strong emotions. The table below shows some commonly used interjections with examples.

Ah! I couldn't succeed.	(expressing sorrow)
Alas! I am undone.	(expressing sorrow)
Bravo! You have done well.	(expressing applause)
Dear! Does it hurt?	(expressing pity)
Damn! I missed the ball.	(expressing anger)
Good God! My result is grand.	(expressing wonder)
Eh! Really.	(expressing surprise)
Fie! Fie! You mean fellow you cheated me.	(expressing hatred)
Hi! How are you?	(expressing greeting)
Hip! Hip! Hurrah! We have won the match.	(expressing joy)
Hello! How are you today?	(expressing greeting)
Hey! Look at that.	(calling attention)
Uh! I don't know the answer.	(expressing hesitation)
Umm! I am not so sure.	(expressing hesitation)
Lo! A snake is coming.	(calling attention)
Ouch! It hurts.	(expressing pain)
Well done! It is a grand victory.	(expressing joy)

Introductory expressions such as *Yes, No, Indeed, Really, Well, Sorry*, etc. are also classed as interjections.

Let's have a look.

Well, it is 7 o'clock. Better go home and spend some time with the kids.

(Homer Simpson)

Indeed, this is not the first time the roof has collapsed.

No, he shouldn't have done it.

Not only the above mentioned expressions but also *'Excuse me'*, *'No, thank you'*, *'Oh Dear'*, *'Hey, that's mine'* and similar ones often serve as interjections.

Truly speaking, an interjection simply conveys strong or mild emotion. It clearly expresses meaning and feeling of the speaker.

EXERCISE-1

Use the following interjections in a meaningful sentence.

Oh No! Alas! Ouch! Well done! Hurrah! Lo!

Hi! Hey! Umm! Good God!

9

Article

What is an Article?

An article is an adjectival particle (determiner) that usually comes before nouns to determine their identity or make a change in their meaning. Look at these sentences.

A. I. He has a red and blue pen.
(only one pen that is partly red and partly blue)

II. He has a red and a blue pen.
(two pens—one is red and the other is blue)

B. I. We know English. (English language)

II. We know the English. (English people)

C. I. The uncle and guardian has come to see Anil.
(One man who is uncle and guardian of Anil)

II. The uncle and the guardian have come to see Anil.
(Two men—one is uncle and the other guardian)

These differences in meaning are due to the use of articles in the above three pairs of sentences.

Kinds of Articles

There are two kinds of articles.

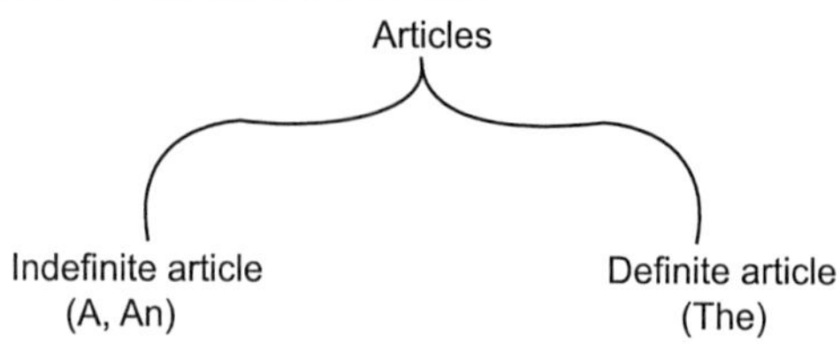

'A and an' are called indefinite articles.

'The' is called a definite article.

'A and an' are called indefinite articles because they come for the first time before (to introduce) an unknown countable noun, for example:

A. There is a king.

She is a girl.

Why is 'the' called a definite article?

'The' is called definite article because it comes to refer to a known noun.

B. The king is kind and honest.

The girl is tall.

Here, the use of indefinite article 'a' in example A and the use of definite article 'the' in B clearly indicate the indefinite and definite functions of the same noun.

Generic and Specific use of articles:

Generic use

When we use an article before a noun to refer to the whole class, this linguistic reference is called the generic use of article, e.g.

A book is a storehouse of knowledge.
(A book means all books)
The book is a storehouse of knowledge.
(The book means all books)

Specific use

When we use an article before a noun to refer to a particular member of a class, this linguistic reference is called the specific use of article, e.g.

I have a parrot. (a parrot means one parrot)

The parrot is in the cage. (the parrot means my parrot)

Use of Articles on the Basis of Number

The use of 'a' and 'an' is related to number system of nouns because it is always used before a singular countable noun. It is never used before a plural countable noun, e.g.

He is a student. (never a students)

But 'the' has no relation with the number system of nouns. It is used with singular and plural nouns, e.g.

He bought the book/books from the market.

The number system of nouns is also followed when certain nouns of uncountable nature are used as countable nouns, e.g.

Tea: I take tea in the morning.
Give me a tea. (a cup of tea)

Paper: I need some paper to prepare an answer.
I need a paper every day.
(newspaper)

Glass: The door is made of glass.
Bring a glass of water. (vessel)

Hair: Her hair is black.
There is a hair on the jacket.
(one thread of hair)

Lamb: I like roasted lamb with bread. (meat)
This is a lamb. (youngone of a sheep)

Pronunciation of Articles

'A' has the pronunciation [ə] weak form, and [eI] strong form, e.g.

About [ə'baut], amuse [ə'mju:z] – weak form,

Cake [keIk], snake [sneIk] – strong form.

'An' has the pronunciation [ən] weak form, and [æn] strong form, e.g.

Announcer [ənaunser], anew [ənju] – weak form,

Fan [fæn], man [mæn] – strong form.

'The' is pronounced in two ways.

a. It is pronounced [ðə] when it follows consonant sound.

The [ðə] book is on the [ðə] table.

b. It is pronounced [ðI] when it follows the vowel sound.

The [ðI] orange is fresh.

It is also pronounced [ðI] when it follows the consonant sound to particularize the object.

This is the [ðI] house in which I live.

Use of Article on the Basis of Sound

Use 'a' when the first letter of the word begins with consonant sound and use 'an' when it begins with vowel sound, e.g.

A book, a chair, a fan, etc.

An apple, an orange, an umbrella, etc.

Why is 'a' Used Before the Word that Begins with Consonant Sound and 'an' with Vowel Sound?

'A' is used before consonant sound and 'an' before vowel sound for the sake of convenience in pronunciation. In English language, 'vowel + consonant' pronunciation is easier than 'vowel + vowel' pronunciation. That's why the Britishers avoid pronouncing an apple, they add 'n' with the vowel and make it consonantal sound like a + napple. But it is not permissible.

In the alphabet of English language, a, e, i, o, and u, are considered as vowel letters, and the rest are consonant letters, not sound. But the initial sound of these letters sometimes varies, and so, we should be particular in the use of 'a' and 'an' before words. The rule of using 'a' or 'an' totally depends on the initial vowel or consonant sound of the words, not on the initial vowel or consonant letter of the word. Look at these words of columns A, B, C and D.

A	B	C	D
A university	An LP school	An hour	A hotel
A European	An MR	An honest man	A humble man
A utensil	An FO	An heir	A historical place
A worthless fellow	An NRI	An honorable man	A horrible sight
A one-eyed man	An HMT watch	An honorary President	A habitual action

In column A, the initial sound of university, European, utensil begin with /j/ consonantal sound. So, they take 'a' before them instead of 'an', whereas worthless and one-eyed begin with /w/ consonantal sound. So, they take 'a'.

The sound /j/ and the sound /w/ are semi vowels. But they are consonants because in the structure of the English language they don't behave like vowels.

In column B, all the acronyms (initial letters) are consonant letters. But they are pronounced with initial vowel sounds. So, they take 'an'. During the pronunciation of acronyms starting with F, H, L, M, N, R, S and X, a vowel sound comes in a natural way. So, they take 'an' before them. But when they are used as words they take 'a', e.g.

A NATO member

A FIFA officer

A CAT student

A GATT director, etc.

In column C, the initial sound of hour, honest, heir, honorable, honorary, doesn't begin with consonant letter 'h'. Here, the first letter 'h' of these words is silent and so, these words start with vowel sound due to which they take 'an'.

In column D, the first letter 'h' of these words hotel, humble, historical, horrible and habitual, is not silent (mute). So, they take 'a' before them.

Finally, it is the sound that determines the choice between 'a' and 'an'.

Position of Article 'a' and 'an'

As 'a' or 'an' is a determiner, so its position usually comes before adjective and adverb, e.g.

A car, an old car, a very old car

A girl, a beautiful girl, an extremely beautiful girl

But in certain constructions such as, what a/many a/quite a/such a/rather a, its position comes after adjective, e.g.

I have never spent such a night before.

There are quite a lot of people there.

Many a ship sank in the sea.

He is rather an idiot.

What a nice day it is!

When the adverbs as, too, how, quite, and so, come before the adjective, the position of 'a' or 'an' usually comes after the adjective.

This is so difficult a question.

This is quite difficult a problem.

It is too big a bottle.

How nice a man he is!

She is as tall a girl as her sister.

Note: 'a or an' may come before so, too and quite but its position after adjective is preferred, e.g.

Too big a bottle (OR) A too big bottle

Quite absurd a question (OR) a quite absurd question

Various Uses of 'a' and 'an'

A/An is used:

1. Before a singular countable noun in the sense of 'one', 'any', 'each', 'every' or 'per'

   I have a book. (one book)

   She comes to see me twice a month. (per month)

   Please, give me a pen. (any pen)

   His salary is £ 500 a month. (every month)

Rice sells one dinar a kilo. (per kilo)

2. With a noun complement including names of profession, religion, e.g.

   I am a student.

   My father is an engineer.

   I am a Muslim, not a Christian.

3. In certain numerical expressions, e.g.

   I bought a dozen of eggs.

   He is an eighteen-year-old boy.

4. In expressions of price, speed, ratio, etc., e.g.

   Apples are three dinars a kilo. (price)

   I drive my car at eight kilometers an hour. (speed)

   I go to Delhi once in a year. (ratio)

5. In exclamations before singular countable nouns, e.g.

   What a lazy boy!

   What a nice day!

   What pretty girls! (no article)

6. Instead of preposition 'on'

   He went a hunting. (on hunting)

   He went a bed. (on the bed)

7. As a substitute for 'the same'

   They were much of a size. (of the same size)

   Birds of a feather flock together. (proverb)

8. To refer to the person whose identity is unknown, e.g.

   A Dr. Sharma is calling you.

   A Mr. Omar wants to talk to you.

9. With abstract noun to show a kind of quality, e.g.

   A working knowledge of grammar is always useful.

   A clear understanding of things gives faithful result.

10. In fraction of amount, weight and distance, e.g.

    He bought one and a half kilos of sugar.

(or a kilo and a half)

We walk two and a half kilometers everyday.

11. Before most as a substitute for 'very'
12. Dr. Thakur is a most distinguished scholar of Linguistics.
13. Before proper noun to show likeness, e.g.

    My son wants to be a Tendulkar.

    (a batsman like Tendulkar)
14. Before a verb used as a noun, e.g.

    We go for a walk in the morning.

    Dr. Sharma gave a talk on Linguistics.
15. In some phrases, e.g.

    In a hurry, have a pain/mind/headache/chance/fever.

    In a rage, make a fun/noise.

    In a temper.
16. Before partitive expressions of uncountable nouns, e.g.

A drop of water	A mark of respect
An ounce of petrol	A piece of work
A slice of bread	A pinch of salt
A day of judgment	A tanker of water
A cup of tea	An item of furniture
A bottle of wine	A piece of news
A kilo of rice	A work of art
A piece of sandwich	A gallon of diesel
A litre of oil	A quintal of sugar

Various uses of 'The'

It is used:

1. Before a noun as a result of being mentioned a second time, e.g.

   They bought a dictionary. The dictionary was cheap.

2. Before a noun which by reason of locality can represent only one particular thing, e.g.

   Please, close the door. (the door of the room)

   The students are in the lab. (the lab of the college/school)

3. Before a noun made definite by the addition of a prepositional phrase or clause, e.g.

   The girl in blue is my fiancée.

   The girl at the door is my daughter.

   This is the book which I told you about.

4. Before the names of planets and heavenly bodies, e.g.

   the earth, the sky, the weather, the world, the moon, the air, the universe, the climate

5. Before ordinal numbers and 'only'

   May is the fifth month of a year.

   He is the only child of his father.

6. Before adjectives used as nouns denoting a whole class, e.g.

   The rich (rich people) should help the poor (poor people).

   The young (young people) must respect the old (old people).

7. Before names of seas, rivers, oceans, canals, channel, etc.

   The Mediterranean sea, the Ganga, the Suez canal, the Nile, the Atlantic ocean, the English channel

8. When the name of a country or state expresses its features, especially the abbreviated forms, 'the' is used before it, e.g.

   the Netherlands, The UK, the Sudan, the USSR, the Transvaal, the Congo, the USA, the Punjab, etc.

   Here, UK suggests that it is a kingdom that has come as a result of unification of states, so, it is United Kingdom.

9. Before comparative adjectives to show the sense of selection, e.g.

   Najat is the wiser of the two sisters.

   Which is the easier to learn—English or Physics?

10. Before the comparative of parallel construction, e.g.

   The more you read, the more you learn.

   The higher you go, the cooler you feel.

   "The richer the cobbler, the blacker his thumb" (proverb)

11. Before superlative adjectives, e.g.

The biggest	The highest	The most
The tallest	The greatest	The least

12. Before physical parts and articles of clothing, e.g.

   He caught me by the tie.

   The boy hit me on the head.

13. Before physical positions related to time and place, e.g.

The right	The middle	The bottom	In the evening
The front	The top	The centre	The present

   For the time being   In the morning   In the beginning

14. Before the names of political parties, e.g.

The Congress Party	The Communist Party
The Democratic Party	The Republican Party

15. Before the names of newspapers, magazines, periodicals, e.g.

The *Times of India*, the *News Week*, the *Newyork Times*, the *Illustrated Weekly of India*, the *Blitz*, etc.

Note: Nowadays, the use of 'the' before the names of magazines and periodicals is dropped due to the increasing tendency of search for newness and style, etc.

16. Before the names of musical instruments, e.g.

The piano	The violin	The guitar
The drum	The flute	

17. Before the names of great books, e.g.

The Koran	The Ramayan	The Divine Comedy
The Bible	The lliad	The Mahabharat

18. Before nouns showing weight, measure, rate, etc., e.g.

    Banana is sold by the dozen.

    Cloth is sold by the meter.

    Rice is sold by the kilo.

19. Before the names of directions and points of compass, e.g.

The south	The middle west
The north	The near east

    He is going to the south. (Noun)

    He is going south. (Adverb)

20. Before the names of groups of islands, chain of mountains, deserts, gulf, bay, etc., e.g.

The Himalayas	The West Indies	The Andaman Nicobar
The Hebrides	The Gobi desert	

Note: 'The' is not used before the name of a singular peak and island.

Mount Everest	Java	Sumatra	Kailash
Snowdon	Malta	Bermuda	Crete

21. Before the names of hotels, shops, institutions, branches of government, where the name is impersonal one, e.g.

The Midland Bank	The army stores	The judiciary branch
The national cinema	The Bombay restaurant	The legislative branch

22. Before the names of clubs, committee, public places, etc.

The Rotary club	The youth committee
The Lion's club	The town hall

23. Before the names of armed forces, e.g.

The army The navy The police
The highway patrol The state militia

24. Before an adjective that qualifies a proper noun, e.g.

The late Mahatma Gandhi
The immortal Shakespeare

25. Before the names of historical places, buildings, e.g.

The White House The Taj Mahal The Red Fort

26. Before title, rank, profession, e.g.

The Governor	The poet	The principal
The President	The clerk	The dean
The postman	The chairman	The secretary

27. Before the names of inventions, e.g.

The radio The wireless The television
The telephone The computer

We usually say television (without the).

We often watch television.

Can you turn off the television? (the television set)

28. Before the following nouns, e.g.

Opera, office, theatre, picture, cinema, cathedral, station, zoo, museum, bus stop, etc.

My brother works in the office.

I visited the museum yesterday.

29. Before the words showing nationality, e.g.

The Indians	The Chinese	The English
The Dutch	The Libyans	The French

30. Before the first noun in noun + of + noun construction, e.g.

The king of Libya The book of grammar

The leg of animals The nature of man

31. Before a common noun used as an abstract noun to show the feeling, e.g.

    The brother in Orlando saved the life of Oliver.

    The mother in her cried out to see the accident of a child.

32. Before the names of trains, ships and planes, e.g.

    The Vaishali Express   The Vikrant

    The Meghdoot

33. Before the names of historical periods or events, e.g.

    The Roman Empire   The Mugal Empire   The French Revolution

    The Civil War   The First World War (but World War I)

34. Before proper nouns to show a comparison, e.g.

    Tripoli is the Delhi of Libya. (Delhi is the capital of India)

    Kalidas was the Shakespeare of Sanskrit literature.

35. Before nouns to show definiteness, e.g.

    The gold of this ring is pure.

    The honesty of Ram can't be doubted.

    The milk in the bottle is sour.

36. Before the dates of a month, e.g.

    The fourth of January, The fifth of March

37. Before few and little in adjective clause, e.g.

    I spent the little money I had.

    I read the few books I had.

38. Before common noun used as apposition to a proper noun, e.g.

    Tripoli, the capital of Libya, is a big city.

    Gandhi, the worshipper of truth and non-violence, was murdered.

39. Before indefinite quantity or number beginning with most, much, all, etc.

    Most of the students have passed.

    All of the books are missing.

    Some of the milk is left in the bottle.

    One-third of the land has been cultivated.

    Both of the students are intelligent.

40. Before ordinal numbers in dates and titles, e.g.

    August . 15 . 1947 (read: August the fifteenth)

    Edward II (read: Edward the second)

41. Before singular countable noun specifying the whole class, e.g.

    The cow is an animal.

    The camel is the ship of the desert.

Zero articles (Ø)

Zero article as symbolized as Ø referring to the absence of a, an, and the, from a noun:

Zero article is used:

1. Before proper names of people, places, country, town, village, etc., e.g.

   Ali, Delhi, Patna, Libya, Asia, Rohit, Salma (but the forbidden city, the Hague, the Vatican are exceptions)

2. Before the names of days, months, festivals, e.g.

   Friday, January, Ramajan, Id, Holi, Christmas

3. Before uncountable nouns and indefinite plural nouns, e.g.

   She likes tea with milk.

   They make butter and cheese from milk.

   Love is blind.

   Dogs are faithful animals.

4. With words like school, college, university, work, sea, hospital, market, mosque, temple, prison, court, chapel, bed, home, class, camp.

   These nouns take no article when we think of the use made of the building or object.

   We go to school to learn.

   He went to market to do some shopping.

   He went to class/college/university to learn.

   He went to work as a worker.

   He went to hospital as a patient.

   He went to temple/mosque/church/chapel to pray.

   He went to bed to sleep.

   He went home. (adverb)

These nouns take an article when they are visited for some other purposes, e.g.

Father came to the school to talk to the headmaster.

Ahmed went to the hospital to visit a friend.

5. Before the names of other stars or planets, e.g.

   Mercury, Mars, Saturn, Jupiter, Venus, Uranus

6. Before the names of games and sports, e.g.

   Hockey, football, cricket, volleyball, etc.

7. Before the names of disease, e.g.

   Cancer, Cholera, Influenza, Fever

   (but the plague, the mumps, the rickets)

8. Before nouns used as objective complements after appoint, make, crown, elect, declare

   They crowned her queen.

   We appointed him manager.

   We were appointed assistant professors.

9. Before names of meals that hardly ever take an article unless specially qualified, e.g.

   Lunch is the meal between breakfast and supper.

   Dinner is ready, sir.

My friend prepared a good lunch yesterday.

The committee has arranged a dinner to welcome the guests.

10. Before the names of languages and subjects, e.g.

    Arabic, English, political science, history, chemistry

11. Before the noun that takes the verb 'turn' instead of 'become', e.g.

    He turned politician. (He became a politician.)

12. Before the noun that follows kind of/sort of/type of/species of, e.g.

    What kind of book is this?

    This is the best kind of pen.

    (but they take article to qualify the noun)

    What kind of a teacher are you?

    What type of a book is this?

13. Before nouns used in vocative case, e.g.

    Ladies and gentlemen, I am going to speak on current economic policy of the world.

    Come here, boy.

14. Before proper nouns used in possessive case, e.g.

    Today's Times of India, Ali's coat

    Shakespeare's Hamlet

15. Before man, woman, mankind, humanity, society, art, science, parliament, nature, God, life, literature, etc.

16. Before 'most' if it is immediately followed by a noun or a prepositional noun phrase, e.g.

    Most of people know Arabic in Libya.

    Most of the students are diligent.

17. Before the names of companies, airlines, etc.

    Indian airways, Kodak, Sony, Fiat, Quatar airways, etc.

18. Before the names of singular lakes, capes, etc.

Lake superior, cape code, cape wrath, lake Constance, etc.

19. Before noun + number construction, e.g.

    platform 11, size 32, room 116, page 105, section A, group 3, flight no. 535, etc.

20. Before means of transport, and communication, e.g.

    By bus, by car, by air, by ship, by road, by train, by plane, on horseback, on foot, by post, by mail, by e-mail, by satellite link, by phone, by fax, etc.

21. If the means of transport or communication is not preceded by the preposition 'by', it takes an article, e.g.

In a red car	On the plane	Off the train
On the train	In the bus	Over the phone

22. Before the nouns that come in pairs. (parallel constructions)

Father and mother	Brother and sister
Face to face	Neck and neck
Arm in arm	Lawyer and client

23. Before some idioms and phrases, e.g.

Part and parcel	From hand to mouth
From pillar to post	From right to left

EXERCISE-1

Use 'a or an' in the blanks.

...... Polite girl	...... Unique site
...... Ink bottle	...... Ewe
...... One sided affair	...... Bottle
...... Dog	...... Honest deal
...... Unilateral agreement	...... Doctor
...... Historic survey	...... Unaninous decision
...... Engineer	...... Unintentional mistake
...... Heir	...... Finance officer

...... Utensil
...... Ear
...... Iron
...... Eulogy
...... Hungry men
...... Youngmen
...... King
...... Xerox machine
...... Hindu
...... Pen
...... Year
...... Ring
...... Umbrella
...... Universal fact
...... Oldman
...... Policeman
...... Queen
...... X-ray
...... Christian
...... Overseer

EXERCISE-2

Use 'a or an' wherever necessary.

...... Ink
...... House
...... Blackboard
...... European language
...... Intelligent student
...... Engine
...... Dust
...... Beautiful girl
...... School
...... Sheep
...... Mango
...... Dictionary
...... Hard nut
...... Sand
...... Uncountable noun
...... Nice guy
...... Big ball
...... Room
...... Vapour
...... Ugly woman
...... Steam engine
...... Donkey
...... Section officer
...... Opportunity
...... Good news
...... Milk
...... Suit
...... 'f'

EXERCISE-3

Use 'a or an' wherever necessary.

1. Do you live in ...... house or ...... flat?
2. ...... apple has ...... sweet taste.

3. ...... orange juice is good for children.
4. ...... bread is made from ...... flour and ...... milk.
5. ...... chain is made of ...... wood.
6. Will you have ...... lunch with me tomorrow?
7. ...... good student is never late for ...... school.
8. He goes there once ...... week.
9. I always drink ...... coffee.
10. I need more ...... information.
11. What ...... beautiful girl she is!
12. ...... English is ...... European language.
13. You must write in ...... ink. Here is ...... pen.
14. It was ...... lovely party.
15. Salma is ...... clever at cooking.
16. She is ...... extremely beautiful girl.
17. Many ...... man has come.
18. I have never seen such ...... scene before.
19. It is quite ...... difficult ...... question.
20. She is ...... eighty year old lady.
21. Mango sells two dinars ...... kilo.
22. Such ...... girl is my fiancée.
23. ...... Dr. Sharma wants to speak to you.
24. Shakespeare was ...... most renowned scholar of literature.
25. He bought ...... kilo and .... half packets of rice.
26. This boy wants to be ...... Maradona.
27. We go for ...... walk.
28. He is in ...... temper.
29. Give me ...... tea, please.
30. He bought ...... bottle of wine.
31. As ...... leader of the opposition Gulam Gaus receives ...... official salary.

32. His father is ...... lawyer and earns £3000 ...... month.
33. Go and buy ...... half ...... pound of sugar.
34. One-tenth of ...... thousand is ...... hundred.
35. I left ...... meat on the table and the dog has eaten it.

EXERCISE-4

Use 'a/an or the' in the blanks wherever necessary.

1. ...... eye is black or brown.
2. ...... cat eats ...... meat.
3. "I wish I had ...... million dinars", Mr. Al-Ashab said.
4. I learn how to play ...... chess.
5. I'd like to learn ...... Chinese.
6. He wants to join ...... university in ...... England.
7. Doctors are paid more than ...... teachers.
8. We must help ...... poor whenever we can.
9. We don't go to ...... school on ...... Fridays.
10. What ...... wonderful surprise!
11. ...... money is ...... root of all evils.
12. This ring is made of ...... diamond.
13. I waited at ...... station for ...... hour.
14. I met ...... old friend, and he invited me to have ...... lunch with him.
15. What is ...... price of this book?
16. I live on ...... second floor in that building.
17. This is ...... oldest building in ...... city.
18. Salma is ...... most intelligent girl in her family.

19. I usually have ...... toast and ...... coffee for ...... breakfast.
20. ...... English fought ...... French.
21. ...... Meghdoot is ...... fastest train for Delhi.
22. ...... Alps is one of ...... famous mountains in ...... world.
23. ...... Taj Mahal is one of ...... seven wonders of ...... world.
24. ...... blind can't see.
25. What kind of ...... book is this?
26. He doesn't like to have ...... biscuit and ...... coffee.

EXERCISE-5

Use 'a/an or the' wherever necessary.

1. ...... earth moves around ...... sun.
2. Please close ...... door and open ...... window.
3. They will catch ...... first train.
4. I joined ...... army in ...... month of ...... July.
5. Only ...... brave succeed in ...... love and war.
6. ...... Malta is ...... island in ...... Mediterranean sea.
7. ...... USA is ...... powerful country of ...... world.
8. ...... more you read, ... more you learn.
9. Turn to ...... left.
10. ...... Koran is ...... holy book of ...... Muslims.
11. ...... Newyork Times is ...... popular daily.
12. ...... sun rises in ...... east and sets in ...... west.
13. ...... mother in her cried out to see ...... road accident of ...... child.
14. ...... President of india is ...... active lady.
15. Can you turn on ...... television.
16. They go to ...... college to meet ...... principal.
17. He plays ...... cricket, he doesn't play ...... piano.

18. Omar is promoted to ...... post of ...... Assistant Professor.
19. We had ...... good dinner yesterday.
20. ...... Keat's poetry is sensuous.
21. ...... most of ...... students attend their classes.
22. ...... horses are strong animals.
23. ...... hungry man is ...... angry man.
24. Progress is ...... mother of problems.
25. ...... faith is ...... force of life.
26. ...... mob has many heads but no brains.
27. His father is ...... teacher. He goes to ...... school at 9 A.M. by ...... car.
28. I read ...... Times of India everyday before going to ...... office.
29. We are going to visit ...... Hague.
30. He goes to ...... bed at 10 P.M. and gets up in ...... morning at 6 A.M.
31. ...... dog is ...... faithful animal.

EXERCISE-6

Use 'a/an or the' wherever necessary.

1. ...... boy over there is ...... worst in the class in English.
2. All ...... work and no ...... play makes ...... jack a dull boy.
3. He became ...... member of parliament, but later turned ...... socialist.
4. Who made ...... most mistakes?
5. ...... cruel Macbeth had murdered Macduff's wife and children.
6. ...... Ganga is ...... holy river for ...... Hindus.
7. ...... Nile is ...... largest river in ...... world.
8. ...... Al-Mergeb university is one of ...... best universities.

9. Generally ...... rich travel by ...... air and not by ...... sea.
10. He was appointed ...... lecturer in ...... new college.
11. ...... English is ...... link language of ...... world.
12. Ahmed is ...... only issue of his parents.
13. ...... richer the cobbler, ... blacker his thumb.
14. Some engineers from ...... sudan have come to attend ...... meeting.
15. I go to ...... college sometimes to meet ...... Dean.
16. We had ...... tasty breakfast at home yesterday.
17. Youth is ...... wonderful thing, what ...... crime to waste on ...... children.
18. ...... business of ...... novelist is not to chronicle great events but to make small one interesting.
19. ...... ass that brays ...... most eats ...... least.
20. I am ...... English teacher in ...... JP University.
21. Faiza is ...... MLA and her brother is ...... MP.
22. ...... friend in need is ...... friend indeed.
23. ...... good example is ...... best sermon.
24. ...... German hate ...... French.
25. What ...... weather we are having and what ...... abominable climate it is.

10

Sentence

What is a Sentence?

A sentence is made up of words which are placed in a grammatical order to give meaning. It starts with a capital letter and ends with a full stop. It has at least a subject and a verb, i.e. a principal clause. It is the largest grammatical unit of a language as it gives a complete idea.

In the light of the aforesaid definition, it can be said that a sentence cannot be made up of one word only. It raises an important question, should we consider the responses like 'yes', 'no', 'go', 'eat', etc. as sentences? Look at this conversation between Amit and Ashok

Amit : What is your father's name?

Ashok : Awadh Narayan Sinha.

Amit : Does he teach English?

Ashok : Yes.

Here the responses given by Ashok are made up of one-word only. Are they sentences?

Strictly speaking, they are not sentences. Though they have some features of sentences. Had Ashok answered like

'My father's name is Awadh Narayan Sinha.'

'Yes, he teaches English.'

Then only the responses would have been sentences. But at the same time we find that these one-word responses give complete meaning. Because of this complete meaning feature of such expressions, we call them utterances, not sentences.

Constituents of a Sentence

Now let us look at the constituents of a sentence. A sentence is made up of phrases and clauses. A phrase is that group of words in a sentence which gives the partial meaning. A sentence may be made up of many phrases. For example,

That boy has run very fast in the field.

This sentence has the following phrases:

That boy	(noun phrase)
has run	(verb phrase)
very fast	(adverb phrase)
in the field	(prepositional phrase)

Each phrase gives a fragment of idea (partial meaning) that collectively gives the complete meaning of the sentence.

On the other hand, a clause is that group of words which has a subject and a verb inside it. This combination of subject and verb may not be explicit in some cases, i.e. it may remain hidden also. Look at these sentences.

A. 'That man met me while I was walking'.

This sentence has got two clauses.

That man met me. (main clause)
Subject verb

While I was walking. (subordinate clause)
Subject verb

This sentence has explicit (clear) subjects and verbs.

B. Though very intelligent, he is lazy.

though very intelligent (subordinate clause)

he is lazy (main clause)

In this sentence, the subordinate clause doesn't have explicit subject and verb. These are hidden as we can say 'though he is very intelligent he is lazy'.

Thus, we see that a sentence can satisfactorily be considered as a combination of phrases and clauses. There can be no sentence without phrase and clause if we consider definitions of phrase and clause in terms of implicit items or their assimilatory capacity. By assimilatory capacity, we mean the ability to accommodate adjectives, determiners, quantifiers, etc. in the case of nouns, intensifier in the case of adverbs, etc. For example, 'a strong man' is a noun phrase with a determiner and adjective. 'Man' alone can be treated as a noun phrase because it can accommodate a determiner or adjective if a context so demands. In order to make a scientific analysis, it is better to make a departure from that traditional concept of phrase which fails to convincingly analyse the underlined patterns of a sentence. Look at this sentence.

'Those people have gone'

If someone asks, how many phrases are there in this sentence?

It will sound surprising to answer—it has two phrases but it is true.

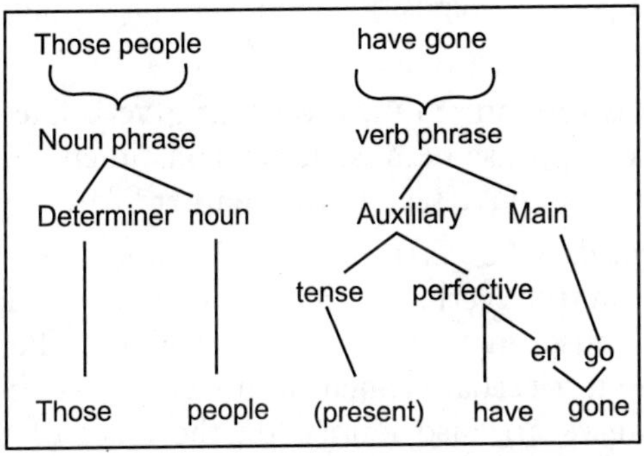

This analysis clearly indicates that both the parts give partial meaning and the whole meaning of this sentence comes in combination only. So these two parts are phrases. Here it is important to note that the meaning of a verb phrase changes with the change of auxiliary. Hence, it is logical to analyse a sentence like this in terms of phrases. On this basis, it can be said that any sentence will have at least two phrases—noun phrase and verb phrase. In addition to it there may be an adjective phrase, an adverb phrase and a prepositional phrase in a sentence. Thus, phrases can be realized in these many forms.

a. Noun Phrase
b. Verb Phrase
c. Adjective Phrase
d. Adverb Phrase
e. Prepositional Phrase

Let us look at some examples.

1.	That tall boy	is running	very fast.	
	noun ph	verb ph	adverb ph	
2.	A man	of France	looks	very handsome.
	noun ph	prepositional ph	verb ph	adjective ph

Here it is relevant to mention that a verb like 'looks' may be treated as a phrase because it has constituents like auxiliary and main that we have seen in the chapter 'Verb'.

As regards the clausal constituents, we know that depending on the verbal elements, explicit or implicit, the number of clauses in a sentence is determined. There can be no clause without a verbal element in it. As we saw in the case of phrases, clauses are also named on the basis of the function that they perform in a sentence.

Let us look at different types of clauses.

1. **Noun Clause:** When a clause functions as a noun in a sentence it is called noun clause. It is found in the form of a subject or an object in a sentence. Ex:
   (a) What he thinks is correct.
   (What he thinks = noun clause (subject))

(b) He knows where I live.

noun clause
(object)

2. **Adjective Clause:** When a clause functions as an adjective in a sentence, it is called adjective clause. It modifies a noun or pronoun like adjectives.

   Ex:

   (a) The boy who comes to me is intelligent.

   adjective clause

   (b) He lives in the house that is very big.

   adjective clause

Adjective clause is called relative clause also as it gives some additional information about nouns or pronouns.

3. **Adverb Clause:** It is that clause which functions as an adverb in a sentence.

Ex:

I go wherever I like.

adverb clause

Classification of the Constituents of a Sentence

We see that a sentence is a group of words that may be classified as phrases or clauses. But each phrase or clause is also divisible into separate grammatical units, i.e. each word of a sentence can be classified into independent units like noun, pronoun, verb, subject, object, etc. In order to make a scientific study of each word that constitutes a sentence, we may follow two approaches—formal and functional.

Formal Approach

It is that approach of studying the words of a sentence in which the grammatical category of a word is determined on the basis of its form, that is to say, we decide the grammatical category of a word just after looking at it independently. Look at these words

boy (noun)	and (conjunction)
he (pronoun)	slowly (adverb)
good (adjective)	go (verb)

After looking at these words, we can say about their grammatical classes as shown above. Here, the form itself indicates the grammatical class. The classification of words according to parts of speech comes under the formal classification. All those words which can be used as substitutes for one another in a sentence at structural level usually belongs to the same formal grammatical category.

For example:

That boy is good.

My pen is short.

His friend is intelligent.

In these sentences, a noun can be substituted for another noun and so is the case with adjectives. That means depending on the ability of substitution, the grammatical category of a word is determined in formal classification. Look at these examples of formal classification.

a. Abhishek is very intelligent.
(noun) (verb) (adverb) (adjective)

b. She likes games.
(pronoun) (verb) (noun)

c. Birds fly in the sky.
(noun) (verb) (preposition) (article) (noun)

d. Man is a social animal.
(noun) (verb) (article) (adjective) (noun)

e. Arti and Anju are friends.
(noun) (conjunction) (noun) (verb) (noun)

Thus we see that in formal classification, the grammatical clause of each word is decided according to its form.

Functional Approach

In this approach, the grammatical clause of a word is determined according to the function that it performs in a sentence. Here, a group of words is also taken as a single functional unit if many words together function as one grammatical category. In this classification, a sentence is divided into five categories—subject, verb, object, complement and adverbial (adjunct).

Let us look at these one by one.

(a) **Subject:** It is that part of a sentence about which anything is said. It usually functions as the doer of an action in a sentence. All the underlined parts are the subjects of these sentences given below.

(i) Alok goes to market.

(ii) That boy plays chess.

(iii) My pen is costly.

(iv) Who is he?

(v) What does Arun like?

(b) **Object:** It is that part of a sentence which receives the effect of an action caused by the subject. It is that word or a group of words which comes after a transitive verb. An object may be direct or indirect depending on the situation. A direct object is usually something that is received, and an indirect object is that which receives. Look at these examples.

(i) He plays football. (object)

(ii) Aman bought a book. (object)

(iii) She gave a present to me.
(direct object) (indirect object)
↓ ↓
the item received the receiver

(iv) He told me (indirect object) a story (direct object).

All the verbs in the sentences given above are transitive.

(c) **Complement:** It is that part of a sentence which completes the meaning. A complement comes after a linking verb. It may be a word or a group of words. Look at these examples.

(i) My friend is tall. (complement)

(ii) Their house is in Patna. (complement)

(iii) The teacher became angry. (complement)

(iv) They made him captain. (complement)

A complement that modifies a subject is subject complement. A complement that modifies an object is an object complement. A complement that modifies a verb is an adverbial complement. A complement that modifies an adjective is an adjectival complement. Look at these examples.

(i) She is beautiful. (subject complement)

(ii) Ajit made him brilliant. (object complement)

(iii) He left me in the park. (adverbial complement)

(iv) It is true that smoking reduces our life. (adjectival complement)

(d) **Adverbial:** It is that part of a sentence which gives some additional information in a sentence. An adverbial may be a word or a group of words. Look at these examples.

(i) They played chess yesterday. (adverbial)

(ii) He was running <u>very slowly</u>.
(adverbial)

(iii) They met me <u>when I was walking</u>.
(adverbial)

As regards a verb, it has already been talked about in detail in the previous chapters.

Thus, according to functional approach, a sentence can be divided into these five categories mentioned above. Any sentence has got a subject and a verb necessarily. Rest of the categories may or may not be found in a sentence. Let us look at these sentences analyzed in terms of the functional categories.

(i) <u>That boy</u> (subject) <u>is</u> (verb) <u>very tall</u>. (complement)

(ii) <u>To write a book</u> (subject) <u>is</u> (verb) <u>very difficult</u>. (complement)

(iii) Shreya (subject) <u>gave</u> (verb) <u>a book</u> (object direct) <u>to me</u>. (object indirect)

(iv) <u>She</u> (subject) <u>made</u> (verb) <u>me</u> (object) <u>nervous</u> (complement) <u>in the class</u>. (adverbial)

Thus, we find that a sentence may have all the functional categories in it, but subject and verb are the essential constituents without which a formal sentence is not possible.

Basic Sentence Pattern

It is that pattern of functional categories which is used for producing different kinds of English sentences. It is called basic because different combinations of these patterns produce multiple kinds of sentences used in English. There are basically five kinds of patterns found in English.

1. Subject + verb
   (Ahmed runs.)
2. Subject + verb + complement
   (She is good.)

3. Subject + verb + object
   (They play chess.)
4. Subject + verb + object (indirect) + object (direct)
   (He gave me a book.)
5. Subject + verb + object + complement
   (People made me president.)

As regards adverbial, its place is changeable and it is usually an optional element as it is used to give additional information in a sentence. Now let us look at some examples.

a.	Binod (subject)	saw (verb)	a dog (object)	in the field. (adverbial)
b.	He (subject)	remained (verb)	puzzled (complement)	for long. (adverbial)
c.	They (subject)	are (verb)	at the door. (complement)	
d.	My friend (subject)	taught (verb)	him (object indirect)	many lessons. (object direct)
e.	They (subject)	turned (verb)	me (object)	red. (complement)
f.	What he does (subject)		is (verb)	good. (complement)

On the basis of these examples, we can understand that the different sentences used in English conform to the basic sentence patterns. Any sentence of English can be analyzed in terms of these functional categories.

Types of Sentences

(A) According to Meaning

(B) According to Structure

(A) Types of Sentences According to Meaning

We use language for communicating different kinds of ideas. The nature of these ideas differs from sentence to sentence depending on contexts. On the basis of these diversities of contexts and meanings, there are basically four types of sentences.

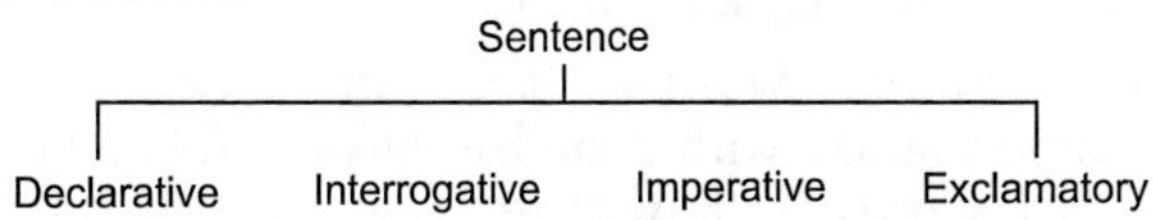

1. Declarative Sentence: Declarative sentences, as the name implies, are those that pass on statements (declarations), information and discourses in general. A declarative sentence is used in affirmative, negative and emphatic forms. Majority of the sentences used in English language are declarative sentences.

(i) *Affirmative*: All those declarative sentences which give positive opinion or remark about any person or thing, are said to be affirmative. An affirmative sentence expresses a reasonable degree of confidence of the speaker in the statement made by him/her.

Examples:

He reads English.

They are interested in games.

(ii) *Negative*: Those declarative sentences which give negative opinion or remark about any person or thing are called negative sentences. They always have negative words (no, not, never, etc.) in them.

Examples:

He doesn't read English.

They are not interested in games.

(iii) *Emphatic*: Those declarative sentences in which additional force is applied on action in order to emphasize it with the help of auxiliary verbs (do, does, did), are called emphatic sentences.

Examples:

He does read English.

They did show interest in games.

2. Interrogative Sentence: Interrogative sentences are those which ask questions. Depending on the nature of questions, they take the following seven forms.

(i) *Question Word Questions*: They seek full information with complete answer. They begin with 'wh-words' or 'how'.

Questions	Answers
What is your name?	My name is Omkar.
What do you do?	I am a teacher.
Where do you come from?	I come from Patna.
How is everything going on?	Everything is going fine.

(ii) *Yes/No Questions*: They begin with auxiliary verbs and require short answers.

	Questions	Short Answers
1.	Is she married?	Yes, she is/No, she isn't.
2.	Does she speak English?	Yes, she does/No, she doesn't.
3.	Did Salma know Arabic?	Yes, she did/No, she didn't.

In Yes/No questions, the answer is given either affirmatively (Yes, she is. or negatively No, she isn't.)

Note: The subject of Yes/No answer is always a pronoun. (see example – 3)

(iii) *Alternative Questions*: They are the questions of choice between two alternatives joined by 'or' and need full answers in both affirmative and negative ways.

Questions	Answers
Do you like fish or chicken?	I like fish. I do not like chicken.

Will they watch TV or play football.	They will watch TV. They will not play football.
Are you a teacher or a doctor?	I am a teacher. I am not a doctor.

(iv) *Rhetorical Questions*: They are questions only in form but statements in sense.

Questions	Statements
Will man not die one day?	Man will die one day.
Can a monkey change his nature?	A monkey can't change his nature.
Should we tell a lie?	We should not tell a lie.

(v) *Question Tags*: They are short questions added to a statement to get confirmation.

Shikha is a clever girl, isn't she?

He is not intelligent, is he?

(vi) *Emphatic Questions*: They are used to express anger or surprise by using either 'ever' or on the earth, in the world, the hell, the devil, etc. with question words.

Who on the earth can change my decision?

Who the devil is he?

Who ever are they?

(vii) *Statement Used as Question*: The rising tone of a statement is also considered a question.

You are going to market?

He is a teacher?

3. **Imperative Sentence:** Those sentences which express command, request, advice, etc. in affirmative, negative and emphatic forms are imperative sentences. These sentences normally begin with a main verb. Sometimes please/kindly is used to make a polite request.

Affirmative	Negative	Emphatic
Do it.	Don't do it.	Do do it.

Come in. Don't come in. Do come in.

Please/kindly is used to express request.

Please help the poor.

Help the poor, please.

Note: '*Please*' is separated by a comma if it is used at the end of a sentence.

4. Exclamatory Sentence: Those sentences which are used to express all on a sudden strong feeling and emotion like anger, pain, delight, surprise, etc. are called exclamatory sentences. An exclamatory sentence ends with the sign of exclamation (!). Such exclamations are mainly expressed in the following ways.

(i) What + noun...........	What a girl she is!
(ii) What + a/an+adj/adv + noun	What a smart boy you are!
(iii) How + adjective/adverb +	How beautiful she is!
(iv) Oh that + clause	Oh that I were a millionaire!
(v) Would that + clause	Would that I had helped him!
(vi) Incomplete sentences	Excellent! Fantastic! Murder!

Note: The subject and the verb in an exclamatory sentence retain their normal word order.

Example:

What a beautiful girl <u>she is</u>!

How old <u>he is</u>!

(B) Types of Sentence According to Structure

We saw that a clause is an important constituent of a sentence. On the basis of functions a clause performs. We classify clauses as noun clause, adjective clause and adverb clause. There is another scope also of classifying clauses in terms of the meaning that they convey in a sentence. The clause that gives the main idea of a sentence is called main or principal clause, whereas the clause that gives additional idea or an idea to support the main idea is called subordinate clause. Look at this sentence and its clauses.

I started for Ranchi when the rain stopped.

main clause	subordinate clause

Here, there are two clauses with separate subjects and verbs. But out of these, one clause gives the main idea and another gives additional information. Thus, we can have many clauses in one sentence and on the basis of the nature of these clauses, we classify sentences. There are four kinds of sentences based on clausal relationship.

1. Simple Sentence: It is that sentence which has one clause only which gives one idea. It has one subject and one predicate. Predicate is that part of a sentence which describes the subject. A predicate may have only one verb or a verb along with some words or phrases.

Examples:

Alok	went.
(Subject)	(predicate)
My teacher	has left for Gaya.
(Subject)	(predicate)
They	went home.
(Subject)	(predicate)

In all of these examples, we find a combination of a subject and a predicate. All of these sentences have one subject and one verb, i.e. one clause only. When there is only one clause in a sentence, it is always a main clause.

2. Compound Sentence: It is that sentence which has two or more than two main clauses joined together with a conjunction. Sometimes, a semi-colon is used in order to join two main clauses. Further, a compound sentence gives more than one idea based on the number of main clauses.

Examples:

A : I was playing	and	she was reading.
main clause	conjunction	main clause

B : He is rich but dull.

C : United we stand; divided we fall.

All of these are compound sentences with certain differences. In sentence A, we find two independent main clauses giving two ideas joined together with the help of a conjunction. In sentence B, we find two clauses but some part of the second main clause is hidden (implicit). It is a contracted form of:

'He is rich but he is dull.'
(hidden)

'But' is the conjunction joining together two separate ideas (features) of richness and dullness of an individual. In sentence C, a semi-colon functions as a conjunction with the help of which two ideas have been put together. Usually, a semi-colon is used in the case of philosophical statements.

3. Complex Sentence: It is that sentence which has one main clause and at least one subordinate clause. Here, the main idea is supported by an additional piece of information given by the subordinate clause. The subordinate clause usually remains attached to the main clause with the help of subordinating conjunctions like if, while, when, before, after, etc.

Examples:

A. I was reading when he came to me.
Main clause subordinate clause

B. Though very young, he has written five books.
Subordinate clause main clause

C. Having done that work, I left for my home.
Subordinate clause main clause

All of these sentences are complex sentences with one main clause and one subordinate clause, but they are different in structures. In sentence A, there are two clear-cut clauses with explicit subject and verb. In sentence B, the subordinate clause does not have explicit subject and verb, but it can be understood with the help of the main clause. Here, 'though very young' is the contracted form of 'though he is very young'. The main clause in this sentence gets more force because of the subordinate clause. A subordinate clause also contains an idea but it is not the main idea that a speaker or writer tries to convey in a sentence. In sentence C, the subordinate clause does not have an explicit subject and a subordinating conjunction, but two ideas in terms of main and subsidiary can easily be derived from this sentence.

4. Compound Complex Sentence: It is that sentence which has at least two main clauses and one subordinate clause. The main clauses give independent ideas supported by subordinate clauses. A compound complex sentence is a comparatively big sentence as it has at least three clauses (two main and one subordinate).

It has the feature of a compound as well as a complex sentence as the name implies.

Examples:

<table>
<tr><td></td><td></td><td></td><td colspan="2">Complex feature</td></tr>
<tr><td>A.</td><td><u>He came</u>
main clause</td><td>and</td><td><u>left shortly</u>
main clause</td><td><u>as he had no time</u>.
subordinate clause</td></tr>
<tr><td></td><td colspan="3">Compound feature</td><td>Complex feature</td></tr>
</table>

In this sentence, 'he came and left shortly' represents a compound sentence with two main clauses in it. Further, 'he left shortly as he had no time' represents a complex sentence with one main clause and one subordinate clause. Thus, a compound complex sentence (mixed sentence) justifies its name. Look at these compound complex sentences to clarify it further.

<table>
<tr><td>A.</td><td>I bought a pen
(1st main cl)</td><td>while going to market
(1st subordinate cl)</td><td>but
(conjunction)</td></tr>
<tr><td></td><td>lost it
(2nd main cl)</td><td>while coming back home.
(2nd subordinate cl)</td><td></td></tr>
<tr><td>B.</td><td>You may fail
(1st main cl)</td><td>if you don't study
(1st subordinate cl)</td><td>and
(conjunction)</td></tr>
<tr><td></td><td>you will top
(2nd main cl)</td><td>if you work hard.
(2nd subordinate cl)</td><td></td></tr>
</table>

C. As you know (1st subordinate cl) I work very hard (1st main cl) but (conjunction) success rarely comes to me. (2nd main cl)

The Concept of Simple and Multiple Sentence

Now we have seen that a simple sentence is made up of one clause and all other kinds of sentences are made up of more than one clause. Further, when we analyze a compound or complex sentence, we find that they are combinations of simple sentences. Look at these examples.

(a) She looks beautiful when she uses specks.

(b) He is tall but weak.

(c) Ahmed is strict and he doesn't favour anyone but none likes him.

A minute analysis of these sentences makes it clear that each sentence is a combination of simple sentences. As for instance, sentence 'a' is made up of 'she looks beautiful' and 'she uses specks': sentence 'b' is made up of 'he is tall' and 'he is weak': sentence 'c' is made up of 'Ahmed is strict', 'he doesn't favour anyone' and 'none likes him'. On this basis, we can say that there are two kinds of sentences in English—'Simple' and 'Multiple'. A multiple sentence is that which is a combination of simple sentences. Hence, compound, complex, and compound-complex sentences are multiple sentences.

When we look at the type of multiple sentences, we find that there are three processes through which simple sentences are joined to produce multiple sentences. These processes are coordination, subordination and embedding.

(a) Coordination: It is that process of combining simple sentences in which two or more than two main clauses are put together with the help of conjunctions. Coordination produces compound sentences.

(b) Subordination: It is that process of combining simple sentences in which one main clause is combined with at least one subordinate clause. Subordination produces complex sentences. In subordination, a subordinate clause functions as an adverbial in a sentence.

(c) **Embedding:** It is that process of combining simple sentences in which one clause is embedded (put inside) in another clause. In the process of embedding, the clause that is embedded usually functions as either the subject or object or complement in a sentence. A big clause that accommodates a small clause (embedded) in it, is called matrix clause. The clause which is embedded as the part of matrix clause, is called embedded clause. Look at this sentence.

subject — verb — complement

(sub) Libya (verb) produces (obj) oil | is | a fact.

embedded clause

Here, 'Libya produces oil' is the subject which is in the form of a clause as it has a subject 'Libya' and a verb 'produce'. This clause is, therefore, an embedded clause which is put inside a bigger clause that runs into the whole sentence. For the bigger clause (matrix clause), the embedded clause functions as the subject. Thus, embedding as a process has put two simple sentences 'Libya produces oil' and 'it is a fact' together. Let us see some more examples.

Matrix clause

(a) He knows what I am.
Sub verb object (embedded clause)

Matrix clause

(b) Ahmed became what he wanted.
Sub verb complement (embedded clause)

Matrix clause

(c) He gave what he brought to all who needed.

Sub verb direct object indirect object

(embedded clause) (embedded clause)

Thus, we see that an embedded clause may function as an object or complement in addition to its function as a subject. We may find more than one embedded clause also in one sentence as shown in the sentence 'c'.

As we know that in English we can produce sentences of any length, we can find a sentence with the matrix clause as well as a subordinate clause.

Matrix clause

He will say what he knows if I ask him.

Sub verb object adverbial

(embedded clause) (subordinate clause)

In this sentence, two processes subordination and embedding are involved. Moreover, we can find sentences with all the three processes involved. Look at this sentence.

Matrix clause

You play when I allow but he, who is my son, plays

(main cl) (subordinate cl) (conj) (embedded cl)

even when I do not allow.

(subordinate cl)

This compound-complex sentence involves co-ordination, subordination and embedding as the processes in its constitution. The above matrix clause functions as the main clause. Matrix clause functions as a main clause especially when it is subordinated as is the case above.

The Relevance of Embedding as a Concept

This concept of embedding has added to the scientificity of sentence analysis to a large extent. It can be seen in such a way. Look at these sentences.

(a) It is true — that Libya produces oil.
main clause — complement

(b) The teacher said that the earth revolves around the sun.
main clause — object

(c) He came out — when it was raining.
main clause — adverbial

In the traditional methods of analysis, we find that all these sentences are complex sentences with two clauses—main and subordinate. But when we look at the features of main clauses, we find a lack of uniformity. The main clauses of the sentences (a) and (b) do not give the main idea of the sentences whereas in the sentence (c), the main clause gives the main idea. Because of this basic difference in the feature of main clauses, it is logical to evolve a different way of analysis. The concept of embedding is a result of such effort that has made the analysis of English sentences more scientific and logical.

The lack of scientificity in the analysis of aforesaid sentences can further be clarified. In sentence (a), the main idea is 'Libya produces oil', in sentence (b) the main idea is 'the earth revolves around the sun', in sentence (c) the main idea is 'came out'. In the first two sentences, main idea comes through subordinate clauses while in the last one, it comes through the main clause. It clearly indicates the shortcoming of the traditional method of analysis of English sentences.

The concept of embedding has solved this problem by introducing matrix and embedded clauses in the analysis of complex sentences. It is reasonable to say that a complex sentence may be a combination of matrix clause and embedded clause as well as main clause and subordinate clause. Herein, lies the justification behind the introduction of the concept of embedding.

EXERCISE-1

1. What do you mean by a sentence? How is it different from an utterance?
2. What are the constituents of a sentence?
3. What is the difference between phrase and clause?
4. Identify the phrases of these sentences and name them.
   (a) Most of my friends have visited the main cities of the world.
   (b) His neighbour works very hard during the winter season.
   (c) A beautiful house has been constructed in my town.
   (d) The students of my college are going for a picnic in the next week.
   (e) A man in need is a friend indeed.
5. Identify the clauses of these sentences and name them.
   (a) What you do is what you like.
   (b) I like the place where she lives.
   (c) She plays chess is known to all who live here.
   (d) While he was young, he wrote five books.
   (e) The doctor who treated me was very gentle.
6. Show the differences between these.
   (a) Formal approach and functional approach
   (b) Noun clause and adjective clause
   (c) Noun phrase and verb phrase
   (d) Adjective phrase and adverb phrase
   (e) Direct object and indirect object.

EXERCISE-2

1. Write down the formal categories of the words of the following sentences.
   (a) They play chess very well.
   (b) Ahmed is an intelligent student of his class.

(c) My father has a beautiful house.

(d) She does not run very fast.

(e) Ambuj and Omkar are good friends.

2. Write down the functional categories of the words of the following sentences.

(a) The doctor who lives in Libya is very gentle.

(b) All the chairs are broken in that room.

(c) They gave me a piece of advice.

(d) Aman is a teacher in that school.

(e) Niraj turned fast.

EXERCISE-3

Make these sentences interrogative.

(a) I am a doctor.

(b) He works hard.

(c) He played football.

(d) You are working hard.

(e) They know me well.

(f) Suraj broke this chair.

(g) He works in this hospital.

(h) Boys learn English in school.

EXERCISE-4

Make these sentences negative.

(a) He does it.

(b) You know it well.

(c) He hit me on the head.

(d) They shut the door.

(e) You write a letter.

(f) People speak Arabic.

(g) You know the place where I live.

EXERCISE-5

Make these sentences (a) negative and (b) emphatic.

(a) Bring a chair.
(b) Inform the police.
(c) Ring the fire brigade.
(d) Write a letter to him.
(e) Come to see me today.
(f) Send money.
(g) Post a letter.
(h) Type a letter.
(i) Draft an application.
(j) Give me ten dinars.
(k) He works hard.
(l) You know Omar.
(m) He teaches English.
(n) Amrit did a good job for me.

EXERCISE-6

Identify whether these sentences are simple, compound, complex or compound-complex.

(a) Most of my friends live in India.
(b) The more you get; the more you want.
(c) He plays when it is hot and studies when it is cold.
(d) She is beautiful but dull.
(e) Although I have interest in games, I do not want to give much time to it.
(f) To err is human; to forgive divine.
(g) They saw a tiger but did not feel scared.
(h) Either you go there or come here.
(i) They left for London even when it was raining heavily.
(j) Having played chess, I decided to study.

EXERCISE-7

Write short notes on these.

(a) Matrix clause
(b) Embedded clause
(c) Co-ordination
(d) Sub-ordination
(e) Embedding
(f) Multiple sentence

EXERCISE-8

Identify the processes involved (sub-ordination, co-ordination, embedding) in the formation of the following sentences.

(a) The man I met in the market was a teacher.
(b) I do not know what he wants.
(c) You go wherever you like.
(d) They gave a book to all who needed it.
(e) The scholar said that the sun rises in the east.
(f) Though very laborious, he could not succeed in the examination.
(g) Where fools reign, it is folly to be wise.
(h) She does not know how to write a sentence but she has written many books.
(i) She likes what I dislike.

11

Time and Tense

What is Time?

Time is a non-grammatical concept that is ever flowing. It neither stops nor ceases even for a single moment.

What is Tense?

Tense is a grammatical term that indicates the time of action and state of a verb.

Kinds of Tenses

According to the traditional school of thought, there are three tenses in English.

(i) Present Tense

(ii) Past Tense

(iii) Future Tense

Each tense has four sub-classes.

(i) Simple

(ii) Progressive

(iii) Perfect

(iv) Perfect Progressive

Now let us talk about all kinds of tense one by one.

Present Simple Tense

Structure:

Affirmative: Sub + v_1 (s/es) + others (obj/comp/adjunct)

Examples:

He reads a book. (object)

Honey tastes sweet. (complement)

We walk in the field. (Adjunct)

Negative: sub + do/does + not + v_1 + others

Examples:

He doesn't read a book.

We don't walk in the field.

Emphatic: sub + do/does + v_1 + others

Examples:

He does read a book.

We do walk in the field.

Interrogative: do/does + sub + v_1 + others

Examples:

Does he read a book?

Do we walk in the field?

A brief description of subject, verb, and object, which have been included under the heading 'others':

(i) *Subject*: The subject of the aforesaid sentences clearly indicates that a singular subject (he, honey) takes singular verb (verb + s/es), and a plural subject takes a verb without 's/es', i.e. a plural verb. Look at these examples.

It rains.	(singular subject, verb with 's')
Lions roar.	(plural subject, verb without 's')

Note: First person singular number pronoun 'I' is an exception to this rule. It always takes plural verb in a sentence of simple present tense.

(ii) *Verb*: As the tense is the form of a verb, it is important to explain the various forms of a verb.

The main verb has five forms.

$Verb_1$—It is the base form of a verb. It is always plural and is in present tense, e.g. go, come, play, etc.

$Verb_2$—It is the past form of a verb. It is found in the same form with singular as well as plural subjects, e.g. went, came, played, etc.

$Verb_3$—It is the past participle form that is 'verb + en/ed' such as gone, come, played, etc.

$Verb_4$—It is the present participle form (verb + ing) such as going, coming, playing, etc.

$Verb_5$—It is the singular form of the verb. It takes s/es at its end such as goes, comes, plays, etc.

Examples:

Plural verb (base form)	Past	Past participle	Present participle	Singular
V_1	V_2	V_3	V_4	V_5
Write	Wrote	Written	Writing	Writes
Do	Did	Done	Doing	Does
Know	Knew	Known	Knowing	Knows

Note: Finite verbs (auxiliary, transitive and intransitive) are always used according to the number and person of their subjects.

The two main constituents of a sentence are subject and verb, without which a sentence can't be framed. Other constituents like object, complement and adjunct are used either to make the meaning clear or to give some additional information.

So far as the use of other constituents in a sentence is concerned, the transitive verb takes an object, intransitive verb takes an adjunct (adverbial), and linking verb takes a complement. So the structure is like this:

Sub + transitive verb + object

Sub + intransitive verb + adjunct

Sub + linking verb + complement

(See all these in detail in the chapter on 'sentence')

Uses of Simple Present Tense

It is used:

(i) to express universal truth

The earth moves round the sun.

The sun rises in the east.

(ii) to express habitual actions

I get up at six o'clock in the morning.

He takes tea every morning.

Note: Adverbs of frequency are normally used: always, after, never, everybody, etc.

(iii) to express planned future action

The college re-opens in September.

Omar leaves for India next month.

(iv) to express natural or inherent qualities

The sun gives us light and heat.

The earth is round.

(v) to express professional activities

A barber cuts hair.

A cobbler mends shoes.

A baker bakes bread.

(vi) to express proverbs/sayings/quotations

A bad carpenter always quarrels with his tools.

One swallow doesn't make a summer.

Keats says, 'A thing of beauty is a joy for ever'.

(vii) to express the running commentary of games and sports.

Maradona heads the ball and puts it into the goal post.

Dhoni hits the ball.

(viii) to describe past events

Italy invades Libya.

Sohrab attacks Rustom and defeats him.

(ix) to express contextual truth

I understand what you mean.

I see what is going to happen.

(x) to express future time in subordinate clause

If she combs her hair she will look better.

Don't release your seat belts until the plane completely stops.

Note: Subordinating conjunctions if, as soon as, when, unless, after, till, until, even if, in case, etc. normally take simple present tense to express future time.

(xi) to express exclamation when the sentence begins with 'here' or 'there'

Here comes the bus.

There goes the train.

Present Progressive Tense

Structure:

Affirmative	-	Sub + am/is/are + v_4 + others (obj/compl/adjunct) I am reading a book.
Negative	-	Sub + am/is/are + not + v_4 + others
		He is not reading a book.
Interrogative	-	Am/is/are + sub + v_4 + others
		Are you going to Tripoli today?
Wh-question	-	Wh-word + am/is/are + sub + v_4 + ?
		Where are you going, son?

The progressive form (verb + ing) is quite common in this tense.

The auxiliary verbs 'am', 'is' and 'are' have the concord with subject like this:

'I' takes 'am'.

We, you, they, and other plural nouns take 'are'.

He, she, it and other singular nouns take 'is'.

Examples:

I am going to London.

He is coming today.

They are reading a book.

Uses of Present Progressive Tense

It is used:

(i) to express present/future action/plan

He is reading a novel. (present action)

The president is coming tomorrow. (future action)

Omar is giving a party next Friday.

I am going to India next week.

(ii) to express such situation that irritates someone

He is always vexing me.

Salma is always demanding new dress.

(iii) to express a change of one state/situation into another, usually become, go, get, grow, etc. are used.

The problems related to university work are getting more and more complicated.

Your body is becoming better day by day.

Static verbs with restrictions:

Usually, static verbs are not used in progressive form except in very limited contexts. They are of five kinds:

(a) Verbs of senses (perception)

see, here, smell, touch, taste, notice, feel.

We see with our eyes.

The flower smells sweet.

But 'he is smelling a flower' expresses a temporary activity.

Here the verb is dynamic (as opposed to static) to express momentary pleasure.

(b) Verbs of emotion

These verbs express feeling.

Love, hate, like, dislike, adore, abhor, detest, care, wish, mind, want, desire, hope.

A cat likes fish.

I wish you a happy journey.

I want to go home.

(c) Verbs of cogitation (knowing)

These verbs express the sense of understanding.

Believe, trust, think, understand, know, recall, mind, mean, forget, remember, realize, suppose.

You know Arabic.

You understand what I say.

(d) Verbs of possession

These verbs express ownership or relationship.

Own, owe, belong, possess, have.

This flat belongs to Ali.

Rahim owes five hundred dinars to me.

I have two cars. (one's property)

Sana has blue eyes. (physical characteristic)

Omar has a very good memory. (mental ability)

I have a beautiful wife. (relation)

But 'have' is used in progressive sense to express the meaning of eat/take.

I am having breakfast and tea.

(e) Verbs of relational qualities

These verbs express the situational conditions.

Appear, seem, look, require, resemble, contain, consist of, suffice, include, equal, fit, matter (keep = continue), concern, signify, remain, deserve.

He appears to be ill.

She deserves respect.

This book includes all important chapters.

But many of these stative verbs are used as dynamic verbs to express deliberate or voluntary activity.

Some of them are used as dynamic verbs with a different meaning.

Look at these examples:

We <u>hear</u> with our ears. (perceive with the ears)

The judge is hearing the case. (in a legal sense)

Why does she appear so sad today? (seem)

When is your book appearing? (publish)

We see with our eyes. (the power of sights)

I am seeing Ahmed today. (meet)

Flowers smell sweet. (the sense of smell)

Ali is smelling the fish whether it is fresh. (inhale the odour of)

You think a lot. (to have an opinion)

Raj is thinking of leaving Libya. (examine the possibility of)

I am thinking about the time I spent in India. (recall)

I feel that she will return by evening. (think)

I am feeling better. (good physical and mental conditions)

Macaroni and chicken tastes delicious. (flavour)

He is tasting the tea whether it is Indian or Lankan. (experience)

Present Perfect Tense

Structure:

Affirmative	-	Sub + has/have + v_3 + others He has done the work.
Negative	-	Sub + has/have + not + v_3 + others We haven't visited Tripoli.
Interrogative	-	Has/have + sub + v_3 + others + ? Have you finished your work? Has she not come to college today?
Wh-question	-	Wh-word + has/have + sub + v_3 + other + ? When have you eaten an apple?

Uses of Present Perfect Tense

It is used:

(i) to express the completion of an action by the time of speaking or writing

Omar has written many books.

(ii) to express continued action of the past

Abdullah has been to England for five years.

I have taught in Libya since 2007.

(iii) with adverbs/preposition of time like these:

just, already, yet, till now, up to now, even now, since.

Has the plan landed yet?

He has just gone out.

I haven't met him since June.

(iv) to express completed action and unfinished time

I have bought two books so far this year.

(It means that I bought two books before the end of the year. I may buy more books this year itself.)

Note: 'Since' and 'for' are also used with present perfect tense.

Present Perfect Progressive

Structure:

Affirmative	-	Sub + has/have + been + v_4 + others + since or for + given time
		I have been learning English since 2007.
Negative	-	Subject + has/have + not + been + v_4 + others + since/for + given time
		She hasn't been cooking food for two months.
Interrogative	-	Has/have + sub + been + v_4 + others + since/for + given time + ?
		Have we not been studying in this college since 2009?
Wh-questions	-	Wh-word + has/have + sub + been + v_4 + others + since/for + given time
		Why have you been playing since Monday?

Use of Since, and For to Denote Time

'Since' is used to denote point of time, e.g. since Monday, since morning, since July, since 1980, since 4 o'clock, etc.

This point of time does not make the duration of any action clear. In all the examples given above we can't guess the duration of action.

'For' is used to denote period of time, e.g. for two days, for a long time, for four months, for twenty years, for an hour, etc. In all these examples, duration of action is given.

Except since and for, other time expressing phrases like all the time, all day, for a long time, etc. are used to express present perfect and present perfect progressive tense.

I have been swimming all morning.

Albert has been working all day.

Uses of Present Perfect Progressive Tense

It is used:

(i) to express continuous action that started in the past and is still going on

The baby has been crying for an hour.

(ii) to express such an action that stopped in the past but the effect of it is still present

Salma feels cold because she has been bathing in the sea for an hour.

(Here, the work of bathing is over but Salma is still shivering with cold.)

Children's clothes are dirty because they have been playing in the dust all day.

(iii) to begin a question with 'since when' instead of when.

Since when have you been waiting here?

We don't say.

When have you been waiting here since?

Past Simple Tense

Structure:

Affirmative: Sub + v_2 + others (obj/comp/adjunct)

Ali wrote a book.

Negative: Sub + didn't + v_1 + others

Ali didn't write a book.

Emphatic: Sub + did + v_1 + others

He did write a book.

Interrogative: Did + sub + v_1 + others + ?

Did he write a book?

Did he not write a book?

'Wh' question: Wh-word + did + sub + v_1 + others + ?

When did he write a book?

Uses of Past Simple Tense

It is used:

(i) to indicate the completion of an action in the immediate or remote past

In such sentences, adverbs of time like ago, last time, yesterday, the other day, etc. are often mentioned.

He came here a month ago.

He met me last night.

She visited the museum yesterday.

(ii) in asking questions to know the past actions

When did you come here?

Why did you cry suddenly?

(iii) to express the repeated actions of the past

When I was a student I went to watch movies.

(iv) to express habitual actions of the past

She always carried an umbrella.

They often came late for class.

Sarah used to play chess.

(v) to express a series of events of the past

Once I went to Delhi, I saw a beautiful house, I bought it.

He come, he saw, he conquered.

(vi) to refer to something of unreal nature and improbable condition and to express present or future time, not past time

I wish I knew him. (but I don't know him)

He speaks as if he knew everything.

I wish I were the president of India.

(vii) to answer the question in the present perfect tense

Have you seen Dr. Francis?

Yes, I have. I saw him just an hour ago.

Past Progressive Tense

Structure:

Affirmative - Sub + was/were + v_4 + others (obj/comp/adjunct)

He was reading a book.

Negative: - Sub + was/were + not + v_4 + others

They were not going to Zliten.

Interrogative - Was/were + sub + v_4 + others?

Were we learning English today?

Wh-question - Wh-word + was/were + sub + v_4 + others?

Where were they going in the morning?

Uses of Past Progressive Tense

It is used:

(i) to express the continuous action of past

Children were crying when I arrived home.

We were playing football when my father came.

A bomb exploded when we were sitting in the café.

(ii) to suggest a gradual development

It was getting dark.

Ahmed was becoming more and more depressed.

(iii) to express two simultaneous actions of the past

When Salma was dining, Saha was dancing.

(iv) to express the past denoting 'point of time' or 'period of time'

Boys were playing football all evening.

At 8 o'clock I was listening to the radio.

(v) to express an action that was in progress in the past

Amina was sweeping the floor.

Girls were reading and writing in the class.

Past Perfect Tense

Structure:

Affirmative	-	Sub + had + v_3 + others (obj/comp/adjunct)
		He had done the work.
Negative	-	Sub + had + not + v_3 + others
		We hadn't finished our Journey.
Interrogative	-	Had + sub + v_3 + others?
		Had she reached here much earlier?
Wh-questions	-	Wh-word + had + sub + v_3 + others?
		Why had she done this work?

Note: When 'had' takes another 'had' after it, its meaning becomes 'take/eat/experience/receive'.

I had had my lunch. (had = taken/eaten)

I had had some additional information. (had = received)

He had had a lot of problem during journey. (had = experienced)

Uses of Past Perfect Tense

It is used:

(i) to express two actions of the past when the first action was complete before the second one was started

Such sentences are usually connected with subordinating conjunctions: after, before, as soon as, till, until, when.

The patient had died before the doctor came.

She got up after the sun had risen.

Omar didn't tell anything till he had read the entire report.

(ii) in conditional clauses to indicate non-fulfilment of a condition

Had I visited Delhi; I would have seen the Delhi gate.

If I had met her, I would have helped her.

(iii) to express an unfulfilled hope, desire, intention

I had hoped to meet him on Friday but I fell ill before that.

She had hoped to get good marks. (but she couldn't get)

(iv) to express two immediate actions that follow one after another in the past

Such simultaneous actions are expressed in simple past form in stead of past perfect.

He washed his hands before he ate.

We arrived at the airport just before the plane took off.

Past Perfect Progressive

Structure:

Affirmative - Sub + had + been + v_4 + others + since/for + given time

They had been working in the field for an hour.

Negative - Sub + had + not + been + v_4 + others + since/for + given time

We had not been cooking since morning.

Interrogative - Had + sub + been + v_4 + others + since/for + given time + ?

Had he been working in this factory for ten years?

Wh-questions - Wh-word + had + sub + been + v_4 + others + since/for + given time + ?

Where had they been living since July?

Note: 'Since/for' is used uniformly in all the tenses in the manner given in present perfect continuous tense.

Uses of Past Perfect Progressive

It is used:

(i) to express repeated action of the past

He had been trying to sell his house since last year.

(ii) to report an action of the past whose effect continued in the past itself

They had been dancing for long when their teacher entered the room.

Future Simple Tense

Structure:

Affirmative - Sub + will/shall + v_1 + others (obj/compl/adjunct)

We shall go there.

They will come here.

Negative - Sub + will/shall + not + v_1 + others

You will not go there.

Interrogative - Will/shall + sub + v_1 + others + ?

Shall we go there?

Wh-questions - Wh-word + will/shall + sub + v_1 + others + ?

When shall we visit the zoo?

Note:

(i) 'shall not' and 'will not' have the contracted form 'shan't' and 'won't' respectively.

(ii) 'He will', 'we shall', 'I shall' and 'you will' have the contracted form 'he'll', 'we'll', 'I'll', and 'you'll' respectively.

(iii) 'Will' is used with I & we, (first person pronouns) instead of 'shall' in declarative sentence.

But it is never used in question.

Shall we do it? (not, will we do it?)

But I/we will go there, is a correct expression.

In modern English, the difference between 'shall and will' is largely ignored as the contracted form 'll is widely used everywhere.

Uses of Simple Future Tense

It is used:

(i) to express an action of future

They will go to Tripoli.

Fatima will do that work soon.

(ii) to express an obstinate habit in an 'if-clause'

If you tell lies, you will fall into trouble.

If you smoke a lot you will suffer from coughing.

(iii) to express conditional sentences in an adverb clause of time

In such sentences, subordinating conjunction takes simple present form.

I shall go when he comes.

If you work hard, you will get good marks.

(iv) to express determination, threat, promise, command, and moral duty. But in such expressions, 'I/we' (first person) takes 'will' and you, they, he, she, etc. (second and third persons) take 'shall'.

One shall not tell a lie. (moral duty)

You shall get the clearance letter. (promise)

Teachers shall submit their passports before Monday. (command)

We will take the examination next week. (determination)

I will beat him. (threat)

(v) to express official announcement/order

In such expressions, 'shall' is used in place of 'will'.

The college shall remain closed till first August.

The examination shall start at 1 p.m.

(vi) to express an imaginary condition

In such expressions, 'would' the past form of 'will' is used. If I were a bird, I would fly in the sky.

She would always come to me and tell me stories.

Future Progressive Tense

Structure:

Affirmative	-	Sub + will/shall + be + v_4 + others
		We shall be reading a story.
Negative	-	Sub + will/shall + not + be + v_4 + others
		You will not be watching the football match.
Interrogative	-	Will/shall + sub + be + v_4 + others + ?
		Shall we not be playing chess?
Wh-questions	-	Wh-words + will/shall + sub + be + v_4 + others + ?
		When shall we be finishing our work?

Uses of Future Progressive Tense

It is used:

(i) to express a future action in progress like present progressive tense

He is writing a book now. (present)

He will be writing a book next month. (future)

(ii) to express possibility in future

I shall be living in Khoms next year.

Future Perfect Tense

Structure:

Affirmative – Sub + will/shall + have + v_3 + others

We shall have finished the work.

Negative - Sub + will/shall + not + have + v_3 + others

They will not have done this work.

Interrogative - Will/shall + sub + have + v_3 + others + ?

Shall we not have finished the work?

Wh-questions - Wh-word + will/shall + sub + have + v_3 + others + ?

Why will they not have signed the paper?

Uses of Future Perfect Tense

It is used:

(i) to express the completion of an action by a given time in future

We shall have done the work by tomorrow.

Raj will have left this country by next month.

(ii) to express a possibility of past

He will have reached home.

(This sentence expresses the possibility of his reaching home but we don't know whether he actually reached home or not. This kind of structure expresses an assumption or deduction about a past action, not about a present or future action. In such cases, 'will' can be replaced by 'may/might'.)

Future Perfect Progressive Tense

Structure:

Affirmative - Sub + will/shall + have + been + v_4 + others + since/for + given time

We shall have been reading a novel since morning.

Negative - Sub + will/shall + not + have + been + v_4 + others + since/for + given time

She will not have been cooking food for two hours.

Interrogative - Will/shall + sub + have been + v_4 + others + since/for + given time

Shall I have been doing my work since Sunday?

Wh-question - Wh-word + will/shall + sub + have been + v_4 + others + since/for + given time + ?

Where will she have been taking breakfast for so many days?

Uses of future perfect progressive

It is used:

(i) to indicate an activity that will continue over a period of time

So, it is generally used with an expression of time.

Examples:

By the end of this week, we shall have been working in Libya for three years.

They will have been doing it since morning.

The above-mentioned tenses have been given according to the traditional approach of grammar. What is scientific and practical regarding them relates to the form of the verb. The verb forms of present tense and past tense are inflected. Only the future tense is indicated with modal verbs 'shall' and 'will' that don't have verbal inflections.

On the basis of the verbal inflections, there are only two tenses—*Present* and *Past*. There is no future tense to express future time. Future time is expressed either by modal auxiliaries like *'shall'*, *'will'*, *'can'* and *'may'* or by *simple present/past or progressive forms* of the verb. Look at the various forms that express future time.

Examples:

1. The aeroplane takes off at 5 o'clock in evening.

2. Omar leaves for London tomorrow.
3. I am to go to India next week.
4. The President is coming tomorrow to attend the meeting.
5. I am going to buy a car next year.

Here, we find that all these sentences express future time by means of present tense.

Keeping this difference between time and tense in mind, Randolph Quirk, a well-known grammarian, says in *A Grammar of Contemporary English*, "English has two tenses: present tense and past tense. As the names imply, the present tense normally refers to present time and past tense to past time."

When we look at sentences minutely, we find that it is auxiliary verb that decides the tense, and auxiliaries have two forms only—present and past.

Look at these sentences.

Amar is going to college. (present tense)

Amar was going to college. (past tense)

Here the difference between the two sentences is seen only on the basis of auxiliary verbs (*is* and *was*), as all other words are the same in these two sentences. Let us see the forms of auxiliary verbs.

Present	**Past**	**Present**	**Past**
Is	was	shall	should
are	were	will	would
am	was	can	could
has/have	had	may	might

There is no third form of these auxiliaries. It supports the view that English language has two tenses only—present and past. Future time is expressed with the help of these two tenses as seen above.

Constructions without Correspondence between Time and Tense

In certain structures, the difference between the verbal form and its meaning shows the lack of correspondence between the form of a verb and the time of an action. Here are some more examples.

1. Could I see Dr. Dinesh?
2. Would you do me a favour?
3. Did you want to meet Aman?
4. I wanted to talk to Ajit.
5. It is going to rain.
6. The sun sets in the west.
7. Gold is yellow.

In the above sentences, 'could', 'would', 'did', and 'wanted' are in the past tense but they express present time. 'Is going to' has the progressive form of present tense but it expresses future time. And the last two sentences indicate no particular time. They inclusively express present past and future time.

Likewise, future simple and future perfect tense also express past and present time.

She will have received the letter.	(Past time showing probability)
Will you have tea or coffee?	(present time)
Salma will be about twenty.	(Probably she is = present time)

The Five Forms of Some Commonly Known Verbs

Simple present	simple past	past participle	present participle	simple present
Plural number v_1	(s+p numbers) v_2	verb+en/d/ed v_3	verb+ing v_4	singular number v_5
be (are)	was/were	been	being	be(is/am)
arise	arose	arisen	arising	arises

awake	awoke	awoken/ awaked	awaking	awakes
bear	bore	born/borne	bearing	bears
beat	beat	beaten	beating	beats
become	became	become	becoming	becomes
begin	began	begun	beginning	begins
bend	bent	bent	bending	bends
bereave	bereaved/ bereft	bereaved/ bereft	bereaving	bereaves
bet	bet/betted	bet/betted	betting	bets
bid	bade	bidden	biding	bids
bind	bound	bound	binding	binds
bite	bit	bitten	biting	bites
bleed	bled	bled	bleeding	bleeds
blow	blew	blown	blowing	blows
break	broke	broken	breaking	breaks
bring	brought	brought	bringing	brings
broadcast	broadcast	broadcast	broadcasting	broadcasts
build	built	built	building	builds
burn	burned/burnt	burned/burnt	burning	burns
burst	burst	burst	bursting	bursts
buy	bought	bought	buying	buys
cast	cast	cast	casting	casts
catch	caught	caught	catching	catches
chide	chided/chid	chided/chid	chiding	chides
choose	chose	chosen	choosing	chooses
climb	climbed	climbed	climbing	climbs
cling	clung	clung	clinging	clings
come	came	come	coming	comes
cost	cost	cost	costing	costs
creep	crept	crept	creeping	creeps
cut	cut	cut	cutting	cuts
deal	dealt	dealt	dealing	deals
dig	dug	dug	digging	digs

do	did	done	doing	does
draw	drew	drawn	drawing	draws
dream	dreamed/ dreamt	dreamed/ dreamt	dreaming	dreams
drink	drank	drunk	drinking	drinks
drive	drove	driven	driving	drives
dwell	dwelt	dwelt	dwelling	dwells
eat	ate	eaten	eating	eats
fall	fell	fallen	falling	falls
feed	fed	fed	feeding	feeds
feel	felt	felt	feeling	feels
fight	fought	fought	fighting	fights
find	found	found	finding	finds
flee	fled	fled	fleeing	flees
fling	flung	flung	flinging	flings
fly	flew	flown	flying	flies
forbid	forbade	forbidden	forbidding	forbids
forget	forgot	forgotten	forgetting	forgets
forgive	forgave	forgiven	forgiving	forgives
forsake	forsook	forsaken	forsaking	forsakes
freeze	froze	frozen	freezing	freezes
get	got	got	getting	gets
give	gave	given	giving	gives
go	went	gone	going	goes
grind	ground	ground	grinding	grinds
grow	grew	grown	growing	grows
hang	hanged	hanged	hanging	hangs
hang	hung	hung	hanging	hangs
have	had	had	having	has
hear	heard	heard	hearing	hears
hide	hid	hid/hidden	hiding	hides
hit	hit	hit	hitting	hits
hold	held	held	holding	holds

hurt	hurt	hurt	hurting	hurts
keep	kept	kept	keeping	keeps
kneel	knelt	knelt	kneeling	kneels
knit	knit/knitted	knit/knitted	knitting	knits
know	knew	known	knowing	knows
lay	laid	laid	lying	lies
lead	led	led	leading	leads
lean	leant/leaned	leant/leaned	leaning	leans
leap	leapt	leapt	leaping	leaps
learn	learnt/learned	learnt/ learned	learning	learns
leave	left	left	leaving	leaves
lend	lent	lent	lending	lends
let	let	let	letting	lets
lie	lay	lain	lying	lies
lie	lied	lied	lying	lies
light	lighted/lit	lighted/lit	lighting	lights
lose	lost	lost	losing	loses
make	made	made	making	makes
mean	meant	meant	meaning	means
meet	met	met	meeting	meets
mislead	misled	misled	misleading	misleads
mistake	mistook	mistaken	mistaking	mistakes
owe	owed	owed	owing	owes
pay	paid	paid	paying	pays
prove	proved	proved	proving	proves
put	put	put	putting	puts
quit	quitted/quit	quitted/quit	quitting	quits
read	read	read	reading	reads
rid	rid	rid	riding	rids
ride	rode	ridden	riding	rides
ring	rang	rung	ringing	rings
rise	rose	risen	rising	rises

run	ran	run	running	runs
saw	sawed	sawed	sawing	saws
say	said	said	saying	says
see	saw	seen	seeing	sees
seek	sought	sought	seeking	seeks
sell	sold	sold	selling	sells
send	sent	sent	sending	sends
set	set	set	setting	sets
sew	sewed	sewn	sewing	sews
shake	shook	shaken	shaking	shakes
shave	shaved	shaved/ shaven	shaving	shaves
shed	shed	shed	shedding	sheds
shine	shone	shone	shining	shines
shoot	shot	shot	shooting	shoots
show	showed	shown	showing	shows
shrink	shrank	shrunk	shrinking	shrinks
shut	shut	shut	shutting	shuts
sing	sang	sung	singing	sings
sink	sank	sunk	sinking	sinks
sit	sat	sat	sitting	sits
slay	slew	slain	slaying	slays
sleep	slept	slept	sleeping	sleeps
slide	slid	slid	sliding	slides
slink	slunk	slunk	slinking	slinks
smell	smelt/smelled	smelt/smelled	smelling	smells
sow	sowed	sown	sowing	sows
speak	spoke	spoken	speaking	speaks
speed	speeded/sped	speeded/sped	speeding	speeds
spell	spelled/spelt	spelled/spelt	spelling	spells
spend	spent	spent	spending	spends
spill	spilled/split	spilled/spilt	spilling	spills
spin	span/spun	spun	spinning	spins

spit	spat	spat	spitting	spits
split	split	split	splitting	splits
spoil	spoiled/spoilt	spoiled/spoilt	spoiling	spoils
spread	spread	spread	spreading	spreads
spring	sprang	sprung	springing	springs
stand	stood	stood	standing	stands
steal	stole	stolen	stealing	steals
stick	stuck	stuck	sticking	sticks
sting	stung	stung	stinging	stings
stink	stank/stunk	stank	stinking	stinks
strew	strewed	strewn	strewing	strews
strike	struck	struck/ stricken	striking	strikes
string	strung	strung	stringing	strings
strive	strove	striven	striving	strives
swear	swore	sworn	swearing	swears
sweep	swept	swept	sweeping	sweeps
swell	swelled	swelled/ swollen	swelling	swells
swim	swam	swum	swimming	swims
swing	swung	swung	swinging	swings
take	took	taken	taking	takes
teach	taught	taught	teaching	teaches
tear	tore	torn	tearing	tears
tell	told	told	telling	tells
think	thought	thought	thinking	thinks
throw	threw	thrown	throwing	throws
thrust	thrust	thrust	thrusting	thrusts
tread	trod	trod/trodden	treading	treads
understand	understood	understood	under- standing	under- stands
wake	woke/waked	woken/woke	waking	wakes
wear	wore	worn	wearing	wears
weave	wove	woven	weaving	weaves

weep	wept	wept	weeping	weeps
win	won	won	winning	wins
wind	wound	wound	winding	winds
wound	wounded	wounded	wounding	wounds
withdraw	withdrew	withdrawn	withdrawing	withdraws
withhold	withheld	withheld	withholding	withholds
work	worked	worked	working	works
write	wrote	written	writing	writes
zero	zeroed	zeroed	zeroing	zeroes

EXERCISE-1

Change the following into negative and emphatic sentences.

1. She knows English.
2. I love children.
3. She wrote a novel.
4. We do it.
5. Boys play in the field.
6. Aman burst into tears.
7. You did it well.
8. They hate each other.
9. She hit me on the head.
10. They go to market daily.
11. I work hard.
12. She does the work.
13. Salma shut the window.
14. Children play football.
15. I feel hungry.
16. Girls did their homework.
17. Teachers come on time to take their classes.
18. We dry our boots in the sun.
19. Students learn the rules of grammar.
20. You hit me on the head.
21. We love our nation.

EXERCISE-2

Change the following sentences into Interrogative.

1. We have finished our lunch.
2. They had been doing it since 2008.
3. Girls always make a noise in the class.
4. Ali and Ahmed will do this work.
5. Omar is sleeping.
6. They have completed their assignment.
7. We came here three years back.
8. They have come to know about it.
9. She hit me on the head.
10. Ali likes tea.
11. Libyans speak Arabic.
12. He does n't speak English.
13. We don't play chess.
14. They fought among themselves.
15. You didn't do it.
16. Ahmed likes coffee.
17. You know me.
18. Boys watch television.
19. A monkey can't change his nature.

EXERCISE-3

Make sentences on the basis of the given structures.

1. sub+v_5+obj
2. sub+v_1+complement
3. sub+v_1+adjunct
4. sub+auxiliary+not+v_3+obj
5. sub+auxiliary+v_4+obj
6. sub+auxiliary+v_4+adjunct
7. sub+will/shall+v_1+obj
8. auxiliary+sub+v_1+obj+?

9. wh-question+auxiliary+sub+v_3+adjunct+?
10. sub+will/shall+have+v_3+obj
11. auxiliary+sub+v_3+obj+?
12. auxiliary+sub+v_4+adjunct+?
13. wh-question+auxiliary+sub+v_4+obj+?
14. sub+v_1+obj.
15. auxiliary+sub+v_1+adjunct+?
16. wh-question+auxiliary+sub+not+v_1+complement+?
17. auxiliary+sub+v_4+obj+?
18. wh-question+auxiliary+sub+v_4+adjunct+?
19. sub+has+v_3+obj, has/have+not+sub+?
20. sub+v_2+obj+do/does/did+not+sub+?
21. sub+auxiliary+v_4+adjunct, auxiliary+not+sub+?

EXERCISE-4

Fill up the blanks with correct forms of the verb given in brackets.

1. He (go) to Tripoli last month.
2. We (live) in Iraq when the war began.
3. We reached the station after the train (leave).
4. I (lose) my watch while I (see) the sights of the city.
5. The train (leave) already.
6. She (not speak) to me for over a year.
7. Marconi (invent) wireless many years ago.
8. The earth (move) around the sun.
9. We (study) English for ten years.
10. Oil (float) on water.
11. He (finish) his work by tomorrow.
12. She (learn) English for the last five years.
13. A thief broke into my house when I (sleep).
14. We (come) here two years back.
15. She will cook rice when I (go) there.

16. I (work) for the last three years.
17. The meeting just (start).
18. Death (come) to everyone.
19. Shakespeare (write) *Hamlet.*
20. Dr. Mukul (come) in 2009.
21. She (visit) the film yesterday.

EXERCISE-5

Fill up the blanks with correct forms of the verb given in brackets.

1. Sana (be) busy for a month.
2. He (go) to college everyday.
3. She (have) a bath now.
4. He will have (have) a letter tomorrow.
5. Ali just (hang) the picture on the wall.
6. You (be) absent since March.
7. Hard work (bring) success.
8. We (study) English when we were at school.
9. I wish I (know) the answer.
10. The train started after the guard (give) the signal.
11. Electricity (light) our house and (expel) darkness.
12. It (rain) for three hours.
13. They (lose) the match if they (not play) well.
14. He talks as if he (know) everything.
15. We (walk) in the evening daily.
16. He said that he (do) it.
17. T.S. Eliot (write) *The Waste Land.*
18. Who (discover) America?
19. When Amina was singing Aisha was (dance).
20. Bad news (travel) fast.
21. Rice and chicken (taste) delicious.

EXERCISE-6

Fill up the blanks with the correct form of the verb given in brackets.

1. Blood (consist) of plasma and cells.
2. I'll phone you if I (get) time.
3. Children often (go) to school by bus.
4. The earth (be) round.
5. I (meet) Ali yesterday.
6. It (rain) heavily last night.
7. I (study) Arabic now.
8. Listen! Someone (call) you outside.
9. Arti broke a plate as she (wash) up dishes.
10. We (watch) a football match at 10 o'clock last night.
11. He (buy) this watch in Libya.
12. Nasir (go) to England next year.
13. These students (work) very hard since July.
14. When evening (come) it (get) dark.
15. What you (do) when the light (go) out half an hour ago.
16. The use of past tense (tell) us that an action (be) complete.
17. Yesterday Ali (get) up at five o'clock and (work) for two hours. He (take) his breakfast before Firoz (come) to meet him.
18. Bimla (sit) in the garden when her brother (come) and (tell) her that Hina (wait) for her outside the house.
19. When Dr. Mukul (be) sixty, Manu will be sixteen.
20. Kiran Desai (write) novels. She (write) a good one. She (write) one now.
21. What would you do if you (meet) a lion?

12

Subject-Verb Agreement (Syntax)

What is Syntax?

Syntax is an art of putting words and phrases together in an orderly manner to form a meaningful sentence. The choice of words depends mainly on the agreement (concord) of number and person between the subject and the verb.

Grammatical Concord of Number and Person

Generally singular subjects take singular verbs and plural subjects take plural verbs.

Subject	Verb
He	*is* a teacher.
singural subject	singular verb
They	*are* students.
plural subject	plural verb

But the number system of nouns and verbs is quite opposite. Nouns ending in '*s/es*' are usually plural, but verbs ending in '*s/es*' are always singular.

Noun + s/es = plural	Verb + s/es = singular
books, boxes, girls, etc.	comes, goes, loves, etc.

The plural form of a verb is used with all persons and numbers except third person singular number.

I, We, You, They, Boys, etc.	go to market.
He, She, Ali, Salma, etc.	goes to market.

Some Exceptions to this Grammatical Concord

(i) Modal auxiliary verbs (*could, may, will, must,* etc.) don't have number and person concord.

I, We, You, They, He, She, Sana, etc. must love children.

(ii) Past and future tense form of the verb except '*was*' and '*were*' don't have any visible concord.

I, We, You, They, He, She, etc. didn't go to market.

I, We, You, They, He, She, etc. went to market.

I, We, You, They, He, She, etc. will go to market.

But '*was*' and '*were*' do have number and person concord.

We, You, They, Girls, etc.	were walking on the road.
I, he, she, Ali, etc.	was watching the football match.

(iii) Semi-modal verbs '*need*', '*dare*' (in the negative form) '*used to*' and '*ought to*' don't have number and person concord.

I, We, They, He, She, etc.	needn't go there.
I, We, You, They, He, She, etc.	daren't insult the principal.
I, We, You, They, He, She, etc.	used to cry in childhood.
I, We, You, They, He, She, etc.	oughtn't tell a lie.

But '*need*' and '*dare*' as main verbs do have number and person concord.

He/She/Ahmed	needs a pen.
I/We/You/They	dare to challenge Ali.

(iv) Sentences expressing subjunctive mood don't have number, person, and tense concord. That's why a singular subject takes plural verbs (*bless/save/help/live*) to express '*wish*' or '*desire*'.

God bless you!

God save the prince!

Heaven help us all!

Long live the king!

(v) Some subjunctives begin with *if, as if, as though, I wish,* etc. and take plural verb (were) with a singular subject to express unreal condition, unfulfilled desire and supposition.

If I were a bird, I would fly in the sky.

I wish I *were* young again.

He behaves as if he *were* mad.

*Note: The past ten*se used in the above sentences is not past but a subjunctive which indicates unreality or improbability.

Concord System in Different Structures

1. When two or more than two nouns or pronouns are joined by '*and*', the verb is plural.

   Anil, Ahmed and Aman are friends.

   Aren't Sujata and Nandini sisters?

   You, he and I were present in the party.

2. When two nouns are joined by '*and*' showing the same notion (food), the verb is singular.

   Rice and chicken is a tasty food.

   Whisky and soda is an intoxicating drink.

3. When two clauses are joined by '*and*', the verb is plural.

   What he does and where he lives are not known to me.

4. When two or more designations of the same person are connected by 'and' the verb is singular.

   The poet and painter has come to see me. (one person)

5. When the article '*the*' comes before each of them to refer to two different persons, the verb is plural.

   The poet and the painter have come to see me. (two persons).

6. When two nouns or pronouns are joined by '*as well as*,' the verb agrees in number and person with the first one.

He as well as I *is* ready to go.

You as well as he *are* going to Tripoli.

7. When words such as, '*with*', '*like*', '*in addition to*', '*except*', '*besides*', '*no less than*', '*along with*', etc. are added to a singular subject, the verb is singular.

   He, along with his wife and children, has gone to Zliten.

   Honesty, in addition to truth, is the finest virtue.

8. When two nouns or pronouns of different number and person are joined by '*or*', '*either...or*', '*neither...nor*' or '*nor*', the verb agrees with the nearer noun or pronoun.

   Either the dogs or *the cat has* eaten fish.

   Neither Ali nor his brothers *have* taken my pen.

   You or I *am* guilty.

9. When '*infinitives/gerunds/phrases/clauses*' are used as subjects, the verb is singular.

   To walk is good for health.

   What to do is a problem.

   What he does these days doesn't concern me.

   Writing makes a man perfect.

10. When '*it*' is used as a subject, it always takes a singular verb.

    It is they who did it.

    It is the boys who have stolen my pen.

11. Dummy '*there*' takes the verb according to the singularity or plurality of the noun that comes after the verb.

    There is a school in this village.

    There are five hundred students in this school.

12. Mathematical calculation or equation normally takes a singular verb when they have a combination of '*and*', '*minus*', '*plus*', '*into*', '*times*', etc.

    Two *and* two is four.

Seven *plus* three is ten.

$(a + b)^2 = a^2 + b^2 + 2ab$ is a common formula in algebra.

Six *times* four is twenty four.

13. *'Weight'*, *'distance'*, *'time'*, *'amount'*, and *'measurement'* take a singular verb whether the noun is singular or plural.

    Four weeks is a short time to learn a language.

    Ten minutes is not enough for a break.

14. *'Everybody'*, *'nobody'*, *'somebody'*, *'anybody'*, *'everyone'*, *'no one'*, *'someone'*, *'anyone'*, *'many a'*, and *'each'*, (indefinite pronouns) take a singular verb.

    Nobody is ready to do the work.

    Everyone has a car.

15. If *each/every/no + noun* is joined by *'and'*, the verb is singular.

    No boy and no girl has come to college today.

    Every man and every woman has to die one day.

16. *Each of, every of, either of and neither of + noun* take a singular verb.

    Neither of the girls is tall.

    Each of the following questions is important.

17. When *'each'* comes after a plural pronoun, it takes plural verb.

    They each want a pen.

    We each have a car.

18. *Not only .... but also* takes the verb according to its nearer noun or pronoun.

    Not only Ali but also *his classmates are* coming.

    Not only the children but also *the baby is* crying.

19. *One of + plural noun or pronoun* takes singular verb.

    One of my friends is a doctor.

20. *None + of + plural noun or pronoun* can either take a singular or a plural verb.

    None of us *is/are* ready to do the work.

21. *Any + noun* may either take singular or plural verb according to the countability or uncoutability of the noun.

    Are there any students? No, there are not any students.

    Is there any hope? No, there is not any hope.

22. *'All'* may take either singular or plural verb.

    It takes a plural verb to refer to plural nouns and a singular verb to refer to either everything or the whole thing.

    All are fine in my family. (all the members)

    All is ready. (everything/the whole thing)

23. *Noun + preposition + noun* takes either a singular or a plural verb according to the singularity or plurality of the first noun.

    The price of rice has gone up.

    The chairs of this hall are new.

24. *Indefinite number/quantity + of* like *the rest of, two-thirds of, lots of, plenty of, a number of, some of, half of, most of, a great deal of, etc. + noun* take either singular or plural verb according to the countability or uncountability of the noun.

    Plenty of books are available in the library.

    Plenty of rice is consumed in my family.

    A number of students have failed.

25. *The number of + noun* takes a singular verb, because '*the number*' denotes a mathematical figure.

    The number of good students is lacking.

26. *The percentage + of + plural noun* takes singular verb.

    The percentage of good people is very rare.

27. *Singular collective noun + of + plural noun* takes a singular verb like *a team of, a bunch of, a gang of, a bouquet of*, etc.

    A bevy of girls is dancing.

    A team of players has gone to South Africa.

28. Collective nouns like these: *government, class, committee, jury, board,* etc. may take either a singular verb (when it is considered a unit) or a plural verb (when it refers to the individual member of the group).

    The government has changed its education policy.

    The government have changed their education policy.

29. *More than + one + singular noun* takes a singular verb.

    More than one pencil is required.

30. *More + plural noun + than + one* takes a plural verb.

    More boys than one have passed.

31. *Subject + noun/pronoun in apposition* takes the verb according to the number and person of its subject.

    I, Dr Samir, *am* speaking to you.

    You, a great scholar, *have* written many books.

32. Relative clause takes the verb after it according to the singularity or plurality of its antecedent (noun/pronoun) that comes before it and not according to the subject of the sentence.

    It is *I* who *am* thinking of going abroad.

    He is one of my *friends* who *live* in England.

33. *The + adjective* denotes plural common noun and takes a plural verb.

    The strong always suppress *the weak.*

    The rich hate *the poor.*

34. Nationality words used as plural common nouns such as *the British, the Irish, the French, the Chinese, the German, the English,* etc. take a plural verb.

The English have a long history.

The French are different.

The German love *the French*.

35. *Nothing but + noun* always takes a singular verb.

    Nothing but trees is here.

    Nothing but sand is there.

36. *Noun + preposition + the same noun* takes a singular verb.

    Ship after ship has sunk.

37. The objects that have two inseparable parts such as *glasses, trousers, scissors, bellows, pants, forceps, shoes*, etc. take a plural verb.

    My glasses are new.

    Your trousers are old.

    But *a pair + inseparable parts* takes a singular verb.

    A pair of shoes has been repaired.

38. If the name of books, countries, places or titles is plural in form, it takes a singular verb.

    '*Hard times*' is a popular novel.

    The West Indies is an island.

39. If the name of a country denotes a team or a group of people, it takes a plural verb.

    India have won the match by two wickets. (Indian players)

    Brazil have lost the football match by one goal. (Brazilian team)

40. Some nouns look plural such as news, measles, mumps, statistics, mathematics, politics, billiards, dominoes, etc. but they take a singular verb.

    Mathematics is a science of number.

    Politics is a dirty game.

    But mathematics, politics, statistics, economics, etc. take plural verb to express different quality.

My mathematics say that this house covers an area of twelve hundred square feet. (mathematical calculation)

The statistics show our poor progress. (numerical information)

41. Some nouns look singular, but they are plural and take a plural verb:

    clergy, cattle, police, people, children, swine, public, gentry, infantry, vermin, poultry, youth, etc.

    The cattle are grazing in the field.

    The police are running after the thief.

42. Plural nouns of foreign origin take a plural verb.

    These *criteria* are not enough.

    New *curricula* have been approved by the government.

    The *data* are correct. (facts)

    Memoranda of instructions have been sent to all the examiners.

43. Agenda and data that are the plural of agendum and datum take a singular verb.

    The agenda of the meeting has been finished.

    The data is ready. (a body of facts)

44. Some nouns are always plural and they take a plural verb as *belongings, clothes, goods, riches, savings, remains*, etc.

    The goods are still in good condition.

    Cheap clothes are sold here.

45. Some nouns are always singular and take a singular verb as: *advice, information, knowledge, scenery, furniture, luggage, wisdom, brick, bread,* etc.

    Luggage is heavy.

    Knowledge is power.

46. *The following/the former/the undersigned* and *the latter* are used as substitutes for a noun. The verb agrees with the noun/pronoun that comes after it.

    The undersigned *request* the pleasure of your company at 7 o'clock in the evening.

    (*Mr. and Mrs. Aman*)

    The undersigned *requests* the pleasure of your company at 7 o'clock in the evening.

    (*Mr. Aman*)

    The following *is the weather report.*
    The following *are the new rates.*

47. Adjectives of quantity take a singular verb.
    Much more is needed.
    Little has been said.
    Not much has been done.

EXERCISE-1

Underline the correct form of the verb.

1. I (am, is) a personal pronoun.
2. There (is, are) a woman at the door.
3. Where (is, are) my trousers.
4. The goods (was, were) shipped yesterday.
5. Look, the police (are, is) coming.
6. Billiards (is, are) my favourite game.
7. The information (is, are) not correct.
8. No frozen poultry (are, is) sold in this store.
9. Two and three (are, is) five.
10. The public (was, were) invited to attend the show.
11. The criteria of admission (is, are) not easy.
12. Not only the players but also the coach (is, are) present.
13. The king, with his ministers, (was, were) present.
14. He as well as I (am, is) going.
15. Not only Ali but also his brothers (was, were) sitting.

16. The crown and glory of life (are, is) character.
17. Two-thirds of the novel (are, is) interesting.
18. All the rules of grammar (is, are) not easy to keep in mind.
19. Half of the apples (is, are) rotten.
20. The number of persons present (are, is) very small.
21. Either of the two girls (are, is) beautiful.

EXERCISE-2

Correct the following sentences

1. He as well as I are going.
2. Ali, like his parents, are gentle.
3. There are nothing but problems in life.
4. Either Salma or Najat have done it.
5. I wish I was a millionaire.
6. It are these boy who do it.
7. Where he lives and what he does is not known to me?
8. Bread and butter are delicious breakfast.
9. The unemployed is looking for a job.
10. The rich hates the poor.
11. Are Ahmed or his friends to blame?
12. She needsn't go there.
13. Bread and butter are our daily need.
14. A series of accidents have taken place everyday.
15. My spectacles is costly.
16. Ten dollars are not much.
17. How to solve it are a problem.
18. The blind is helpless.
19. More books than one has been published.
20. We each likes to take tea.
21. I, Mohammad, is speaking to you.

EXERCISE-3

Supply a verb in agreement with its subject.

1. One of the books ..... missing.
2. There ..... ten girls in this batch.
3. I like a man who ..... laborious.
4. Ten dinars ..... enough for me.
5. Nobody ..... helping me.
6. Either of the two boys ..... willing to work.
7. The jury ..... divided in their opinion.
8. Neither he nor I ..... criminal.
9. The horse and carriage ..... ready.
10. Many a man ..... present there.
11. The French ..... good food.
12. None of the candidates ..... appeared for an interview.
13. The blind ..... helpless.
14. Half of them ..... rotten.
15. The vermin ..... harmful.
16. A herd of cattle ..... in the field.
17. The number of persons present ..... very small.
18. The rest of the novels ..... interesting.
19. Your clothes ..... very expensive.
20. No one ..... to be criticized.
21. The colour of these shirts ..... wonderful.

13

Transformation

What is Transformation?

Transformation, as the name implies, is a process of changing the form of a sentence without changing its basic meaning. In other words, the same idea is expressed through a different kind of structure/sentence in transformation.

Look at these sentences in which the same meaning has been expressed with different types of sentences.

(i) Transformation of simple, compound and complex sentences.

Work hard to get good marks. (simple)

Work hard and you will get good marks. (compound)

If you work hard, you will get good marks. (complex)

(ii) Transformation of degree of comparison:

Very few universities are so popular as Cambridge. (positive)

Cambridge is more popular than most other universities. (comparative)

Cambridge is one of the most popular universities. (superlative)

(iii) Transformation of voice:

He killed a bird. (active)

A bird was killed by him. (passive)

(iv) Transformation of speech:

He said, "I am reading a book". (direct)

He said that he was reading a book. (indirect)

(v) Transformation of rhetorical question:

Can a monkey change its nature? (question)

A monkey can't change its nature. (statement)

(vi) Transformation of imperative sentences:

Please lend me your book. (request)

Will you please lend me your book? (polite request)

Would you mind lending me your book? (form of question)

(vii) As soon as I reached the station, the train left. (affirmative)

(viii) No sooner did I reach the station than the train left. (negative)

All the above-mentioned examples show that English language has a variety of structure for expressing the same meaning.

Some Important Methods of Transformation

A. Transformation of the Degree of Comparison

We can change one degree of comparison into another without changing the basic meaning.

1. Positive into Comparative

Do the following changes:

(i) Omit 'as ... as'

(ii) Use 'than' after comparative degree of adjective/adverb.

(iii) Change affirmative sentence into negative and the negative into affirmative.

(iv) The first noun/pronoun is replaced by the last noun/pronoun.

Examples:

Akash is as tall as Ahmed. (positive)

Ahmed is not taller than Akash. (comparative)

He is not as intelligent as you. (positive)

You are more intelligent than him. (comparative)

2. **Comparative into superlative**

Do the following changes:

(i) Omit any other/all other.

(ii) Change the comparative adjective/adverb into superlative.

(iii) Use 'the' before superlative degree and in/of before noun.

Examples:

He is older than any other man in the village. (comparative)

He is the oldest man in the village. (superlative)

Mount Everest is higher than all other peaks. (comparative)

Mount Everest is the highest peak. (superlative)

1. Most other + noun

Do the following changes:

(i) Change the comparative adjective/adverb into superlative.

(ii) 'Most other' is replaced by 'one of the + plural nouns.'

Examples:

He is better than most other boys. (comparative)

He is one of the best boys. (superlative)

3. Positive into Superlative

1. No other + noun ....

Do the following changes:

(i) Omit no other and as .... as.

(ii) Change the adjective/adverb into superlative degree.

(iii) The last noun of the sentence comes in the beginning and the first is placed at the end.

Examples:

No other flower is as lovely as rose. (positive)

Rose is the loveliest flower. (superlative)

No other metal is as costly as gold. (positive)

Gold is the costliest metal. (superlative)

2. very few + noun ....

Do the following changes:

(i) Omit 'very few.'

(ii) Change positive degree into superlative.

(iii) As .... as is replaced by 'one of the + plural noun'

Examples:

Very few dramatists are as great as Shakespeare. (positive)

Shakespeare is one of the greatest dramatists. (superlative)

B. Transformation of Different Kinds of Sentences

(i) Rhetorical questions into statements

(ii) There are some sentences that are questions in form but statements in meaning. They are called 'rhetorical questions' (statements). Basically, they are used to make a statement more emphatic and forceful.

(iii) It is relevant to note that affirmative (rhetorical) question is like affirmative statement.

Do the following changes:

(i) Change the affirmative question into a negative statement.

(ii) Change a negative question into an affirmative statement.

(iii) Change 'who' into 'none' or 'everyone' according to affirmative or negative question.

Examples:

Who doesn't recall God? (question)

Everyone recalls God. (statement)

Who wouldn't run to see a tiger? (question)

Everybody would run to see a tiger. (statement)

Doesn't the sun rise in the east? (question)

The sun rises in the east. (statement)

Can a man live forever? (question)

A man can't live forever. (statement)

(ii) Negative into affirmative

or

Affirmative into Negative

The transformation of such kinds of sentences takes the opposite form of certain pronouns, adjectives, verbs and adverbs that are listed below:

Affirmative	Negative	Affirmative	Negative
Always	Never	Doubtful	Not sure
Any	No	As soon as	No sooner than
All	None	Cruel	Not kind
Everybody	Nobody	Love	Not hate
Everyone	None	Just	Not unjust
Anyone	No one	Innocent	Not guilty
Only/alone	None but	Sweet	Not sour
A few	Not many	Bad	Not good
Sometimes	Not always	Great	No mean
Bound to	Can't but	For the last time	Never again
Possible	Not impossible	Admit	Not deny

Do the following changes:

(i) Change the affirmative into negative statement.

(ii) Use the opposite keywords.

Examples:

This is not impossible. (negative)

This is possible. (affirmative)

I am not sure about the new salary. (negative)

I am doubtful about the new salary. (affirmative)

It is no mean achievement. (negative)

It is a great achievement. (affirmative)

(iii) Exclamation into statement

Sentences that express sudden, strong feelings of joy, sorrow, surprise, shame or wish, are changed into statement.

(a) *O that/would that/Oh that/O to be/if only + clause express wish + regret*

Do the following changes:

(i) O that/if only, etc. is replaced by I wish + clause.

(ii) Use full stop in place of sign of exclamation.

Examples:

Would that I had not left my home! (exclamation)

I wish I had not left my home. (statement)

O that I were a king! (exclamation)

I wish I were a king. (statement)

O to be a magician! (exclamation)

I wish I were a magician. (statement)

If I only could meet him once! (exclamation)

I wish I could meet him once. (statement)

(b) *What + noun/how + adjective/adverb* show surprise and wonder.

Do the following changes:

(i) 'What + noun' changes into adjective + noun.

(ii) 'How + adjective/adverb' changes into 'very + adjective/adverb + noun'.

(iii) Omit what/how and begin the sentence with subject + verb.

(iv) Add subject + verb (it/he/she + is/was) if it is not mentioned in the sentence.

Examples:

What a pleasure to see you! (exclamation)

It is a great pleasure to see you. (statement)

What a rose it is! (exclamation)

It is a lovely rose. (statement)

How foolish you are! (exclamation)

You are very foolish. (statement)

What an idea! (exclamation)

It is a great idea. (statement)

(c) *How + adjective + of + other words show surprise.*

Do the following changes:

Use subject + verb + adjective + enough + infinitive.

Or

Use: It + is/was (be) + adjective + of + object + infinitive.

How wise of you to do the work! (exclamation)

You were wise enough to do the work. (statement)

Or

It was wise of you to do the work. (statement)

(d) *Infinitive + other words Show the Sense of Surprise.*

Do the following changes:

(i) Use it is + adjective (strange) + that + clause.

(ii) Begin the clause with subject + should if there is no separate clause.

Examples:

To imagine meeting you here! (exclamation)

It is strange that I should meet you here. (statement)

To think he was once a rich man! (exclamation)

It is strange that he was once a rich man. (statement)

(e) *Fie! fie! well done, bravo, hurrah, (interjection) + sentence show the sense of contempt, anger, joy,* etc.

Do the following changes:

(i) Omit the words of interjection.

(ii) Begin the sentence with *It is a matter of + surprise/joy/anger/delight,* etc. according to the meaning of interjection.

Examples:

Well done! We have won the match. (exclamation)

It is a matter of joy that we have

won the match. (statement)

Ah! He's badly hurt. (exclamation)

It is a matter of sorrow that he's badly hurt. (statement)

C. Transformation of simple into complex sentence

Sentences expressing excess of any feature/thing

(i) Subject + verb + adjective/adverb

Do the following changes:

(i) Remove too.

(ii) Change adjective/adverb into comparative degree.

(iii) Adverb clause begins with than + it is/was proper/it/he/she should (be).

Examples:

He is too old. (simple)

He is older than it is proper/he should be. (complex)

She is too angry. (simple)

She is more angry than it is proper/she should be. (complex)

(ii) Sentences expressing cause

Subject + verb + too + adjective + adverb + infinitive

Do the following changes:

(i) 'Too' is replaced by so/such.

(ii) Change the infinitive (to + v_1) into that + negative adverb clause.

Note: Negative adverb clause is used to show the negative sense of 'too'

Examples:

He is too weak to walk. (simple)

He is so weak that he can't walk. (complex)

It was too boring a speech to attract the audience. (simple)

It was such a boring speech that it couldn't attract the audience. (complex)

(iii) Subject + verb + too + adjective/adverb + for + noun/pronoun

Do the following changes:

(i) 'Too' is replaced by such/so.

(ii) 'Too much' is replaced by so bad/so shocking.

(iii) Use that + negative adverb clause.

Examples:

He is too dull for a runner. (simple)

He is so dull that he can't be a runner. (complex)

It is too much boring to bear here. (simple)

It is so shocking that he can't bear it. (complex)

(iv) Sentences expressing ability

Subject + verb + adjective/adverb + enough + infinitive

Do the following changes:

(i) 'Enough' is replaced by 'so'.

(ii) Change the infinitive into that + positive adverb clause of result.

Examples:

He is competent enough to write a book. (simple)

He is so competent that he can write a book. (complex)

I am strong enough to lift the box. (simple)

I am so strong that I can lift the box. (complex)

D. Transformation of Different Parts of Speech

Sentences expressing time

(i) Use the preposition (at/in/since)

Do the following changes:

(i) Change past simple into present perfect tense.

(ii) Change the affirmative into negative sentence.

(iii) Use since in place of at/in.

Examples:

I saw him at 4 o'clock.

I haven't seen him since 4 o'clock.

He met me in April.

He hasn't met me since April.

(ii) Use of adverb

When + clause and since + clause

Do the following changes:

(i) Use past simple tense after since.

(ii) Use negative form of present perfect tense before since.

(iii) 'Last ... when' is replaced by since.

Examples

I last saw her when I went to Tripoli.

I haven't seen her since I went to Tripoli.

Use of preposition 'for' in place of adverb 'ago'.

Do the following changes:

(i) Remove 'last' and use 'for' in place of 'ago'.

(ii) Use the negative form of present perfect tense.

Note: 'Ago' is always used with past tense. 'Last' is not used with 'for'.

Examples:

He last saw me a month ago.

He hasn't seen me for a month.

I last wrote him a week ago.

I haven't written to him for a week.

Use of adjective/adverb/verb/noun and vice versa

Examples:

1. One shouldn't be proud of one's knowledge. (adjective)
   One shouldn't take pride in one's knowledge. (noun)
2. There are clouds in the sky. (noun)
   The sky is cloudy. (adjective)
3. He succeeded in the examination. (verb)
   He was successful in the examination. (adjective)
4. The boy intentionally insulted his teacher. (adverb)
   The boy intended to insult his teacher. (verb)
5. He gave her a warm treatment. (adjective)
   He treated her warmly. (adverb)

EXERCISE-1

Change these into negative sentences.

1. As soon as I entered the classroom, everyone became silent.
2. You alone were to be blamed for this.
3. She is innocent.
4. Only a coward would say so.
5. I found a few spectators.
6. All must admit that he was a great writer.

EXERCISE-2

Change these into comparative degree.

1. She is as smart as you.
2. He is as brave as I.
3. You are as good as he.
4. Mohan is not as tall as Sohan.
5. Gold is not as costly as diamond.
6. Salma is as clever as Sabia.

EXERCISE-3

Change these into statement.

1. O that I were young again!
2. To think winning a lottery!
3. Alas! She is dead.
4. How kind of you to help me!
5. How attentively he listens!
6. How foolish of him to throw stones.
7. How happily he sings.
8. What an idiot you are!
9. Hurrah! we have won.
10. Ha! Ha! what a story.

EXERCISE-4

Change the form of the following sentences as directed.

1. Actions speak louder than words. (positive degree)
2. She is as tall as you are. (comparative degree)
3. This novel is more expensive than any other in the market. (superlative)
4. A lion is stronger than all other animals. (superlative)
5. Who cares for small insects? (statement)
6. Spring is the best season. (question)
7. He last sent me money a year ago. (use for)
8. None but the brave deserves victory. (affirmative)

9. Everybody feels that Harshad Mehta is guilty. (negative)
10. I am doubtful about his success. (negative)
11. Everybody wants to live long. (question)
12. Did I not warn you? (statement)

EXERCISE-5

Change these sentences as directed.

1. Would that I were a king! (statement)
2. Does man live by bread alone? (statement)
3. Very few poets are as great as Milton. (superlative)
4. Mango is the sweetest fruit. (positive)
5. She is one of the best girls. (comparative)
6. He is cleverer than all other men. (superlative)
7. He is too poor to buy a book. (remove 'too')
8. He is too weak. (remove 'too')
9. She is as poor as you. (comparative)
10. He is wise enough to answer well. (complex sentence)
11. A wife loves her husband. (question)
12. Isn't honestly the best policy? (statement)
13. What a fine picture it is! (statement)
14. He runs very fast. (exclamation)
15. How important a question! (statement)
16. O to be a prince! (statement)
17. She last saw me in summer. (use 'since')
18. If you prick us don't we bleed? (statement)
19. Who doesn't know Tendulkar? (statement)
20. I last saw her when I visited Kolkata. (use 'since')
21. He is honest. (negative)

14

Narration (Speech)

What is Narration?

Narration is an art of the expression of ideas and emotions in a formal and lively way.

There are two kinds of narration:

1. Direct speech
2. Indirect speech

A direct speech is conveyed directly by a speaker putting the exact words within the inverted commas, e.g.

He says, "I have lost my book".

An indirect speech is conveyed indirectly involving the third person in communication with certain changes in direct speech, e.g. the sentence given above can be said in indirect form like this.

He says that he has lost his book.

Now let us see some important points that help in identification of direct and indirect speeches.

1. A direct speech has two clauses separated by a comma and inverted commas, whereas indirect speech doesn't have any comma and inverted commas.
2. The two clauses of direct speech are named reporting clause and reported clause which are also called reporting verb and reported speech respectively.

He says, "I have lost my book".

He says = reporting clause/verb

I have lost my book = reported clause/verb.

3. The reporting clause may take initial, medial or final position in a sentence, e.g.

   He says, "I am fine". (initial)

   "A thing of beauty" says Keats, "is a joy for ever". (medial)

   "I am fine", says he. (final)

4. The main verb of the reporting clause is also called introductory verb or introducing verb.

From grammatical point of view, we should know how to change a direct sentence into an indirect sentence. Here are the general rules regarding the change of speech.

These Rules are Commonly Used with All Kinds of Sentences

(A) Change of Personal Pronoun /Possessive Adjective

When the subject of the reported speech has the first person pronoun, it is changed according to the subject of the reporting verb, e.g.

She says, "I do my work". (Direct)

She says that she does her work. (Indirect)

When the subject of the reported speech has the second person pronoun, it is changed according to the object of the reporting verb, e.g.

He says to me, "you are my friend". (Direct)
He tells me that I am his friend. (Indirect)

Reporting verb without object

If the reporting verb doesn't have an object and the reported speech has second person pronoun, in such cases it takes either third or first person pronoun according to the sense of the sentence, e.g.

The teacher says, "You must work hard".
The teacher tells him/me that he/I must work hard.

If the subject of the reported speech has third person pronoun it requires no change, e.g.

You say, "he is an utter fool". (Direct)
You say that he is an utter fool. (Indirect)

We can conclude it in this way, e.g.

First person changes according to subject.

Second person changes according to object.

Third person requires no change.

First	Second	Third
1st	2nd	3rd
Subject	object	no change

Note: The pronouns of the reported speech are changed into the same number and case.

(B) Change of Verb (tense)

If the reporting verb has present and future tense structures, the verb of the reported speech does not change, e.g.

I shall say to him, "You never do your duty punctually". (Direct)

I shall tell him that he never does his duty punctually. (Indirect)

If the reporting verb has past tense structure, the verb of the reported speech takes the following changes in tense, e.g.

(i) Present simple changes into past simple.

He said, "I write a book". (Direct)
He said that he wrote a book. (Indirect)

(ii) Present continuous changes into past continuous.

I said, "I am going to market". (Direct)

I said that I was going to market. (Indirect)

(iii) Present perfect changes into past perfect.

They said, "We have done it". (Direct)

They said that they had done it. (Indirect)

(iv) Present perfect continuous changes into past perfect continuous.

He said, "I have been playing football since evening". (Direct)

He said that he had been playing football since evening. (Indirect)

(v) Past simple changes into past perfect.

Ahmed said, "I wrote a letter". (Direct)

Ahmed said that he had written a letter. (Indirect)

(vi) Past continuous changes into past perfect continuous.

He said, "I was cooking". (Direct)

He said that he had been cooking. (Indirect)

Note: Past perfect and past perfect continuous tenses don't change.

Modal and other auxiliary verbs expressing present and future time take the following changes, e.g.

Will	would
Shall	should
Can	could
May	might
Has, have	had
Am, is, are	was, were
Was, were	had been
Must	had to or would have to

(But 'must' related to any rule or principle doesn't change.)

Note: Ought to, used to, could, might, should, would, had better and would better don't change.

The above-mentioned rules regarding the change of verb are not followed in the following conditions.

(1) When the reported speech expresses a proverb, universal fact, scientific fact or habitual action, the tense doesn't change e.g.

a. He said, "Man is mortal".

He said that man is mortal.

b. The teacher said, "The early bird catches the worm".

The teacher said that the early bird catches the worm.

(2) When the verb of the reported speech expresses wish, unfulfilled desire or adverb clause of time, it is not changed, e.g.

He said, "I wish I were prince".

He said that he wished he were a prince.

She said, "When I worked/was working in a factory I faced a lot of problems".

She said that when she worked/was working in a factory she faced a lot of problems.

(3) When the present tense expresses definite future action it is not changed into past tense rather future expressing modal verbs are used, e.g.

She said, "My husband leaves for London tomorrow".

She said that her husband would leave for London tomorrow.

(C) Change of Other Parts of Speech

Words denoting 'nearness' change into words 'denoting remoteness' because the time and the place have changed since the words were already spoken.

Direct		*indirect*	*direct*		*indirect*
This	-	that	hence	-	thence
These	-	those	now	-	then
Here	-	there	today	-	that day
Thus	-	so	tomorrow	-	next day
Ago	-	before			
next day/month	-	following day/month			
Yesterday	-	previous day			
Last night/week	-	previous night/week			

Some Special Rules

(1) *Declarative Sentence (Statement)*

Do the following to change a statement from direct to indirect:

(i) Start the sentence with the subject and the reporting verb.

(ii) Change say + to + object into tell + object.

(iii) Don't change "say", "said" into "tell", "told" without an object.

(iv) Use 'that' as conjunction before the indirect speech.

Note: We often leave out 'that' specially after common verbs like say, think, admit.

Examples:

a. Ali said, "I am tired".

Ali said that he was tired.

b. He said to me, "you are my friend".

He told me that I was his friend.

Note: When noun or pronoun is used in reported speech as a term of address, it is usually made the object of the reporting verb, but words of expressions such as well, o, now, you know, see, etc. are left out, e.g.

He said, "Well, Ali, I shall do the work".

He told Ali that he would do the work.

NB. When we use past tense in the reporting clause we can use either a present or past tense in the 'that' clause, e.g.

a. He said, "I am living in Delhi".

He said that he is/was living in Delhi.

b. I said to her, "I don't like going to the party".

I told her that I don't like going to the party.

Using present tense in the 'that' clause emphasizes that the situation being reported still exists or is still relevant when we report it.

(2) *Interrogative Sentence (Question)*

Do the following to change a direct question into a statement.

(i) Change "said", "said to" into "asked".

(ii) Use 'if' or 'whether' as a conjunction.

(iii) Change the question into a statement by placing the subject before the verb and replacing the question mark with a full stop.

(iv) When the question begins with a question-word, use the same question-word as a conjunction.

Examples:

a. He said to me, "Do you read English?"

He asked me whether I read English.

b. She said, "Where is the police station?" She asked where the police station was. (Question tags)

Do the following changes:

(i) Omit the statement and expand the tag to a full question.

(ii) Change the question tags like Yes/No (direct) questions.

Examples:

1. He said, "You don't like fish, do you?" (Direct)

He said, "Do you like fish?"

(Full tag-question)

He asked me if I liked fish. (Indirect)

The Change of yes/no in Indirect Speech

Yes/No part of direct speech is changed as such:

Use 'sub + auxiliary verb' to answer Yes/No.

Examples:

a. The baby said to me, "Do you love me?" I said, "Yes". (Direct)

The baby asked me if I loved her and I said that I did. (Indirect)

b. I said, "Can I use your pen?" he said "No".

I asked if I could use his pen and he said that I couldn't.

(3) *Imperative Sentence (Command or Request)*

Make the following changes:

(i) change "said", "said to" into "asked", "told", "requested", commanded, ordered, advised, begged, urged, warned, suggested + object, according to the meaning of the reported clause.

(ii) Change the verb of the reported clause into infinitive (with 'to').

Examples:

a. He said, "Stand up on the bench".
He asked me to stand up on the bench.

b. He said to me, "Give me some money, please".
He requested me to give some money.
(Omit please/kindly and use requested)

c. He said to her, "Do come tomorrow".
He asked her to come next day.
(Omit do/does/did of emphatic command)

d. He said to me, "Don't run in the sun".
He asked me not to run in the sun. (Negative command)

Note: The use of forbade + infinitive and prevented/ prohibited from + present participle, also expresses negative command.

He forbade me to run in the sun.

He prevented/prohibited me from running in the sun.

(Forbid/prevent and prohibit express negative meaning)

Imperative Question Tags and Rhetorical Questions

Do the following changes:

Omit will you, would you, could you, etc., i.e. the part that seeks yes/no response and follow the rules given above under the heading Imperative sentences.

Examples:

a. She said, "Would you take tea, please?"
She requested me to take tea.

b. Open the window, will you? The teacher said to me.

The teacher ordered me to open the window.

Imperatives Expressing Advice or Request

Do the following changes:

(i) Omit 'sub + must/might/ought to/should/had better and better'

(ii) Follow the above mentioned rules

Examples:

a. He said, "You must walk in the morning".

Ha advised me to walk in the morning.

b. She said, "You might attend the conference on my behalf".

She requested me to attend the conference on my behalf.

Imperatives with proposal or suggestion beginning with let me/let's

Do the following changes:

(i) Change "said", "said to" into "proposed" or "suggested"

(ii) Use 'that' as a conjunction

(iii) Change let into should

(iv) Change objective case pronoun (me/us) into subjective case pronoun (I/We)

Examples:

a. I said, "Let's go for a walk".

I proposed/suggested that we should go for a walk.

Imperatives Beginning with Let him/her/them

Do the following changes:

(i) Change said, said to into ordered, asked or requested

(ii) Use 'that' as a conjunction

(iii) Change "let" into should

(iv) Change objective case pronoun (him/her/them) into subjective case pronoun (he/she/they)

Examples:

He said, "Let her do it".

He ordered that she should do it.

(4) *Exclamatory Sentence*

Do the following changes:

(i) Change "said", "said to" into "exclaimed" with joy/sorrow/surprise/anger, etc.

(ii) Use that as a conjunction

(iii) Omit interjections (Ah!, Alas!, Bravo!, etc.)

(iv) Omit *what/how* and change *what* + *noun* into *adjective* + *noun* and *how* + *adj* + *adv* into *very* + *adj* + *adverb*.

(v) Use he/she/it + is/was as a subject + verb of incomplete sentences

Examples:

a. He said, "I am ruined".

He exclaimed with sorrow that he was ruined.

b. She said, "How smart he is!"

She exclaimed with surprise that he was very smart.

c. I said, "Oh, enough".

I exclaimed with disgust that it was enough.

Exclamatory Sentences of Incomplete Structure

Do the following changes:

(i) Change the reporting verb (said, said to) into wished/called or a suitable transitive verb

(ii) Use the words of reported speech as an object of the transitive verb

Examples:

a. He told me, "Happy Id".

He wished me a happy Id.

b. She said to me, "Thank you!"

She thanked me.

c. She told me, "Congratulations!"
   She congratulated me.

d. He said, "Fool!"
   He called me a fool.

Expression of Wish/Desire

Do the following changes:

(i) Change *'said'*, *'said to'* into *wished/prayed/cursed/blessed*

(ii) Use 'that' as a conjunction

(iii) Change *may* into *might*

(iv) Change the sentence into a statement

Examples:

a. Ha said, "May she be happy!"
   He wished that she might be happy.

b. People said, "Long live the king!"
   People prayed that the king might live long.

(Such sentences are called optative sentences in traditional grammar.)

EXERCISE-1

Change the following into indirect speech.

1. He said, "I am going to have my hair cut".
2. The teacher said, "The early bird catches the worm".
3. The man says, "The train always arrives late".
4. Dad said to me, "I will be pleased if you get high marks".
5. He said to me, "I saw your brother at the party last night".
6. Salma says, "I'm not coming to work tomorrow".
7. Girls always say, "We don't like washing up dishes".
8. The teacher said, "The earth is smaller than the sun".
9. "I hope that my passport was lost on my way to work", said the lady.

10. He said to me, "I lost your phone number".
11. They said to us, "We are your friends".
12. He said, "Ali, you know, I am your cousin".

EXERCISE-2

Change the following into indirect speech.

1. The tourist said, "Is this the way to museum?"
2. He asks, "Is the boss in?"
3. The secretary said to him, "Do you want to see the manager?"
4. "Where are you going, boys?" said the headmaster.
5. What did you study in the UK? I asked him.
6. The teacher asked them, "Why were you absent yesterday?"
7. I asked the policeman, "Which way leads to the bus station?"
8. They said to me, "Did Ali come here yesterday?"
9. "Have you seen my son anywhere?" she said to me.
10. He said to her, "Are you married?"
11. The teacher said to me, "What is your name?"
12. He said to me, "Why did you not give me money?"
13. He told me, "You are my friend, aren't you?"
14. She told me, "Shall I go to visit the film tonight?"
15. The passenger said to the guard, "How far is Kolkata from New Delhi?"

EXERCISE-3

Change the following into indirect speech.

1. The teacher said to us, "Copy these notes into your note-books".
2. He said to me, "Wait for me at the bus-station".
3. She said, "Don't make a noise".
4. He said, "Help me, please".
5. He said to me, "Open the door, will you?"

6. The doctor said, "You should take medicine in time".
7. The teacher said, "Will you bring a board marker?"
8. He said, "Let them go out".
9. I said, "Let's go to visit a picture tonight".
10. The commandant said, "Let the army march ahead".

EXERCISE-4

Change the following into indirect speech.

1. He said, "May God bless you!"
2. She said, "Alas! Her husband is dead".
3. The saint said, "May you be blessed with a son!"
4. I said, "Enough!"
5. He said, "What a fool!"
6. He said, "How lovely this girl is!"
7. He said to me, "Good morning".
8. He said, "What a snake!"
9. He said, "How foolish I am!"
10. He said to me, "Thank you!"

EXERCISE-5

Change the following into indirect speech.

1. "What do you want?" asked he "Tell me, please". I am ready to help you.
2. He said to me, "What can I do for you" you are a good looking boy.
3. The saint said to the old man, "Where are you coming from and what is your problem" Do you need my help?

15
Voice

What is Voice?

Voice is that property of a verb which shows whether the subject is performing or experiencing an action.

He writes a letter.
A letter is written by him.

Here, in both the sentences, the doer of the action is '*he*' and the object affected by the action is a '*letter*'. Thus, we can say that voice is a kind of transformation of grammatical constituents, and not of the basic meaning of sentences.

There are two kinds of voice.

(i) Active voice (ii) Passive voice

Active voice is used to emphasize the doer of the action, e.g.

They broke the window.

Passive voice is used to emphasize the action rather than the doer or when the doer is vague or unimportant, e.g.

The window was broken.

Here, who broke the window is unimportant, and how is the window, whether broken or not, is important.

Now let us talk about the change of Active voice into Passive.

Rules for the Formation of Passive Structures

There are two kinds of passive constructions—Agentive and Non-agentive, depending on the presence or absence of the doer/agent.

1. Agentive Passive (Passive with Agent/Doer)

(i) The active subject becomes the passive object.

(ii) The active object becomes the passive subject.

(iii) Verb 'be' (am, is, are, was, were, be, been, being) + past participle (v_3) come before 'by' followed by the agent.

(iv) Personal pronouns of nominative case change into accusative case, e.g.

I – me		We – us
He – him		She – her
They – them		Who – whom

Other personal pronouns '*you*' and '*it*' don't have distinct case forms.

(v) The verb of the passive sentence agrees with number and person of its subject.

I am beaten by him.

(vi) Negative and interrogative sentences of the active voice have the same structure in the passive.

Note: Only *transitive verbs* can be changed into their passive forms. *Linking verbs* or *intransitive verbs* can never be passivized.

Basic Patterns of Voice

Tense

Simple Present - Sub + v_1/v_5 + object. (Active)

Sub + am/is/are + v_3 + by + doer. (Passive)

Example: He reads a letter. (Active)

A letter is written by him. (Passive)

Present progressive - Sub + am/is/are + v_4 + obj. (Active)

Sub + am/is/are + being + v_3 + by + doer. (Passive)

She is singing a song. (Active)

A song is being sung by her. (Passive)

Present perfect - Sub + has/have + v_3 + obj. (Active)

Sub + has/have + been + v_3 + by + doer. (Passive)

Ali has done the work. (active)

The work has been done by Ali. (Passive)

Simple Past - Sub + v_2 + obj. (Active)

Sub + was/were + v_3 + by + doer. (Passive)

They wrote many letters. (Active)

Many letters were written by them. (Passive)

Past progressive - Sub + was/were + v_4 + obj. (Active)

Sub + was/were + being + v_3 + by + doer. (Passive)

Boys were playing football. (Active)

Football was being played by boys. (Passive)

Past perfect - Sub + had + v_3 + obj. (Active)

Sub + had been + v_3 + by + doer. (Passive)

We had solved the sum. (Active)

The sum had been solved by us. (Passive)

Simple future - Sub + will/shall + v_1 + obj. (Active)

Sub + will/shall + be + v_3 + by + doer. (Passive)

He will beat me. (Active)

I shall be beaten by him. (Passive)

Future progressive-

Sub + will/shall + be + v_4 + object. (Active)

Sub + will/shall + be + being + v_3 + by + doer. (Passive)

He will be writing a book. (Active)

A book will be being written by him. (Passive)

Future perfect-

Sub + will/shall + have + v_3 + obj. (Active)

Sub + will/shall + have been + v_3 + by + doer. (Passive)

He will have finished the work. (Active)

The work will have been finished by him. (Passive)

Note: The passive forms of *present, past* and *future perfect progressive* tenses are possible. But they are not usually passivized in order to avoid repetitive pattern of 'been + being' in the same construction, e.g.

They have been doing the work. (Active)

The work has been being done by them. (Passive)

2. Non-Agentive (Agentless) Passive

If the active subject is *vague* or *obvious*, it is usually omitted in the passive, e.g.

Someone has stolen my watch. (Active)

My watch has been stolen. (Passive)

People speak English all over the world. (Active)

English is spoken all over the world. (Passive)

The *police* arrested the thief. (Active)

The thief was arrested. (Passive)

The *doctor* operated the patient. (Active)

The patient was operated. (Passive)

Here, it is relevant to mention that *someone* refers to a person whose identity is unknown (*vague*), and *people, police* and *doctor* refer to the persons whose identities are known (*obvious*) in terms of actions they perform.

Miscellaneous Kinds of Passive Constructions

1. Passives with Infinitive

A- Sub + be (am/is/are/was/were) + infinitive + obj:

Students are to clean the rooms. (Active)

The rooms are to be cleaned by the students. (Passive)

They were to help me. (Active)

I was to be helped by them. (Passive)

B- Sub + (have) have, has, had + infinitive + obj:

Salma has to cook food. (Active)

Food has to be cooked by Salma. (Passive)

C- Sub + modal + v_1 *+ obj:*

He can speak English. (Active)

English can be spoken by him. (Passive)

You must do it. (Active)

It must be done by you. (Passive)

2. Passives as per the Nature of Verbs

A- Monotransitive verb:

It contains only one object.

Girls like chocolates. (Active)

Chocolates are liked by girls. (Passive)

B- Ditransitive verb:

It contains a direct and an indirect object. Either of the two objects can be used as subjects for passive.

IO DO

She gave me a pen. (Active)

I was given a pen. (Passive)

A pen was given to me. (Passive)

IO DO

He bought me a new car (Active)

I was bought a new car. (Passive)

A new car was bought for me. (Passive)

Only indirect objects take '*to*' or '*for*' before it when it comes as the object of the passive.

C- Complex transitive verb:

It contains a direct object and an objective complement.

They elected him leader. (Active)

He was elected leader. (Passive)

Samir called her foolish. (Active)

She was called foolish. (Passive)

Note: Objective complement may be a noun or an adjective. But it can't function as a subject of the passive voice.

3. Passive with Cognate Object

A - Sub + verb + cognate object:

Cognate object is a *verbal noun*.
He dreamt a sweet dream. (Active)
A sweet dream was dreamt. (Passive)
We ran a race. (Active)
A race was run. (Passive)

4. Passive with Objects of Preposition

A- Sub + verb + preposition + object:
He laughed at me. (Active)
I was laughed at by him. (Passive)
Ali looked into the case. (Active)
The case was looked into by Ali. (Passive)

5. Passive with Negatives

Negative sub + verb + object is passivized by making the sentence negative and omitting the active subject.

Nobody can do it.
It can't be done.
No one heard the sound.
No sound was heard.
No one answered the question.
The question was not answered.

6. Passive with Bare Infinitive

Sub + verb + obj + bare infinitive (without 'to') is used with full infinitive (with 'to') in the passive.

I saw her sing a song.
She was seen to sing a song.
He made me weep.
I was made to weep.
But *let* doesn't take *'to'* in the passive.
I let her go.
She was let go.

7. Passive with 'there'

There + verb (be) + noun (subject) + infinitive:
There was no time to waste.
There was no time to be wasted.
There are no books to distribute.
There are no books to be distributed.

8. The formation of the get passives

The *'get'* passives are occasionally used with some typical verbs instead of 'be' passive in spoken English.

The *'get'* passives take *sub + get + past participle* (v_3) form of the verb. The verbs that usually take get in the passive construction are; *married/hit/involved/stuck/paid/tired/worried/finished/lost/engaged/invited*, etc.

In most cases, *'get'* passives have the same meaning as *'be'* passive sentences have.

The mail gets delivered everyday. (get passive)

The mail is delivered everyday. (be passive)

I got invited to his wedding party.

I was invited to his wedding party.

She got married in her early twenties.

She was married in her early twenties.

9. Passive with Vague Subjects

Sub (vague) + verb + clause:

If the subject of the main clause is vague like *someone/people/we/they/*followed by the verb *believe/know/say/report/think/understand/consider/hope/want,* etc. it is changed into *it is/was* + v_3 + *the rest of noun clause.*

People believe that the earth is round. (Active)

It is believed that the earth is round. (Passive)

Someone says that honesty is the best policy. (Active)

It is said that honesty is the best policy. (Passive)

10. Passive of complex sentences

A- Main clause + that + noun clause (object)constructions

It is changed into the following two ways.

(i) Sub + verb (be) + v_3 + infinitive.

or

Sub + verb (be) + v_3 + to be + noun (Adjective).

(ii) It + is/was + v_3 + that + clause.

A. Someone believes that girls grow young early.

Girls are believed *to grow* young early. (Infinitive)

It is believed that girls grow young early.

B. People think that he is intelligent.

It is thought that he is intelligent.

He is thought to be *intelligent.* (Adjective)

Thus, the above sentences are changed in the following ways.

(i) Use the subject of noun clause as the subject of main clause.

(ii) Omit the subject of the main clause.

(iii) Never use by + obj.

or

It is/was + v_3 + that + clause.

B. Main clause + that + noun clause (passive form)

Main clause + to be + v_3

She hopes that she ought to be praised. (Active)

She hopes to be praised. (Passive)

They consider that they should be

treated as teachers. (Active)

They consider to be treated as teachers. (Passive)

Such sentences are changed by omitting some parts of noun clause (*that + subject + auxiliary*) using to *be + v_3* after the main verb.

11. Passive of Compound Sentences

Compound sentences which can be passivized, have more than one transitive verb. All the transitive verbs are changed into past participle (v_3) form of the verb.

(i) Passive subject takes the first object only. Others are left out.

He wrote a letter and posted it. (Active)

A letter was written and posted. (Passive)

She took a book and torn it into pieces. (Active)

A book was taken and torn into pieces. (Passive)

12. Passive Sentences with Other Than 'by' Agent

(i) When material or substance is used as an object of the passive it is preceded by *with* phrase.

Mud covered his shoes. (Active)

His shoes were covered with mud. (Passive)

Smoke filled the room. (Active)

The room was filled with smoke (Passive)

(ii) There are certain verbs that take a different preposition instead of *'by'*, e.g.

know/marry – to

amaze/astonish/surprise/shock – at

pleased/displeased/satisfied/dissatisfied – with

interest – in

I know you. (Active)

You are known to me. (not 'by me') (Passive)

This book interests me. (Active)

I am interested in this book. (Passive)

13. Passive of Interrogative Sentences with Auxiliary Verbs

Do/does/did of the active sentences changes into *am/is/are/was/were* in the passive. Other auxiliary verbs don't change.

Does he write a letter? (Active)

Is a letter written by him? (Passive)

Can you do it? (Active)

Can it be done by you? (Passive)

14. Passive of Interrogative Sentences with wh-Questions (as Object) (why/when/how/where/what)

Why do you not read English? (Active)

Why is English not read by you? (Passive)

When did they do it? (Active)

When was it done by them? (Passive)

15. Passive of Interrogative sentences with who/what /which (as subject)

Who did it? (Active)

By whom was it done? (Passive)

Or

Who was it done by? (Passive)

Note: These days the use of *'by whom'* is avoided.

What caused the accident? (Active)

What was the accident caused by? (Passive)

What will interest you? (Active)

What will you be interested in? (Passive)

Which boy disturbed her? (Active)

Which boy was she disturbed by? (Passive)

16. Passives of Interrogative with Indirect Question

We simply use the object of the reporting verb as *passive subject + to be +* v_3 *+ the rest of the sentence.*

I asked Mariam if she was well. (Active)

Mariam was asked if she was well. (Passive)

He asked me where I was going. (Active)

I was asked where I was going. (Passive)

17. Imperative sentence with order/command

We use *let + obj +be + pp* (v_3).

Open the window. (Active)

Let the window be opened. (Passive)

Clean the room. (Active)

Let the room be cleaned. (Passive)

In the sentences of *request* and *advice*, the structure of the passive is like:

Obj + should + be + v_3.

Take medicine in time. (Active)

The medicine should be taken in time. (Passive)

Help the needy. (Active)

The needy should be helped. (Passive)

In the sentences of request beginning with *please/kindly*, we generally use '*you are requested to*' + *the rest of the sentence* omitting *please/kindly*.

Please help me. (Active)

You are requested to help me. (Passive)

When such a sentence has double objects, either of the two may be made the subject of the passive and *please/kindly* is placed between *may* and *be*.

Please give me some money. (Active)

Some money may please be given to me. (Passive)

or

I may please be given some money.

18. Passives of Imperative Sentence with Indirect Command/ Advice

The object of the reporting verb is changed into subject.

The verb is changed into *be* + v_3 and the rest of the sentence remains the same.

She told me to write a letter.	(Active)
I was told to write a letter.	(Passive)
He advised me to read attentively.	(Active)
I was advised to read attentively.	(Passive)

Some important uses of the passive:

(i) Passive sentences are used in official notices and procedures, e.g.

Original documents should be forwarded for admission.

Students are informed to deposit their fees immediately.

(ii) Passive sentences are used in making objective description of anything like industrial and scientific processes, e.g.

A thermometer is used for measuring temperature.

Some parts of the motors are being made of plastic.

(iii) Passive constructions are used for passing instructions and guidelines, e.g.

Smoking is not allowed here.

(iv) Passive constructions are used in advertisements and headlines of newspapers.

Candidates are supposed to come with all testimonials in the interview.

Robbers were arrested.

Two cabinet ministers were forced to resign.

EXERCISE-1

Change the voice.

1. Girls don't play football.
2. He didn't do it.
3. They take him to hospital.
4. The doctors ordered me to stay in bed.
5. Do they grow tea in China?
6. How can I open the box?
7. Where do they grow rice?
8. Has she broken the vase?
9. Do it.
10. Why did they punish the old man?
11. They gave him a prize.
12. A company is repairing the dam.
13. Shakespeare didn't write *The Oldman and the Sea.*
14. They don't sell fruits here.
15. You ought to open all the windows.
16. We use computers for designing the houses and offices.
17. I can't open this window.
18. Why have they arrested the girl?

19. He damaged his car in an accident?
20. Close all the windows.
21. Smoking causes cancer.
22. What will satisfy you?
23. Who invented wireless?
24. Some students left these books in the classroom.
25. They will close the waterways for three days.
26. People write Arabic from right to left.
27. No one has found the lost child.
28. Rabia typed the letter and posted it.
29. Shakespeare wrote *Hamlet* in 1601.
30. Will they build a laboratory in the college?

EXERCISE-2

Change the voice.

1. They let me go.
2. There is no money to waste.
3. We heard her sing.
4. No one can solve this problem.
5. She looks after the baby.
6. We slept a sound sleep last night.
7. People think that labour never goes in vain.
8. The teacher told the students to listen to him patiently.
9. Kindly grant me two days' leave.
10. Obey your parents.
11. Let him do it.
12. I asked her if she was fine.
13. They asked me where I lived.
14. Which book do you take interest?
15. What causes the crack?
16. Her behaviour pleased me.

17. Gas filled the courtyard.
18. He made many mistakes.
19. The performance shocked the audience.
20. The dog chased the cat.
21. Shefali hit the ball with force.
22. Ravi opened the door with a key.
23. Did she buy a book yesterday?
24. We must wait for him.
25. Paint covered the lock.
26. You must shut these doors.
27. They were carrying the injured player off the field.
28. Helicopters fascinate children.
29. This news will amaze you.
30. Water surrounds an island.
31. Mr. Hopkins invited me to dinner.

EXERCISE-3

Change the voice.

1. Boys were taught English by the teacher.
2. She thinks to be admired.
3. How are the dolls destroyed by the boys?
4. Shut the window.
5. Take it for granted.
6. I told you not to run in the sun.
7. She took a sound sleep.
8. A song was sung by me.
9. I filed a case against the government.
10. I named the child Yusuf.
11. The teacher is being given a prize by the President.
12. Salma sent for a doctor.
13. What questions did Dr Ashok set?
14. We have not been invited to dinner today.

15. I overheard her talk.
16. You do it.
17. My mobile has been stolen.
18. Football is played all over Libya.
19. Did she impress Basam?
20. Why has she not done it?
21. We must write to him.
22. Who raised this question?
23. Read this book to improve language skill.
24. The doctor brought the dead child back to life.
25. Bear this trouble with patience.
26. The police will have to look into the matter.
27. Who wrote the *Bible*?
28. Omar sent letters of thanks to his Indian friends.
29. One looks up a word in the dictionary to know the meaning.
30. When did she do her Ph.D?
31. Is he writing a novel or a drama?

EXERCISE-4

Change the voice.

1. I had to challenge him.
2. Who offered you a job?
3. She prevented me from doing it.
4. I sent him four chapters.
5. Ali painted the box green.
6. They obliged us to go.
7. The baby forced me to buy a balloon.
8. She makes me laugh.
9. No one likes fish in my family.
10. We believe that patience pays in the long run.
11. They proved me wrong.

12. She prepared food and gave it to her children.
13. Poverty drives a man to desperation.
14. Kindly pay me the fee first.
15. Iron my dress immediately.
16. How did he steal a pen?
17. The angry man threw away my bag.
18. I have to teach English grammar in the class.
19. We hang the picture on the wall.
20. Let me note it down.
21. Please pay attention to what I say.
22. She wants that she should be admired.
23. I am surprised at his behaviour.
24. I promised her a rich reward.
25. Credit the salary to my account.

16

Question Tag

What is a Question Tag?

A question tag or tail question is a question attached to the end of a statement, command or proposal for the clarification of doubt and confirmation of opinion in conversational English. It is formed with the help of auxiliary verbs taking only a 'pronoun' or 'there' as a subject of the tag. But it lacks the force of a direct question. For example:

They are good students, aren't they?
There is a book on the table, isn't there?

Here, it is relevant to note that 'there' comes as an introductory or expletive grammatical subject when the real subject of the sentence comes after the verb instead of coming before it. Look at these examples.

There is a page missing from my notebook, isn't there?
There are five hundred students in this college, aren't there?

In the above two sentences the real subject is 'a page' and 'five hundred students'. But such type of sentences can't be framed without the use of 'there' as grammatical subjects. One can't write like this:

Is a page missing from my notebook.
Are five hundred students in this college.

So, 'there' becomes an essential existential subject that is used in simple and interrogative sentences. It is used in question tags.

There was a king?	(simple)
Was there a king?	(interrogative)
There was a king, wasn't there?	(question tag)

There are Some Common Rules to Make a Question Tag.

1. A negative tag is added to an affirmative statement.

   An affirmative tag is added to a negative statement, e.g.

   He is a student, isn't he?

   She is not a doctor, is she?

2. Auxiliary verbs are repeated in the tag. Other verbs of simple present or past tense have do, does or did in the tag, e.g.

   You are my teacher, aren't you?

   She works hard, doesn't she?

   You like fish, don't you?

   They wrote a letter, didn't they?

3. It takes a pronoun even though the subject of the statement is a noun or a command. (without a subject)

   Ali is a good boy, isn't he?

   Open the window, will you?

4. Usually, the contracted form of auxiliary verbs is used to shorten the length of speech, e.g.

Will not = won't	cannot = can't
Shall not = shan't	are not = aren't

There are some special forms of question tag that need special care at the time of speaking or writing.

1. When 'used to' comes in the sentence it takes either 'didn't' or 'usedn't' in the tag, e.g.

   She used to play tennis, didn't she or usedn't she?

2. When 'had rather', 'had better', 'would rather' or 'would better' comes in the sentence, it takes 'hadn't' and 'wouldn't' respectively, e.g.

   They had better go there, hadn't they?

She would rather consult a doctor, wouldn't she?

3. When few, little, no (adjectives); no one, none, nobody, nothing, neither (pronouns); barely, rarely, scarcely, hardly, never, seldom, too (adverbs); contain semi-negative meaning, and are treated as negative sentences, they take positive tag, e.g.

   I have little idea in this regard, have I?

   There is too much sugar in tea, is there?

   We rarely go to the cinema, do we?

   Few people of this place would help us, would they?

4. When 'few' contains positive meaning, it takes a negative tag, e.g.

   Alok is a man of few means, isn't he?

5. But 'a few', 'the few', 'a little' or 'the little' contains a positive meaning and takes a negative tag, e.g.

   A few students have passed, haven't they?

   He ate the few apple he had, didn't he?

   He wasted the little time he had, didn't he?

6. When anybody, somebody, everybody, anyone, someone, everyone (pronoun) come as subjects, the pronoun in the tag is "they" because there is no possessive adjective in English that can stand for both masculine and feminine, singular and plural nouns, e.g.

   Everybody is present, aren't they?

   Everyone of my class can do it, can't they?

7. When anything, something or everything (pronoun) comes as a subject, it takes singular pronoun 'it' in the tag, e.g.

   Anything can be possible, can't it?

8. If 'this' or 'that' comes as a subject, it takes singular pronoun 'it'. But 'these' or 'those' takes 'they', e.g.

   These books are expensive, aren't they?

   This coat is cheap, isn't it?

9. When a positive sentence begins with 'I am' it takes 'aren't I' in the tag but the negative sentence beginning with 'I am not' takes 'am I' in the tag, e.g.

   I am a teacher, aren't I?

   I am not a student, am I?

Here it is relevant to note that 'I am' changes into 'aren't I' in conversational (colloquial) English but 'amn't I' is the formal form of expression when direct question is formed, e.g.

Am I not strong enough to lift this box?

Aren't I strong enough to lift this box?

10. When the main clause is an imperative sentence showing request or command, it usually takes 'will you' in the tag, e.g.

    Pass me the salt, will you?

11. When the main clause expresses invitation, offer or suggestion, it takes 'won't you' in the tag to show urgency, e.g.

    Take medicine in time, won't you?

    Have a seat, won't you?

12. When the main clause expresses impatience showing the force of a rebuke, it takes 'can't you?' in the tag, e.g.

    Mind your own business, can't you?

13. Negative command always takes a positive tag, e.g.

    Don't make noise, will you?

14. When 'let's' come in the main clause showing the sense of proposal or suggestion, it takes 'shall we' in the tag, e.g.

    Let's go for a walk, shall we?

15. When let them/him/her/me come in the sentence showing the sense of permission, it takes 'will you' in the tag, e.g.

    Let me go now, will you?

    Let them finish the work, will you?

16. When needn't or daren't comes in the main clause, it takes positive tag, e.g.

    She needn't go there, need she?

    You daren't do it, dare you?

17. When 'need' or 'dare' comes as main verbs in the clause, it takes 'don't', 'doesn't' or 'didn't' in the tag, e.g.

    They need our support, don't they?

    She needs a pen, doesn't she?

    You dared to speak the truth, didn't you?

18. When the subject of the main clause is 'all of us', 'some of us', 'many of us', 'none of us', 'one of us' or 'most of us', it takes 'we' in the tag, e.g.

    All of us have seen the Taj Mahal, haven't we?

19. When the subject of the main clause is 'all of you', 'some of you', 'none of you', 'many of you', 'most of you' or 'one of you', it takes 'you' in the tag, e.g.

    Many of you are diligent, aren't you?

20. When the subject of the main clause is 'all of them', 'some of them', 'many of them', 'most of them', 'none of them' or 'one of them', it takes 'they' in the tag, e.g.

    Most of them were present, weren't they?

    None of them know it, do they?

21. When 'some of us' comes as a subject and includes the speaker, it takes 'we', but it takes 'they' when it does not include the speaker himself, e.g.

    Some of us wanted to attend the marriage, didn't we?

    Some of us were to take a bath in the sea, weren't they?

22. When impersonal pronoun 'one' comes as a subject, it is repeated in the tag, e.g.

    One can't play here, can one?

But it may take either he or you in the tag, e.g.

One should read seriously, shouldn't he? shouldn't they?

EXERCISE-1

Add question tags.

1. Mr. Rakesh is a farmer.
2. You can speak English.
3. Your friends will come with you.
4. He ought to know the answer.
5. You know the answer.
6. Your father speaks English.
7. I am not late.
8. Akhilesh is never late.
9. Sudha doesn't want to go.
10. The children broke the window.
11. The teacher didn't explain the lesson well.
12. There is no one in the house.
13. This is not your book.
14. Ali loves fishing.
15. You'll have some more tea.
16. They arrived yesterday.
17. They didn't see you.
18. You like coffee.
19. You don't like sugar.
20. Adel won't come to the party.
21. Surely you'll come.
22. One should read seriously, shouldn't he/should not you?
23. I am not wrong.
24. Everybody knows you.
25. Your uncle leaves here.

26. Abhishek is never late for work.
27. Come and see tomorrow.
28. Let's have a look.
29. Let's go together.
30. There is an engineering college in khoms.
31. Nothing is clear.
32. You needn't go there.

EXERCISE-2

Add question tags.

1. You can do this exercise without help.
2. Sana is a clever girl.
3. She speaks English.
4. There are a dozen eggs in the basket.
5. Open the door.
6. She used to play tennis.
7. Mahesh doesn't like English food.
8. You won't be late tomorrow.
9. Aniket didn't come on time.
10. Girls like to be admired.
11. I am late.
12. Ashok has been here.
13. Bees die when they sting someone.
14. You can't do it.
15. Not all the students are clever.
16. The children will go to Leptis magna.
17. They have never been there.
18. We shan't be able to push the car.
19. Health is wealth.
20. Come to the meeting.
21. The man spoke to you in English.
22. Everybody is ready.

23. Let me help you.
24. He ought to follow my advice.
25. She needs chocolates.
26. We dare to say it.
27. She daren't go there.
28. He seldom goes to church.
29. You must go there.
30. Come in.
31. You had better talk to him.
32. She would rather resign.

17

Punctuation

What is Punctuation?

Punctuation is an established code of signs used in written and printed forms to separate words, phrases and sentences from one another to give clarity of meaning.

Look at the importance of punctuation marks in the following sentences to notice how a comma completely changes the meaning.

Mary Robinson says, Mrs Abington is the greatest actress in London.

Mary Robinson, says Mrs Abington, is the greatest actress in London.

Punctuation Marks with Symbols

i. Comma (,)
ii. Full stop/period (.)
iii. Question mark (?)
iv. Exclamation mark (!)
v. Quotation mark/inverted commas (‘ ’) (“ ”)
vi. Apostrophe (’)
vii. Colon (:)
viii. Semicolon (;)
ix. Parenthesis/brackets (( ))
x. Dash (—)
xi. Hyphen (-)

xii.	Ellipsis/dots	(....)
xiii.	Slashes/oblique	(/)
xiv.	Square brackets	([ ])
xv.	Underlining/italics	(____)

Comma (,)

A comma is used:

A. To separate items in a list, but it is often not used between the last two items, e.g.

- Ahmed, George, Rakesh and Jayant are friends.
- She ate her food speedily, noisely and greedily.
- Early to bed and early to rise makes a man healthy, wealthy and wise.
- He is a tall, intelligent, handsome and submissive student.

B. After the words yes, no, when they are used in an answer to a question, e.g.

Did you understand this?

Yes, I did.

No, I didn't.

C. After the words well, as you know, by the way, etc... when they come in the beginning of a sentence (asides), e.g.

As you know, this lesson is very important in writing.

Well, let's review it together.

By the way, will there be an exam tomorrow?

D. Before a question tag, e.g.

Health is wealth, isn't it?

E. Between two main clauses (independent) joined by and, but, for, or, etc., e.g.

He went to England, but he couldn't improve his English.

Study hard, or you will fail.

I read the lesson twice, but I couldn't understand it.

F. After an 'adverbial clause' when it comes first in a sentence, e.g.

If you help me, I'll help you.

When I went home, I didn't find you.

Although he is poor, he is happy.

G. To mark off direct speech, e.g.

He said, "I will go to the cinema."

"I am busy now", said Nuri.

H. In addressing a noun/pronoun in vocative case, e.g.

May I come in, sir?

Ali, please close the window.

I. To separate words from the rest of the sentence, e.g.

I met our teacher, Dr. Samir, this evening.

Your uncle, Ramesh, asked for you.

The workers, young and old, are always busy.

J. In dates where order is month, day and year, e.g.

I was born on May 10, 1960.

(but it is not used with dates where order is day, month, year)

I was born on 10 May 1960.

K. In letters after salutation, e.g.

Dear father,

Respected sir,

(but in application it doesn't come except yours faithfully, sincerely yours, etc...after the complimentary close in letters)

To

The principal,

....

Sir/Madam,

....

Yours sincerely,

L. After adverbial phrase, absolute phrase and participial phrase, e.g.

At last, he managed to pass.

Having finished the work, he went home.

The sun having risen, the fog disappeared.

M. Between noun, pronoun in apposition.

Tripoli, the capital of Libya, is a big city.

Shakespeare, the greatest dramatist of the Elizabethan age, was a genius.

I, Dr. Seikh Ahmed, am speaking to you.

N. Before 'please' when it comes at the end of the sentence, e.g.

Give me some money, please.

Help her, please.

O. Before and after the parenthetical expression when it comes in the middle of a sentence.

He is, to tell the truth, is an honest man.

Your suggestion, in my opinion, is not logical.

P. After the following expressions:

In fact, obviously, of course, in short, too, moreover, therefore, etc..., e.g.

In fact, he is an honest man.

I, therefore, request you to grant me leave.

Q. To separate a non-restrictive relative clause, e.g.

My son, who is an engineer, is still single.

R. Between names and titles or degrees, e.g.

Dr Martin, M.Sc., Ph.D.

Mr Abdullah, M.B.B.S.

S. After a non-finite or verbless construction, e.g.

When in Libya, do as Libyans do.

To know a language, we must work hard.

T. In figures to separate thousands between the third and the fourth digits from the right

1,000 2,000

U. To separate the same verbs which may be mistakenly read together.

What he did, didn't impress anyone of us.

What he is, is not known to me.

What I know, know well.

V. To indicate contrast by the use of 'not' in the sentence.

Ali, not Ravi, is going to receive the guest at the airport.

Not Rabia, but her sister, is going to get married.

W. In addresses when it is written in the same line, e.g.

Hospital road, Rajendra Nagar, Patna

20 street, Khoms, Libya

Full stop (period) (.)

It is used:

i. At the end of a sentence except optative, exclamatory and interrogative sentences, e.g.

He needs your help.

Help him.

ii. At the end of an indirect question, e.g.

He asked me where I was going.

iii. To separate hours from minutes, e.g.

They reached there at 8.30 in the morning.

She will get back at 5.15 in the evening.

iv. To separate dates from months and years, e.g.

16.2.2009

5.10.1960

v. In sentence fragments and short polite statements, e.g.

Okay. Yes.

See you.	Sorry.
No.	Nice to see you.

vi. In abbreviated words, e.g.

etc. (etcetera)	a.m. (ante meridiem)	i.e. (id est)
viz. (videlicit)	e.g. (exempli gratia)	N.B. (nota bene)

vii. To indicate decimal points (said points), e.g.

3.8 (three point eight)

4.6 (four point six)

0.245 (zero point two four five)

viii. In the internet and e-mail addresses (said dots)

e-mail: raj1972@yahoo.com

http: www.oed.com

ix. At the end of a question to express polite request in a formal way, e.g.

May I call on Dr Joseph to inaugurate the session.

x. With initials for personal names and degrees, e.g.

R.K. Sharma M.A., Ph.D.

Though there are some common sets of initials or acronyms with which stops are not used, e.g.

RSVP	OED	VIP	CNN	PM
UK	USSR	BBC	ISD	MLA

xi. Without stops in acronyms pronounced as a word, e.g.

ASEAN VAT AIDS UNESCO CAT

xii. Without stops in abbreviation formed with few letters and syllables of the word

TV (television)	Bus (minibus/omnibus)
Flu (influenza)	Phone (telephone)
TB (tuberculosis)	Memo (memorandum)
Ad (advertisement)	Exam (examination)

xiii. Without stops in the abbreviations of number/ weight/measure, e.g.

3 yds and 5 ins (three yards and five inches)

2 kgs (two kilograms)

kph (kilometer per hour)

cm (centimeter)

1 m dollars (one million dollars)

xiv. Without stops in abbreviation formed with the first and the last letter, e.g.

Dr	Doctor	Mrs	Mistress
Mr	Mister	St	Saint
Ms	Miss	Ltd	Limited

xv. Without stops in the newspaper headlines, heading and subheading of books, magazines, etc., e.g.

War and Peace (book)

Punctuation (heading)

Question marks and exclamation marks (subheading)

Three boys kidnapped (news headlines)

Probe (magazine)

xvi. Without stops with superscript and normal script, e.g.

1st (superscript)	1st (normal script)
2nd (superscript)	2nd (normal script)
4th (superscript)	4th (normal script)

Question Mark (?)

It is used:

i. At the end of a direct question, e.g.

Where is your book?

Is he here?

(but not before indirect question)

He asked me where my book was.

He asked if he was there.

ii. At the end of elliptical question, e.g.

Why worry now?
So what?
Why not?

iii. At the end of question tag, e.g.

They like it, don't they?
He was there, wasn't he?

iv. To indicate doubt, e.g.

Shelley was born in 1865 (?) and died in 1894.

Exclamation Mark (!)

It is used:

i. At the end of exclamatory sentence or after interjections. To express surprise, anger, applause, etc., e.g.

Alas! She is dead.

What a lovely garden it is!
Fie! Fie! Go away.
There goes our train!

ii. At the end of optative sentence to express wish, desire, etc., e.g.

May lord help us!
Long live the king!
May she die!

Quotation Mark (Inverted Commas)

There are two types of quotation marks.

(i) Single inverted commas ('.........').

(ii) Double inverted commas (".........").

Both single inverted commas and double inverted commas are the acceptable forms in writing.

He said, 'I know English.'

He said, "I know English."

But usually single inverted commas are preferred to emphasize a word or a group of words within a quotation.

The teacher said, "What is the meaning of 'education' in life?"

It is used:

i. To enclose a quotation, proverb, maxim, etc., e.g.

Keats says, "A thing of beauty is a joy for ever".

ii. To enclose words, lines, sentences, titles of articles, essay, poems, stories, etc., e.g.

Tennyson's 'In Memoriam' is a long poem.

The word 'rest' has been used to express different meanings in the poem 'The Gift of God'.

Apostrophe (')

It is used:

i. To form the possessive of a singular noun, add an apostrophe and (s), e.g.

Ali's book

Shakespeare's Hamlet

Ahmed's handwriting

ii. To form the possessive of a plural noun ending in an (s), add only an apostrophe, e.g.

Students' books

Tourists' luggage

iii. To form the possessive of a plural noun not ending in an (s), add an apostrophe and an (s), e.g.

Women's hostel

Children's toys

iv. In contracted forms, to indicate that a letter or letters have been omitted, e.g.

I've (I have) don't (do not) o'clock (of the clock)

v. To indicate joint possession by two or more persons, add an apostrophe and an (s) at the end of the last word, e.g.

Ali, Ahmed and Amiri's apartment.

vi. To indicate individual possession by two or more persons, add an apostrophe and an (s) at the end of all the words, e.g.

Ali's, Ahmed's and Amiri's flats.

vii. To form the plural of letters and figures, e.g.

There are more S's than P's in Mississippi.

Five 4's and four 5's are forty.

viii. To form the possessive of a compound word, add an apostrophe and an (s) at the end of the last word, e.g.

This is my son-in-law's car.

His brothers-in-law's property are unlimited.

ix. To form the possessive of names that end with 's', add an apostrophe with or without an (s), e.g.

Yeats's poetry	Williams's drama
Yeats' poetry	Williams' drama

Colon (:)

It is used:

i. To separate two sentences of which the second half explains more fully the meaning of the first, e.g.

Hiba's work is unsatisfactory: her answers are thoughtless, her spelling is incorrect and her writing is bad.

My life has changed: I have a job, a house and a family.

ii. To introduce a list of things, e.g.

To make a cake you need the following: sugar, eggs, flour, etc.

I visited four Arab countries: Dubai, Libya, Jordan and Kuwait.

iii. To introduce a quotation, e.g.

J.L. Nehru writes: there must be a coordination between thought and action.

iv. After the name of the character in a drama, e.g.

Turner: a flirt!

Ann: yes, a flirt.

v. Between titles and its parts of books and theses, e.g.

Mulk Raj Anand as a Short Story Writer: A Critical Study.

vi. To separate hours from minutes, e.g.

5:30 A.M.

11:20 P.M.

Semicolon (;)

It is used:

i. To join sentences instead of conjunction, e.g.

He is careless; his brother is a hard working student.

I am not going to the meeting tonight; I have a headache.

ii. To separate connectives like therefore, besides, however, moreover, otherwise, nevertheless, e.g.

Some of the members are present; therefore, the president has extended the date of the meeting.

She doesn't like to swim in the sea; besides, it is a risky exercise.

iii. To join sentences with internal commas, e.g.

If you are brave, fight bravely; if you are a coward, surrender calmly.

Parenthesis/brackets (( ))

It is used:

i. To separate additional information from the rest of a sentence, e.g.

William Wordsworth (1770-1850) was a great romantic poet.

ii. To enclose cross reference, e.g.

The use of zero article is mentioned in this book. (see chapter nine)

The result of the recent election has affected the stock market. (see diagram B)

iii. Around numbers or letters in texts, e.g.

Our aims and objectives are (1) to improve the standard of education (2) to provide quality education and (3) to train the students properly.

Dash (—)

It is used:

i. To indicate an abrupt break in thought, e.g.

I spoke to Mariam—you know, Joe's sister—and told her what you said.

ii. To express an unexpected turn in the sentence, e.g.

There is only one thing wrong with the information regarding salary—it is never correct.

To express the conclusion of what has been said earlier, e.g.

iii. The teacher was teaching, some students were listening, some were writing—everyone was busy.

Hyphen (-)

It is used:

i. To separate an incomplete word of the same line, e.g.

The entire population of Libya is two hundred times smaller than that of India.

ii. To form a compound from two or more than two words, e.g.

Father-in-law	Editor-in-chief	Ink-pot
Hard-hearted	Engineer-in-chief	

iii. In writing compound numbers between 21 and 99 in words and fractions used as adjectives, e.g.

Thirty-two

Seventy-four

Two-thirds of the land...

One-fourth of the students...

iv. Between two numbers to indicate inclusion, e.g.

Open at page 5-8 (read: five to eight)

v. Within modifiers, e.g.

He is an eighteen-year-old boy.
It is a five-man committee.

vi. To separate dates from months and years, e.g.

19-2-2009

vii. With all the prefixes before a proper noun or proper adjective, etc...

Anti-social	Ultra-modern	Un-Indian
Co-operation	Non-cooperative	Sub-division
Ex-MP	Pre-medical	Neo-classicism
Pro-government	Post-independence	Counter-revolution
Vice-chancellor	Mini-taxi	Multi-purpose

viii. To prevent combination or awkwardness, e.g.

Semi-invalid (avoids the awkwardness of semiinvalid)
Re-form (prevent confusion with reform)

Ellipsis (...)

It is used:

i. To indicate incompletion of a quotation or a sentence, e.g.

"poetry is an spontaneous overflow of powerful feelings and emotions, recollected..."

ii. To omit words or lines of a poem, e.g.

A few paternal...

Slash (oblique) (/)

It is used:

i. To separate alternative words or phrases, e.g.
Are you single/married/divorced?

ii. In e-mail and Internet addresses, e.g.

e-mail: raj1972@yahoo.com/elt/
http:/www.oed.com

Square brackets ([ ])

It is used:

i. To enclose explanation within parenthesis, e.g.

Five cabinet ministers have resigned. (read the news on page 4 [column A] of the times of India)

ii. Around the words inserted to make a statement grammatically correct, e.g.

India in [those] days was without nuclear power.

Underline and Italics

These are used:

i. To highlight something in a corpus of writing such as, titles of books, monuments, etc., e.g.

Shakespeare's Macbeth, *Macbeth*

Bronte's Wuthering Heights, *Wuthering Heights*

The Taj of India, *The Taj*

ii. To indicate words of other languages, e.g.

Example *(exempli gratia)* latin.

A meal offered at a fixed time *(prix fixe)* French.

iii. To show emphasis

I am not going to visit the movies.

The Use of Capital Letters

i. Capitalize the first letter of every sentence, line of a poem, quotation, direct narration, etc., e.g.

They are teachers.

This is my book.

Our teacher always says, "No gains without pains".

Keats says: "A thing of beauty is a joy for ever".

Happy those early days when I

Shined in my angel – infancy! (but some modern poets disregarded this convention)

ii. Capitalize the pronoun 'I' and the interjection 'O', e.g.

Help us, O mightiest of all!

May I use your pen?

iii. Capitalize the first letter of a proper noun and proper adjective, e.g.

Delhi, Khoms, Libya, American, Libyan, Osama, Indian, Chinese, Egyptian, etc.

iv. Capitalize the first letter of the name of religion, festival, year, month, e.g.

Holi, Diwali, Muslim, Hindu, July, October, Ramadan, Id, Christianity, Monday, Friday, etc.

v. Capitalize the first letter of the name of historical events, period and government bodies, e.g.

World War I, Battle of Waterloo,

National Open Golf Championships,

Mugal Empire, Sepoy Mutiny,

House of Commons, Congress,

Human Resource Development Ministry, etc.

vi. Capitalize the first letter of the name of political parties, institutions and degrees, e.g.

The Communist Party of India,

Oxford University, MA, MBBS, Department of English, etc.

vii. Capitalize the titles of books, newspapers, magazines, films, plays, poems, television and radio programs, special events, etc.

The Mayor of Casterbridge, The Times,

The Retreat, Outlook,

Note: Avoid writing 'article', 'preposition' or 'conjunction' in capital letter if it doesn't come in the beginning, e.g.

'A Tale of Two Cities'

'The Fall of the House of Usher'

'Sons and Lovers'

viii. Capitalize the words referring to the Deity, e.g.

God, Allah, Lord, The Almighty

Pronouns referring to God (He, Him, Whom) are often capitalized.

God gives His heat and light equally to all worldly creatures.

The word God when used to refer to ancient mythology is not capitalized.

Peasant's mother asked the gods to help her son.

ix. Capitalize the names of streets, roads, colonies, e.g.

National Highway, Harati Street,

Sahja Nand Colony, Serpentine Road, etc.

x. Capitalize the words of salutation, designation and complimentary close of a letter or application, e.g.

My Dear Rakesh   Khoms
                              20.2.2009

Respected Father,

                              Yours affectionately,

To

The Principal,

                              Yours faithfully,

xi. Capitalize the personified words of poetry, e.g.

O Wild West Wind, thou breath of Autumn being

If Winter comes, can Spring be far behind?

(Shelley)

EXERCISE-1

Use capital letters and punctuation marks wherever necessary.

1. we learned many new words from his book
2. where are mr and mrs kripal
3. how do you like your tea aman
4. he writes slowly deliberately thoughtfully

5. this is salmas bag
6. yes I know what you were talking about
7. if you are right then i am wrong
8. he is absent today isn't he
9. my brother is a ph d in english from delhi university india
10. the Hindustan times has wide-circulation in india
11. I've been to the new library but i haven't been to a new shopping mall
12. dr raj our english teacher took his linguistics classes at 8 30 on Monday last week
13. the university of kolkata is situated by the side of the river hugli
14. the Rotary club of tripoli has established an office in the taj hotel
15. according to professor hilton wordsworths lyrical ballads was published in 1778 the same year that saw the publication of other literary works
16. the faculty of arts has a number of facilities a language lab two meeting rooms a fast food café and a big library
17. it was getting really tense she said and everybody was shivering with cold why don't you go home

EXERCISE-2

Use capital letters and punctuation marks wherever necessary.

1. our head of the department of english who often loses his temper even at trivial things is the calmest person at home
2. while i was going to college i came across a twenty year old student of medical college
3. your appearance pleased my friend it delighted me i have watched your behavior in strange circumstances that's why i invited you to lunch last Friday

4. i can't understand it said mr williams oh what can't you understand said his friend well said mr williams just look at this suit I am wearing the wool was grown in australia the cloth was woven in yorkshire the buttons were made in india the suit was made in london and I bought it in cairo

18

Idioms and Phrases

What is an Idiom?

An idiom is a group of words that gives a figurative meaning and not the literal meaning of the individual words.

Look at the given examples:

1. At sixes and sevens: This idiom does not refer to the numeral meaning of *six* and *seven* but gives the meaning of "badly organised or difficult situation".

   The books are lying at sixes and sevens. It means that books are scattered, not kept in an orderly manner.

2. Rain cats and dogs: This idiom has nothing to do with the literal meaning of *cats* and *dogs* that belong to animal species but has a figurative meaning which means "heavily or torrent".

   It is raining cats and dogs.

What is a Phrase?

A phrase is that grammatical concept which has neither the subject nor the predicate but a sequence of words that acts as a single grammatical unit in a sentence.

Look at the given examples:

1. All in all (*vested with all power*): The Vice-chancellor is all in all in the university.
2. At any rate (*anyhow*): I will get your work done at any rate.

3. As a rule (*generally*): As a rule, a common noun takes an article in singular number.

What is the difference between an idiom and a phrase?

The difference between an idiom and a phrase lies in the fact that every idiom is a phrase but every phrase is not an idiom. It is like every father is a man but every man is not a father.

In other words, an idiom is a phrase that gives figurative meaning whereas a phrase functions as a single unit in the syntax of a sentence. For example, 'all in all' is an adjective, 'at any rate' and 'as a rule' are adverbs.

Some commonly used idioms

A bird's eye view (*a view at a glance*) You can have a bird's eye view of Patna from an aeroplane.

A fish out of water (*restless*) The postmaster felt like a fish out of water in that remote village.

A good Samaritan (*a kind and charitable person*) Let him be a good Samaritan in this corrupt world.

A lame excuse (*unsatisfactory reason*) Headache is merely a lame excuse for absence.

Acid test (*decisive or critical test*) Qualifying in the UPSC examination is an acid test of one's intelligence.

A beast of burden (*an animal for carrying loads*) Donkeys are the best beast of burden.

A man of letters (*a scholar*) Rabindra Nath Tagore was a man of letters.

Apple of one's eyes (*dearest*) Children are the apple of their mothers' eyes.

Apple-pie order (*systematic*) Everything is in apple-pie order in the drawing room.

A snake in the grass (*secret enemy*) A secret foe may be called a snake in the grass.

A wolf in sheep's clothing (*a wicked man going about with innocent looks*) Many thieves are wolves in sheep's clothing.

Achilles' heel (*a weak point*) Macbeth's vaulting ambition was his Achilles' heel.

An axe to grind (*to have a selfish motive*) I have no axe to grind in helping the students.

A red letter day (*a memorable day*) Republic day is a red letter day in the history of India.

A bone of contention (*unsettled point of disagreement*) Sometimes a fence becomes a bone of contention between two brothers.

A good for nothing fellow (*a useless person*) A good for nothing fellow is not liked by anyone.

A litmus test (*a method which clearly proves something*) The parliamentary election in Bihar is a litmus test for Nitish government.

A cock and a bull story (*false story*) A liar tells a cock and a bull story to attract the children.

A fresh lease of life (*recovery from serious illness*) She has got a fresh lease of life after a fatal disease.

A queer fish (*a strange fellow*) His father is a queer fish indeed.

A bird of prey (*that kills and eats other creatures*) An eagle is a bird of prey.

A slip of the tongue (*slight mistake in speaking*) A slip of the tongue cost him his job.

At arm's length (*at a distance*) We must keep dishonest people at arm's length.

At one's wit's end (*puzzled or confused*) When I saw a huge snake in my room, I was at my wit's end.

At one's finger's end (*fully known*) The main dates and events of Indian history are at his finger's end.

At the eleventh hour (to *be too late*) Dr. Daman came to examine the patient at the eleventh hour.

Add fuel to fire (to *give another cause of anger*) The arrest of the union leader added fuel to the fire among the employees.

An eyewash (*a deception*) The members of the interview board had already made their choice; the interview was only an eyewash.

At beck and call (*at one's disposal*) I am always at your beck and call.

A wet blanket (*one who discourages others*) Your father is a wet blanket; he never permits you to do what you like.

Back the wrong horse (*to support someone weak*) Wise people do not back the wrong horse in the election.

Bag and baggage (*with all personal property*) The renter left the house bag and baggage.

Beat about the bush (*to tell something without having clarity*) Please don't beat about the bush while answering during an interview.

Black and blue (*severely beaten*) The thief was beaten black and blue.

Be on cloud nine (to *be very happy*) He is on cloud nine to get a government job.

Be ill at ease (to be *uncomfortable*) The naughty boy felt quite ill at ease before the principal.

Bed of roses (*a state of comfort and luxury*) Life is not a bed of roses.

Bell the cat (*perform a daring act*) Who will bell the cat?

Between the devil and the deep sea (*in a difficult situation where there are two equally unpleasant choices*) He is between the devil and the deep sea.

Bid fair (to make *promises*) The business deal bids fair to be very profitable to us.

Birds of the same feather (*men of same nature*) Birds of the same feather flock together.

Blow one's own trumpet (*praise oneself*) No one likes a person who blows his own trumpet.

Bone of contention (*subject matter of the fight*) Kashmir is a bone of contention between India and Pakistan.

Bolt from the blue (*sudden mishap*) The news of her husband's death came as a bolt from the blue.

Bring to book (*punish*) Children were brought to book for telling lies.

Burn the midnight oil (*to study till late of night*) Nitu is burning the midnight oil to secure good marks.

Bury the hatchet (*to forget enmity*) We all want Pakistan to bury the hatchet and live in peace with India.

By leaps and bounds (*rapidly*) China is progressing by leaps and bounds.

By fits and starts (*irregularly*) If you work by fits and starts, you will never succeed.

By hook or by crook (*by fair means or foul*) Dr. D.N. Sinha will get the work done by hook or by crook.

Call a spade a spade (*speak exactly as one thinks*) Honesty and boldness enable a man to call a spade a spade.

Cards are stacked against (*luck is against someone*) Cards are stacked against me these days.

Castle in the air (*a fanciful hope or daydreaming*) Do not build castle in the air.

Cat and dog life (*a quarrelsome life*) Many people lead a cat and dog life.

Chicken-hearted (*timid*) He is a chicken-hearted fellow.

Close-fisted (*miser*) The shopkeeper is a close-fisted man.

Come to blows (*fight*) Children usually come to blows even for a chocolate.

Crocodile tears (pretentious *tears*) Ravi was not really sorry for his fault, he was shedding crocodile tears.

Cut a sorry figure (*create a bad impression*) If you do not perform well in the interview you will cut a sorry figure.

Cut no ice (*fail to impress*) The maid tried to prove her innocence but cut no ice.

Cut to the quick (*very sorry*) He was cut to the quick by the news of his father's death.

Cut and dried (*well prepared*) There is no cut and dried policy to improve the sale of books.

Dances to the tune (*to do what someone tells you to do*) He dances to the tune of his boss.

Dog in the manger (some sort of policy in which *one prevents you from enjoying something that he himself does not need*) A dog in the manger policy is not good in one's life.

Don't wash your dirty laundry in public (*making private issues public*) Generally men don't wash their dirty laundry in public.

Dress up to the nines (*wearing fancy clothes*) She is dressed up to the nines.

Face the music (*accept punishment*) Do your duty honestly or be ready to face the music.

French leave (*to be absent without permission*) The peon was scolded for taking French leave.

From cradle to the grave (*whole life*) Man longs for health, wealth and happiness from cradle to the grave.

Eye for an eye (*to take the same in revenge*) Usually, criminals get eye for an eye treatment from their rivals.

Eyes are bigger than one's stomach (*insatiable desire or hunger*) Sonu's eyes are bigger than his stomach.

Fair and square (*just*) He has been fair and square in all his dealings.

Fair weather friend (*a friend in prosperity only*) It is better to be friendless than to have a fair weather friend.

Fast and loose (*deceitful*) I do not like a fast and loose policy with anyone.

Fan the flame (*aggravate*) The new taxes may fan the flame of discontent.

Fight shy of (*avoid*) Don't fight shy of healthy criticism; it will help you to improve.

Fool's paradise (*a false sense of happiness or success*) For long I lived in a fool's paradise, and then the hard struggle of life made me return to earth to face facts.

From bad to worse (*decreasing position*) Things went from bad to worse in a couple of months.

Get a raw deal (*not treated equally*) He got a raw deal in partnership.

Get off the hook (*free from all obligations*) One cannot get off the hook in one's life.

Gift of the gab (*talent of speaking*) A few of our leaders have the gift of the gab. Most of them are very boring speakers.

Give up the ghost (*die*) He gave up the ghost yesterday.

Give me a hand (*help*) A few will give you a hand in bad days.

Get the slap on the wrist (to *give little punishment*) The baby gets the slap on the wrist for her minor mistake.

Grease the palm (to *bribe*) Nowadays one cannot get anything done without greasing the palm of somebody or the other.

Have ants in your pants (to be *excited and worried*) Are there ants in your pants?

Hard and fast (*strict*) There are some hard and fast rules in every walk of life, and we must abide by them.

Hard nut to crack (a *difficult task*) Climbing Mount Everest is a hard nut to crack.

Heart and soul (*work honestly*) Let us work heart and soul.

Hit below the belt (*strike unfairly*) A victory by hitting below the belt is no victory at all.

Hit the nail on the head (*do the thing correctly*) People will praise you if you hit the nail on the head.

Hole and corner (*secret*) Someone has adopted hole and corner policy to harm me.

Hope against hope (unachievable *hope*) It is hoping against hope to recover the lost bag.

Hue and cry (*noise*) The government wakes up only after people raise a great hue and cry.

Hold one's tongue (*become silent*) Hold your tongue and get out from here.

In the doghouse (*be in disgrace and disfavour*) Our country is in the doghouse after opposing the WHO scheme.

In black and white (*in writing*) Give your statement in black and white.

In vogue (*in force*) Purdah system is still in vogue among the Muslims.

Ins and outs (*details*) I know the ins and outs of the matter.

In season and out of season (*at all times, right or wrong*) He tries to be humorous in season and out of season.

In high spirits (*cheerful*) Every team remains in high spirits before the match.

Jack of all the trades (*one who knows something of everything*) A jack of all the trades is usually master of none.

Jaundiced eye (biased *view*) A judge should never have a jaundiced eye.

Jersey justice (*severe punishment*) Rapists deserve jersey justice.

Just for the heck of it (*without a good reason*) One should not do something just for the heck of it.

Keep an eye on (*watch carefully*) The best teacher keeps an eye on the activity of the students.

Keep body and soul together (*earn money just to meet basic needs*) He earns as much as to keep his body and soul together.

Kith and kin (*friends and relations*) He invited all his kith and kin to the wedding party.

King of terrors (*death*) Who does not fear the king of terrors?

Leave no stone unturned (*spare no pains*) I will leave no stone unturned to get a job.

Leave in the lurch (*to desert when help is needed*) Never leave your parents in the lurch.

Lion's share (*a major share*) The naughty boys took the lion's share of the sweets at the picnic.

Loaves and fishes (undue *material gains*) One should not care for the loaves and fishes of the office.

Let the cat out of the bag (*reveal the secret*) The servant let the cat out of the bag before his master.

Like a sitting duck (*totally unaware*) *Shreya* should not be like a sitting duck about her future.

Make neither head nor tail (*understand nothing*) Dull students make neither head nor tail of the lecture.

Make a clean breast of (to *confess/admit*) The accused made a clean breast of his guilt in the court.

Make both ends meet (*fulfil the needs of life*) My neighbour is too poor to make both ends meet.

Miss the bus (*lose a chance*) Try hard to get a job or you will miss the bus.

Nook and corner (*everywhere*) I searched for my dictionary in every nook and corner, but could not find it.

Null and void (*invalid*) The old rules become null and void when they are replaced by new ones.

Nip in the bud (*destroy in the beginning*) We must nip our bad habits in the bud.

No love lost (*a situation of animosity/dislike*) Now there is no love lost between the two sisters.

No smoke without fire (*valid cause for suspicion*) There is no smoke without fire.

On the horns of a dilemma (*in a very difficult position*) I was on the horns of a dilemma when my teacher told me to stand up on the bench or go out of the classroom.

On the spur of the moment (*to be without previous planning*) The teacher made some clever remarks on the spur of the moment during the debate.

Open secret (*secret but known to all*) Corruption in government offices is an open secret.

Over head and ears (*fully*) She is over head and ears in love.

Put paper over the cracks (*try to hide something*) It is not proper to put paper over the cracks all the time.

Pick someone's brains (*ask someone for advice*) The bursar must pick accountant's brains in financial matter.

Pieces of the same cake (*having the same qualities*) The deficit granted teachers of my college are the pieces of the same cake.

Pandora's box (*a source of many unforeseen troubles*) If you open a pandora's box, you will invite all sorts of troubles that you had never anticipated.

Pick holes in others (*find faults*) Generally people pick holes in others instead of paying attention to their work.

Pocket an insult (*tolerate an insult*) He had to pocket the insult of his boss.

Poke one's nose into (i*nterfere*) One should not poke one's nose in the affairs of others.

Pros and cons (*everything in favour of or against*) The Education Minister thought over the pros and cons of the matter.

Part and parcel (integral *portion*) Kashmir is the part and parcel of India.

Point blank (*directly*) He told me point blank that he won't be able to help me.

Poison the ear (*give false report*) Someone is poisoning the ear of the secretary against the principal.

Quiet as a mouse (*silent*) Why are you quiet as a mouse?

Red carpet (*special treatment and hospitality*) The dignitaries were given the red carpet treatment in military camp.

Rhyme and reason (*valid cause*) He turned out his driver without any rhyme and reason.

Root and branch (*totally*) Corruption must be removed root and branch.

Showing the door (*asking someone to leave*) It is not good to show the door to everyone.

Song of the sirens (*sweet words that are dangerous*) Students must not listen to the songs of sirens of the politicians.

Stuff and nonsense (*irrelevance*) His lecture was full of stuff and nonsense.

Sum and substance (*gist*) Tell me the sum and substance of the story.

Take to task (*punish*) The student was taken to task for his misconduct.

Take to the heels (*flee away*) The robbers took to the heels to see the police van.

The whys and the wherefores (*reason*) I don't know the whys and the wherefores of my dismissal.

Through thick and thin (*in all conditions*) My wife stood by me through thick and thin.

Throw dust in one's eyes (*deceive*) By showing loyalty, he tried to throw dust in my eyes.

Throw cold water (*discourage*) Don't throw cold water upon my plan.

To all intents and purposes (*in the real sense*) The secretary is, in all intents and purposes, the head of the Governing Body.

Toil and moil (*work seriously*) The farmers toil and moil in the field to yield good crops.

Turn over a new leaf (*start a fresh life*) Sometimes even robbers turn over a new leaf.

Turn a deaf ear (*to ignore/avoid*) The director turned a deaf ear to my request.

Under the nose (*openly before one's eyes*) Sometimes serious crimes are done under the nose of the police.

Upon one's sweet will (*on one's own desire*) It depends upon my sweet will whether I do the work today or tomorrow.

Upset the apple cart (*to create trouble*) Don't upset the apple cart at the cash counter.

Under lock and key (*safe*) I keep my valuable documents under lock and key.

Weal and woe (*joy and sorrow*) I assure you that I'll stand by you in weal and woe.

With open arms (*warmly*) Indian troops were welcomed in Bangladesh with open arms.

With might and main (*with full power*) One should work with might and main.

Will and pleasure (*sweet will*) The section officer does everything according to the will and pleasure of the bursar.

Vicar of bray (*one who changes his beliefs and principles to stay popular*) A clever politician is a vicar of bray.

Yellow bellied (*coward*) A yellow bellied man easily surrenders before the enemy.

Yeoman's service (*help in the hours of need*) Yoeman's service is always praised.

Zip your lip (*shut up*) Zip your lip otherwise I will send you out of the class.

Some Common Phrases in Use

Noun Phrases

Abc (*the basic facts of a subject*) He does not know the abc of English.

A freelance (*a non-committed independent person*) There are a few freelance politicians in every party.

A friend in court (*a person in high position*) A friend in court rarely helps the needy these days.

A fly in the ointment (*someone or something that spoils the situation*) The barking of the dog was a fly in the ointment.

A henpecked husband (*women who dominate and harass their husband*) Some married men turn out to be henpecked husbands.

A gala day (*one day festival*) Dipawali is a gala day for the Hindus.

A light sleeper (*one who sleeps for a few hours*) My old father is a light sleeper.

A man of spirit (*courageous*) Bhagat Singh was a man of spirits.

A big gun (*powerful and influential*) Indira Gandhi was a big gun in international politics.

A blue ribbon (*a symbol of high honour*) The Gnanpith award is a blue ribbon for a writer.

A casting vote (a *deciding vote*) The victory of the chairman was declared by a casting vote.

A cold blooded murder (*showing no sympathy or mercy*) A cold blooded murder of the child stunned the villagers.

A curtain lecture (*a private reprimand of wife*) A curtain lecture is an unpleasant marital confrontation.

A gentleman at large (*a rich man with time on his hands*) A gentleman at large passes his days in mirth and merriment.

Fair hand (*good writing*) Students are encouraged by the teacher for a fair hand.

Apple of discord (*an object of quarrel*) The post of secretary has always been an apple of discord among the members of affiliated colleges.

A slip of the pen (*A mistake in writing*) The teacher wrote 'smile' in place of 'simile' on the whiteboard that was a slip of pen.

A dead certainty (*that which is sure to happen*) It is a dead certainty that she will be proved guilty.

A wet blanket (*a person or thing that dampens one's enthusiasm*) My father's presence in the party threw a wet blanket on my dancing programme.

A white elephant (*a burden in some ways*) A horse is a white elephant for a farmer.

A wild goose chase (*a foolish, profitless attempt*) The effort to provide government job to every graduate is a wild goose chase.

Bosom friend (*close friend*) Vinay is my bosom friend.

Blue blood (*member of a socially prominent family*) It is the duty of the men of blue blood to ensure the uplift of the masses.

Capital punishment (*death sentence*) Capital punishment is rare in our country.

Drag one's feet (*to act with reluctance/delay*) The governing Body is dragging its feet in distributing the grant.

Easy virtue (*someone with loose moral*) She is a woman of easy virtue.

Fair sex (*woman*) Modesty is the beauty of fair sex.

Fast life (*cosy life*) He leads a fast life.

Forty winks (*a slight sleep in the day*) Everyone likes to have forty winks after meal in summer.

Hair breadth escape (*a narrow slip*) She had a hair breadth escape in the firing.

Hush money (*bribe*) Many officers take hush money these days.

Laughing stock (*an object of ridicule*) His wrong reply made him a laughing stock in the meeting.

Maiden speech (*the first speech of a member in a public body*) Her maiden speech was really very impressive.

Maiden name (*the title before marriage*) Mrs Singh's maiden name was Miss Jolly.

Moot point (*an issue open to discussion*) The distribution of grant is a moot point among the employees.

Oily tongue (*a smooth talker*) She has an oily tongue, but bad heart.

Odds and ends (*miscellaneous items*) This cabin is meant for odds and ends.

Petticoat government (*dominance of woman in the house*) A petticoat government runs in almost every house in India.

Raw spirits (*highly intoxicating liquor*) Many workers die due to the frequent use of raw spirits.

Sleeping partner (*an inactive shareholder*) I could not prosper in business due to my sleeping partner.

Slow coach (*dull and foolish person*) A slow coach never takes a wise decision.

Sheet anchor (*a person or thing to be relied upon in emergency*) Religion is the sheet anchor of life.

The long and the short (*summary*) The long and the short of the story is interesting.

Three R's (*reading, writing and arithmetic*) The illiterate are ignorant of the three R's.

Ups and downs (*rise and fall*) I have seen many ups and downs in my life.

White collar (*one who does not do manual work*) Our country does not need only white collar officials but also workers.

Witch hunt (*search to punish the disloyal person*) The police led a witch hunt to catch the dreaded criminal.

Adjective Phrases

At one's best (*showing one's best*) He is at his best only among his admirers.

At large (*free, not confined*) The robbers are still at large.

At home (*comfortable*) I feel quite at home in my new building.

At stake (*in serious danger*) My life was at stake; so I resigned.

At sea (*confused*) She is quite at sea to see the stranger in the house.

Behind time (*late*) Many trains are running behind time.

Double-minded (*fickle*) A double-minded man wavers between two or more courses of action.

High and low (*everywhere*) She searched for her scarf high and low in the house.

Open handed (*generous with money*) An open handed man helps the poor and the needy.

Open hearted (*frank, not cunning*) Our principal is an open hearted man.

Out of the way (*secluded*) It is not safe to pass night in an out of the way place.

Wide awake (*to be quite alert*) I was wide awake all night after hearing the barking of the dog.

Well-to-do (*rich*) He comes of a well-to-do family.

Verb Phrases

Abide by (*act according to someone's rules, commands or wishes*) Everyone should abide by the rules.

Account for (*give reasons for/be the reason or explanation for*) The dealing clerk must account for the contingency fund.

Answer back (*a quick reply to a remark*) It is not good for anyone to answer back unnecessarily.

Back away (*retreat/withdraw*) They gradually began to back away from their earlier opinion.

Back off (*back down*) Now that the time for action has arrived, it is too late to back off.

Back out (*withdraw from a promise*) He backed out of his promise to help me.

Back up (*support*) He was backed up by the union to fight for the rights.

Bank on (*depend*) Students should not bank on guess papers only.

Bear out (*support/confirm*) The evidence does not bear out the charge against him.

Blow out (*put out*) Blow out the candle.

Blow up (*explode*) The maoist blew up the bridge before the polling.

Break out (*appear suddenly*) A fire broke out during the night.

Break off (*stop speaking*) The teacher broke off in the middle of his lecture.

Break through (*make a way through*) The cattle have broken through the fence.

Break into (*enter by force*) The dacoits broke into the house in the broad daylight.

Break up (*dissolve/disperse/cause to separate*) The meeting will break up soon.

Break down (*stop operating or functioning/fall apart/lose control of one's emotions*) The car we travelled in broke down on the way to Patna.

Bring about (*cause to happen, occur or exist*) The new health superintendent will bring about a change in the health care system.

Bring out (*publish/reveal clearly*) When will you bring out my new book of grammar?

Bring up (*educate*) If we do not bring up our children carefully, they will go for bad ways.

Brush aside (*bar from attention or consideration*) The principal brushed aside all objections.

Brush up (*bring to a highly developed, finished and refined way*) Brush up your English if you are planning to go abroad.

Call back (*telephone again*) Could you call back tomorrow please?

Call off (cancel) The workers called off their strike.

Call on (*pay a visit to*) While I was in Libya, I called on my friend.

Call out (*utter aloud*) The teacher called out the roll numbers in the class.

Carry out (*put in effect/execute the decision*) My son carries out my orders.

Come up (*raise*) This question must come up in the meeting of the committee.

Come back (*return*) He will come back soon.

Come in (*enter*) May I come in, sir?

Come of (*belong to*) She comes of a respectable family.

Come off (*happen*) The marriage did not come off.

Cook up (*make up something artificial or untrue*) She is expert in cooking up stories.

Count on (*rely on*) I count on your promise.

Conjure up (*summon into action or bring into existence*) Everyone may conjure up images of the past.

Crop up (*appear suddenly or unexpectedly*) Many problems crop up at a time in bad days.

Cut down (*reduce*) Gandhi Jee cut down his expenses to lead a plain life.

Deal in (*do business*) The shopkeeper deals in grain.

Die out (*become extinct*) Old fashion is dying out fast.

Do away with (*put an end to or abolish/kill*) The bluebeard did away with all his wives.

Do up (*repair*) Your house needs doing up.

Do with (*tolerate*) I cannot do with it.

Do without (*difficult to survive*) We cannot do without food.

Draw up (*prepare*) He drew up a routine.

Drop in (*to visit casually*) Why do not you drop in at my place?

Eat out (*have meal in a restaurant*) Let's eat out for a change.

Egg on (*urge on*) My mother egged me on to appear for the interview.

Fade away (*disappear or die soon*) Dews fade away in the sunshine.

Fall down (*lose an upright position suddenly*) He fell down and broke his hand.

Fall in with (*agree to*) I could not persuade the chairman to fall in with my suggestion.

Fall through (*fail to take place*) The project fell through for want of adequate funds.

Fill in (*complete*) Fill in the blanks with appropriate preposition.

Get at (*reach*) I don't understand what you are trying to get at.

Get back (*return*) I shall get back very soon.

Get down (*come down*) She got down from the train.

Get into (*investigate*) I don't want to get into the whole matter at the moment.

Get off (*alight from*) I got off the bus at the stop.

Get out (*go away*) Get out from here.

Get over (*recover*) She got over with grief very soon after her mother's death.

Get through (*succeed in the examination*) He could not get through the written test.

Get up (*rise from bed*) I get up early in the morning.

Give up (*stop taking something*) He gave up drinking wine.

Go back (*return*) Go back to your house immediately.

Go down (*sink/fall/become worse*) Your health has gone down.

Go up (*move upward*) Prices have gone up.

Go in (*enter*) The key does not go in the lock.

Go on (*continue*) He went on speaking.

Grow up (*become an adult*) My son has grown up young.

Hold forth (*talk at great length*) He always holds forth on political issues.

Hold on (*wait on the phone*) Could you hold on for a moment, please?

Hold up (*cause to slow down or delay*) The robbers held up the car and assaulted the passengers.

Hush up (*cover up a fault or error*) He hushed up the matter from the principal.

Insist on (*put pressure*) Don't insist on playing in the scorching sun.

Jot down (*write in haste*) The examinees jotted down the answer five minutes before the time.

Keep in (*cause to stay indoors/have a good relation*) It was difficult to keep in the sick child in bed.

Keep on (*continue*) Keep on trying to achieve your goal.

Knock down (*meet an accident*) The old lady was knocked down by a speeding truck.

Keep off (*refrain from something*) The notice said, "Please keep off the lawn."

Lay up (*amass/be ill*) The old lady has laid up enough money for future.

He is laid up with fever.

Let down (*disappoint*) I will never let you down with my performance.

Let on (*reveal one's true feeling*) He is terrified at the prospect, but did not let on.

Let off (*allow to go with little punishment*) The police let off the youth with a reprimand.

Look after (*care*) The nurse is looking after the patient.

Look up (*seek information in a book*) Look up the word in the dictionary.

Look for (*seek*) He is looking for a good job.

Look forward to (*wait for something with pleasure*) The principal is looking forward to getting a positive reply.

Make for (*go towards*) The sailor made for the boat.

Make up (*compose/adjust for*) He made up the loss by selling his old car.

Make room (*find a place for*) When the principal entered the hall, all made room for him.

Make out (*find out/comprehend*) I do not make out the meaning of this poem.

Put aside (*put out of use for sometime*) I have put aside your proposal to consider it later.

Put up (*stay*) I was put up in a hotel for a month in Tripoli.

Put up with (*tolerate*) I cannot put up with such an insult.

Run out (*come to an end*) It seems that petrol has run out.

See after (*attend to, take care of*) Will you please see after my plants while I'm away.

See off (*to take leave of someone setting out on a journey*) There was nobody to see her off at the station.

See through (*comprehend*) We could easily see through his clever tricks.

Set in (*begin*) The rain has set in early today.

Set out/off (*begin journey*) We set out for the picnic.

Set up (*establish*) My plan is to set up a new college.

Set aside (*make inoperative or stop*) The court has set aside many of the acts passed by the government.

Take after (*resemble*) She takes after her mother.

Take down (*write*) Take down my name and address.

Take over (*seize and take control*) All deficit granted colleges were taken over in 1986 except P.R. College, Sonpur.

Take up with (*occupied*) I am very much taken up with my new book.

Tell upon (*affect*) Hard work will tell upon your health.

Touch upon (*refer the points only*) Politicians touch upon many topics in canvassing before election.

Turn down (*refuse*) He turned down my proposal.

Turn into (*change*) The dacoit turned into a gentleman.

The caterpillar turned into a butterfly.

Turn up (*appear*) He did not turn up for the interview.

Turn on (*cause to operate by flipping a switch*) She turned on the television.

Wind up (*conclude/arrange in order*) I wind up my watch in the morning.

She wound up her lecture in five minutes.

Work off (*lose/dispose/pay by working*) He worked off his debt by doing odd jobs.

Write down (*note down*) Please write down the answer in an hour.

Write out (*fill in the blank of a printed paper or communicate in writing*) The principal wrote out many cheques during examination.

Adverb Phrases

Above all (*before any other consideration*) Above all, be careful about your studies.

After all (*in spite of every fact to the contrary*) After all she is a good lady.

Again and again/Time and again/Over and over again (*very often*) Language learners should pronounce a difficult word time and again.

As a matter of fact (*really*) She lives in a fine style, but as a matter of fact she is a woman of easy virtue.

As far as (*to the extent possible*) As far as I know, she is a practical lady.

As it were (*as if*) A teacher is, as it were, the father of the child.

At all (*completely*) The dumb does not speak at all.

At last (*in the end*) He attempted many times and at last he succeeded.

At most (*maximum*) At most I can lend you ten thousand rupees only.

At once (*immediately*) He came at once.

At present (*in the ongoing time*) At present Narendra Modi is the Prime Minister of India.

At random (*without any aim*) He kicked the ball at random.

Before long (*soon*) I shall return before long.

By and by (*after an interval*) You will feel better by and by.

By far (*decidedly*) Dr. Singh is by far the best teacher of zoology.

By no means (*in no way*) He can, by no means, take away my laptop.

By the by (*incidentally*) By the by he told me something about his love affairs.

Hither and thither (*to and fro*) The mad man is walking on the road hither and thither.

Far and away (*by a considerable margin*) It was far and away the best meal I had ever taken.

Far and wide/Far and near (*everywhere*) He searched for his lost son far and wide.

First and foremost (*before anything else*) First and foremost one should learn to obey one's superiors.

For certain (*definitely*) I know for certain that she will be back in an hour.

For good (*forever*) The English left India for good.

For long (*for a long time*) You cannot stay in a hotel for long.

In a body (*together*) A majority of the students approached the principal in a body.

In the least (*at all*) She does not read at the least.

In the long run (*eventually*) He succeeded in the long run.

In time (*at proper time*) Students should go to school in time.

In vain (*with no tangible result*) She studied seriously to pass the examination but her effort went in vain.

Just now (*right away*) He has gone just now.

Little by little (*gradually*) If you study regularly, you will learn many things little by little.

Now and then (*occasionally*) I go to the post office now and then.

Of course (*certainly*) Of course, he is the best student in the class.

Off and on (*irregularly*) I visit the pictures off and on.

On and on (*continuously*) She worked on and on for many years.

Once again/Once more/Over again (*anew*) The actors rehearsed the scene once again.

Once for all (*once for ever*) I tell you once for all that you should never drink again.

On the alert (*watchful*) Invigilators are on the alert in the examination hall.

On the contrary (*rather*) I do not like her, on the contrary, I dislike her.

On the morrow (*the next day*) I reached Delhi in time and on the morrow I set out for Agra.

On the whole (*taking everything into consideration*) On the whole, he appears to be a good man.

Over and above (*In addition to/besides*) The boy left the bag in school and was beaten over and above for his carelessness.

Out and out (*fully*) He is out and out a vegetarian.

So far as (*as far as*) So far as I know, he is poor.

Sooner or later (*eventually*) A thief will be caught sooner or later.

Then and there (*at that very time and place*) The rebel was caught then and there by the police.

The other day (*not long ago*) I met him the other day in the mall.

Through and through (*completely*) She was drenched through and through.

To and fro (*backward and forward*) A thirsty crow was flying to and fro in search of water.

To the contrary (*to the opposite effect*) The witness had nothing to say to the contrary.

Prepositional Phrases

As to (*that*) He did not say anything as to what he wanted.

So as to (*in order to*) I took off my shoes so as to avoid scratching on the floor.

At enmity with (*not on friendly terms*) The two neighbours are at enmity with each other.

At home in (*expert*) He is at home in English grammar.

At variance with (*opposed*) Your action is at variance with your word.

According to (*in accordance with*) The student acted according to the instruction of the principal.

At the top of (*at the highest place/position*) The girl shouted at the top of her voice.

Because of (*owing to*) She could not appear at the test examination because of illness.

By dint of (*with the help of*) He topped the list by dint of hard labour.

By means of (*by the use of*) He went to the fifth floor by means of lift.

By virtue of (*on the ground of*) She got promotion by virtue of her merit.

By the side of (*beside*) The dog is sitting by the side of its master.

For fear of (*be afraid of*) She could not tell the name of the criminal for fear of assult.

In connection with (*concerning/relating to*) Give the statement in writing in connection with the case.

In consequence of (*as a result of*) Crops failed in consequence of the heavy rains.

In consideration of (*considering*) The intelligent students deserve free-studentship in consideration of their merit.

In course of (*while progressing*) The teacher cited many examples in course of his lecture.

In defence of (*in protection of*) The lawyer argues in defence of his client.

In defiance of (*in violation of*) The police rebelled in defiance of law.

In favour of (*on the side of*) The government took many decisions in favour of teachers.

In front of (*opposite*) There is a garden in front of my house.

In honour of (*as a mark of respect*) The school was closed in honour of the President's visit.

In hot haste (*in great haste*) Don't write your answer in hot haste.

In a fix (*in an indecisive condition*) Being in a fix; I need her advice.

In keeping with (*suited to/harmonizing with*) His action is in keeping with his character.

In lieu of (*as a substitute for*) She gave me a book in lieu of a pen.

In the name of (*under the designation or excuse of*) Some men commit crime in the name of religion.

In opposition to (*against*) The girl married a criminal in opposition to her father's will.

In point of (*in respect of*) Dr. P.N. Singh is senior to me in point of age.

In prospect of (*in the hope of*) She is trying hard in prospect of getting a job.

In quest of (*in search of*) The saint always appeared to be in the quest of a job.

In spite of (*notwithstanding*) She failed at the examination in spite of hard work.

Instead of (*in place of*) You went to that city instead of coming to this city.

In view of (*considering*) He deserves help in view of his poverty.

In the event of (*in case of*) One should try again in the event of failure.

In the face of (*in presence of*) One must be brave in the face of danger.

In the guise of (*in false dress*) Sometimes thieves rob the people in the guise of saints.

In the rear of (*in the hindmost position*) The old man was going in the rear of the procession.

In order to (*with an objective to*) Study seriously in order to get through the examination.

In proportion to (*in relation to*) She is more intelligent in proportion to her age.

In regard to (*in connection with*) He has nothing to do in regard to his promotion.

In unison with (*in accordance with*) His views are not in unison with my views.

On behalf of (*from the side of*) The monitor spoke to the principal on behalf of the students.

On account of (*due to*) Jolly did not appear at the examination on account of illness.

On the brink of/On the point of/On the verge of (*about to/near*) The old man is on the verge of death.

On the ground of (*showing cause*) Medical leave is granted on the ground of illness.

On the part of (*from the side of*) Idleness on the part of the students is not good.

On the score of (*on the ground of*) Many people get government pension on the score of old age.

On the pretence of (*on the false ground*) She did not cook on the pretence of headache.

With a view to (*with the aim of*) I served in Libya with a view to earning money.

With an eye to (*keeping in view*) One must lay by something with an eye to the future.

With reference to/With regard to/With respect to (*in connection with*) Have you got anything to say with regard to her character?

Conjunctional Phrases

According as (*as much as*) She will obtain high or low marks according as she labours hard.

As long as (*throughout a specified period of time*) As long as I am here you need not worry.

As soon as (*just after*) Please call me as soon as dinner is ready.

As well as (*and*) He as well as I is going.

In as much as (*because*) He must be punished in as much as he has neglected the task.

In case (*If*) Take an umbrella in case it rains.

In so much that (*to such degree or extent as*) The riot continued all day, in so much that it was risky to go out of the house.

In order that (*so that*) (it denotes purpose) Pratyush regularly attends the interview in order that he may get a job.

So long as (*during the time that*) So long as we were neighbours, they never invited us to dinner.

Miscellaneous Phrases

Above board (*open, beyond doubt*) His dealings are always fair and above board.

As usual (*as in the ordinary practice*) I went there in the evening, as usual.

And so on (*et cetera*) I like reading poetry, drama, novel, newspaper and so on.

As for (*regarding*) As for his ability so many recommendations have come to me.

All the same (*of equal importance*) It is all the same whether you do it or I.

At all costs/At all events (*in all conditions*) He should stick to the truth at all events.

At a stretch (*in one continuance*) He can speak one hour at a stretch.

At stake (*in danger*) My prestige is at stake.

At times (*occasionally*) At times I go for a long drive.

Anything but (*not at all*) Her manners are anything but agreeable.

As such (*therefore*) He is ill, and as such he has applied for leave.

At a blow (*at a stroke*) The brave man killed two soldiers at a blow.

Broad daylight (*during day*) The burglar entered the house in the broad daylight.

Below the mark (*inferior in quality*) His remark is below the mark.

Child's play (*very easy*) It is not a child's play to get a job.

From head to foot (*from top to bottom*) The pig is drenched with mud from head to foot.

For the time being (*for some time*) Give me some money for the time being.

From time immemorial (*from a long time*) Purdah system is in vogue from time immemorial.

Happy-go-lucky (*haphazard*) This is a happy-go-lucky plan.

Hand in hand (*together*) All must work hand in hand for the uplift of the nation.

In a temper (*angry*) My wife seems to be in a temper.

In a trice (*very quickly*) He finished the work in a trice.

In no time (*soon*) He finished his work in no time.

In preference to (*more than*) I accept this post in preference to that.

In full swing (*fully running*) Classes are in full swing from July to December.

In a nutshell (*in brief*) Tell me the story in a nutshell.

Let loose (*to set free*) She lets her dog loose at night.

Look blank (*look confused*) He looked blank to get the information of theft in his house.

Muster strong (*to assemble in a large number*) People mustered strong to listen to the speech of Narendra Modi in Varanasi.

Neck and crop (*fully*) My brother was turned out of the office neck and crop.

Other than (*except*) No one other than a Ph.D. holder will apply for the post of Principal.

On a large scale (*extensively*) Anjani Kumar runs schools on a large scale.

Put to the sword (*kill*) Many Indian soldiers were put to the sword in the Kargil war.

Red-handed (*while committing crime*) The robber was caught red-handed.

Sterner sex (*male*) Men are the sterner sex.

To be taken aback (*to be surprised*) I was taken aback when the police arrested the principal.

To the letter (*strictly as directed*) She followed my orders to the letter.

To be in a dilemma (*between two different thoughts*) I am in a dilemma; I do not understand whether I should stay here or go there.

To beggar description (*beyond description*) The scenery of Jammu beggars description.

To get off scot-free (*to escape unpunished*) The five culprits got off scot-free.

To pass a poor night (*to be restless at night*) The patient passed a poor night.

To be at one (*to agree*) He is at one with me on this point.

To idle away time/To fritter away time/To trifle away time (*to misuse time*) Students should not trifle away their time.

Foreign Phrases

Ab initio (*from the beginning*) My case was taken up ab initio in the Supreme Court.

Ad hoc (*for the special aim*) An ad hoc committee is examining the demand of the teachers.

Ad infinitum (*up to infinity*) The old woman keeps on telling old stories ad infinitum.

Ad interim (*in the meantime*) The college employees have been allowed an increase of one thousand rupees ad interim.

De facto (*really, in fact*) Gandhi was the de facto ruler of India after independence.

De jure (*be right in law*) The de jure transfer of post in office is the de facto transfer.

De novo (*afresh*) As my file is missing I have to prepare my case de novo.

En masse (*in a body*) The students met the principal en masse to put pressure on him.

En route (*on the way*) He broke journey at Aligarh en route to Delhi.

In memoriam (*in the memory of*) The Taj Mahal was built by Shah Jehan in memoriam Mumtaz Mahal.

In toto (*entirely*) All demands were refused by the government in toto.

Lingua franca (*language spoken by different races*) Hindi is the lingua franca of our country.

Locus standi (*place for standing*) Although politicians have no locus standi in the affairs of students, they keep on interfering.

Modus operandi (*mode of doing*) The modus operandi of the smugglers in Bihar is not common.

Nota bene (*take notice*) I wrote nota bene at the end of my letter to add something.

Par excellence (*by way of eminence*) Keats was a poet par excellence.

Post mortem (*autopsy*) Post mortem report revealed that Ravi had been poisoned.

Sub judice (*under consideration in a court of law*) My case is sub judice.

Summum bonum (*the highest good*) Gandhi's policy of truth and non-violence was the summum bonum of his life.

Ultra vires (*illegal*) The Supreme Court alone has the authority to decide whether a certain law is ultra vires.

Vice versa (*the term being exchanged*) It does not really matter whether the written test follows the oral or vice versa.

Via media (*a middle course*) A via media has to be found between rising prices of diesel and rationing them.

Vis-a-vis (*opposite to*) My brother's stand vis-a-vis his company is well known.

Viva voce (*oral examination*) Pradeep performed well in the viva voce.

EXERCISE-1

Explain the difference in meaning of the following phrases by using them in sentences of your own.

1. Back out, back up, back off
2. Come of come across, come down
3. Hold on, hold up, hold forth
4. Let down, let off, let on
5. See off, see through, see after
6. Turn down, turn up, turn into
7. Go on, go up, go in
8. Break up, break into, break out
9. Get out, get over, get up
10. Call on, call off, call back

EXERCISE-2

Match the expressions with meaning.

1. get off	a. succeed
2. look forward to	b. get down from
3. look for	c. seek information in a book
4. look up	d. wait with pleasure
5. get through	e. seek
6. back up	f. telephone
7. call back	g. support
8. turn down	h. finish
9. wind up	i. disappoint
10. let down	j. refuse

EXERCISE-3

Use the following idioms in sentences.

Add fuel to the fire, fight shy of, hit below the belt, face the music, cut to the quick, An eyewash, in high spirits, a good Samaritan, a red letter day, sum and substance, hole and corner, in black and white, cock and bull story

EXERCISE-4

Write the meaning of the following idioms and phrases with examples.

Abc, take after, come down, write out, at the eleventh hour, at stake, cook up,

In black and white, a wild goose chase, first and foremost, with a view to, look forward to, bury the hatchet, so that, vice versa, viva voce, as well as, with reference to, in lieu of

EXERCISE-5

Fill in the blanks with the given idioms and phrases.

With open arms, ins. and outs, sum and substance, in a nutshell,

In vogue, a red letter day, hit below the belt, in spite of

I. ....many failures, he succeeded at last.

II. The............................of the Principal's speech was that all must be honest.

III. On its return, the victorious cricket team was received ....

IV. The 15th August is.........................in the history of India.

V. I don't know the...............of the matter.

VI. Jeans are still............

VII. Narrate the incident..............

VIII. It is not justified to..................................

19

Paragraph Writing

What is a Paragraph?

A paragraph is simply an elaboration of ideas related to a single topic.

In a paragraph, sentences are so organised that they look to be well-knit into an organic whole. The idea, the theme, the argument or the main point of the topic is sufficiently described in the body of a paragraph. It can stand by itself because it is the development of a single idea or experience.

How to write a paragraph

There are some essential features that a good paragraph is supposed to contain. They are as follows:

1. Unity: All the sentences in a paragraph must bring out only one main idea, thought or fact. That single controlling idea is expressed only with the supporting sentences in a sequence.
2. Order: Order relates to the way in which you organise your supporting sentences. It helps the reader grasp your meaning and avoid confusion.
3. Coherence: Coherence is the quality that makes your writing understandable. Sentences within a paragraph need to be connected to each other and work together as a whole. One of the best ways to achieve coherence is to use a consistent verb tense and point of view along with suitable adverbs that may reflect logical growth of the paragraph.

4. Emphasis: Each sentence should be given due importance and emphasis in order to have a proper impression. The key sentence should be preferably the first sentence to make the paragraph interesting. The paragraph must have a striking conclusion.
5. Completeness: It means all round development of the paragraph from the topic sentence to the concluding sentence. If all sentences clearly support the main idea, it means that the paragraph is complete.

Tips for an effective paragraph

Kindly bear in mind the following facts while writing a paragraph.

1. Give proper time to think over and grasp the exact meaning, implication and significance of the topic.
2. Arrange your ideas to develop them in a logical sequence.
3. Begin the paragraph with a striking sentence to express the main idea.
4. Arrange the sentences in a logical order to reach the climax towards the end.
5. Develop the sentences with coherence.
6. Avoid mentioning irrelevant ideas that give scope for digression.

Finally, it should be read as a complete and coherent piece of composition conveyed in a polished style.

Sample Paragraphs

1. A child is the father of man

A man's childhood decides the future of his life. His character, behaviour and action of early years usually form the basis of the man on which he develops. Gradually, the impact of one's upbringing gets reflected in one's tendencies and attitudes that develop with passage of time. If we take a glimpse of life of some great men of the world, we come to know that the seed of greatness was sown in their very childhood. Napoleon, Nelson and Nehru as children gave clear signs of their future greatness. Their greatness was manifest even in their childish fun and frolic. The courage of Napoleon, the strong will power of the great naval commander, Nelson, and the keenly sharp brain of Nehru showed their ability. True, it is the seed that grows into a tree and it is conditionally a healthy seed that grows into a healthy tree. Herein, lies the justification of this Wordsworthian proverb.

2. Rome was not built in a day

Rome, the greatest city of the ancient world, was not built in a short time. It took several years to build this city and bring it to the state of glory. This is applicable in the case of each great achievement. When we wish to achieve something, we can't expect success in a moment. We should not be impatient. We must stick to the work till it is finished. We must keep in mind the saying similar as above: "If at first you don't succeed, try, try, and try again." An important task can't be done without patience and perseverance. Truly, there is no short cut to success. Any professional who succeeds in his field undertakes a long and arduous journey full of hard work. Then only success embraces such people. A fruit attains maturity after it passes through the phases of flower and bud. A sportsperson earns name and fame only after a long drawn practice. Therefore, we should keep in mind this didactic quotation that is highly inspiring.

3. A true citizen

A true citizen is a member of a disciplined and civilized society of a nation. The relationship between the citizen and the state is based on the rights that the citizens enjoy and the duties that they do for the state. Usually, a citizen has the tendency to enjoy his rights and neglect his duties. A society in which the citizens have this tendency does not prosper well. A true citizen supports and defends his country in all conditions. He obeys his country's laws and behaves towards others in such a way that proper human relationship is maintained. It should be noted at the same time that the most valuable contribution a citizen can make towards service to nation is upholding high moral character. To be honest, open-minded and altruist is the best thing that a man can do for his country. A nation with citizens having these virtues will always stand ahead of other nations in every respect.

4. A rolling stone gathers no moss

A stone which lies at the same place for a long time collects moss, while a stone which is always rolling from one place to another does not. A man who keeps on changing his occupations and pursuits and never settles down steadily to anything is like the rolling stone. He must be careful in choosing a profession and stick to the profession if he is to achieve success. It is applicable to studies, too. A student who aims to become a scholar must stick to one subject. The student who chooses mathematics, and then takes up chemistry, and tiring of it, goes in for physics, and drops this again for engineering, will never succeed in his life. It shows fickle mindedness and escapism of an individual. This proverb teaches us a great lesson of life.

5. No pains, no gains

Only those who work hard get glory and success in life. Nothing great can be achieved without effort. It is also true that God helps those who help themselves. There is no royal road to success. A student can never come out with flying colours unless he really works hard throughout the year. A farmer can't reap a good harvest without putting his all efforts while working in the fields. A lawyer can't defend his clients if he doesn't work hard at his law books. A businessman has to work hard to earn fat profits. Scientists keep on toiling and moiling for years and then they make great inventions. Always keep in mind that there are 'no gains' in life without 'pains'. In this highly competitive modern world, one has to embrace pains to ensure gains. A glance at the life of all the successful and great men stands witness to the truthfulness of this wise saying.

EXERCISE-1

Fill in the blanks with suitable verbs given below to make it a meaningful paragraph.

We are happier than our forefathers

Life.......comfortable and worth living in the world of today. If our forefathers.......to visit us today, they.......wonderstruck to notice the significant changes.......by the advancement in science and technology. In the absence of medical facilities our forefathers.......premature deaths. Their movement.......restricted, as there.......no means of communication and conveyance. Being superstitious and illiterate, they.......that calamities.......a result of the fury of gods. Today with the advancement of science, we.......leading a luxurious life and enjoying all the amenities like television, air-conditioners, refrigerators, etc. Which.......a gift of science. With the invention of fast moving planes the entire world has.......easily accessible to us. Education has.......man to think rationally so that he.......easily..........any problem related to life. Medical science and hygienic conditions...........helping him to enjoy a longer span of life. Thus the man of today......definitely in a better position and......far happier than his forefathers.

(is, is, is, are, are, are, become believed, brought about, can, died, enabled, happened, solve, was, were, were, would be)

EXERCISE-2

Complete the sentences with the words given below to make your paragraph a perfect one.

My first attempt at making a cup of tea

When I was ten, my father..........me to.........tea for him as..........not feeling well. I..........very..........because..........he never allowed me..........in the kitchen.........., I felt it was a child's play.......... I poured half a.........., half a cup of milk along with a..........in the saucepan, I..........the gas and put it.......... The tea kept..........for about ten minutes..........I took it.........., I burnt my fingers. I was horrified..........that it was..........and only.......... With tears in my eyes, I took it to.........., for I..........that the tea must have become..........contrary to my expectation,..........drank the..........and was..........for me.

(bitter, all praise, felt, asked, cup of water, to work, and when, on fire, off the gas, spoonful of sugar, half a cup, my father, prepare a cup of, the whole of it, On entering the kitchen, boiling, excited, felt, he was, before that, to prepare a cup of tea, lighted)

EXERCISE-3

Write short paragraphs on the following topics.

a. A picnic
b. Friendship
c. Courage
d. Patriotism
e. Love
f. A journey
g. Mobile Phone
h. Education
i. Technology
j. Computer
k. Selfishness

EXERCISE-4

Write a paragraph on each of the following proverbs.

a. Honesty is the best policy.
b. Health is wealth.
c. A pen is mightier than a sword.
d. Might is right.
e. Where there is a will there is a way.
f. Fortune favours the brave.
g. Slow and steady wins the race.
h. All that glitters is not gold.
i. United we stand, divided we fall.
j. A guilty mind is always suspicious.
k. A little knowledge is a dangerous thing.

20

Précis Writing

What is a Précis?

A précis is a brief summary of an original passage. It is written in a precise, clear and coherent manner. In other words, it is a condensed restatement of the central idea of a passage in an integrated form.

How to Write a Précis

There are several steps that can be followed in order to write an effective précis. They are as follows:

- First of all, read the passage to have a clear-cut understanding.
- Read again to guess the heading and underline the main points.
- Read a third time to confirm the correctness of the heading you have chosen.
- Delete repetitions, illustrations and comparisons.
- Summarize the passage.
- Arrange the main points in a natural way so that it may mirror the passage.

Tips for an Effective Précis

The following are the essential features to keep in mind while writing a précis:

Give a suitable heading.

- Use one-third of words of the given passage or as directed.

- Be as concise as possible but include all important points logically.
- Use third person pronoun to write the précis.
- Avoid rhetorical expressions.
- Avoid using words of the original passage as far as possible.
- Cut out the number of words by using active voice and coordinating conjunctions.
- Use indirect form of narration.
- Restate the passage in your own words but don't include your opinion.
- Mention the number of words used in the précis in the end.

Use single words for phrases and long expressions like

Contemporaries for those living in the same period
Feminist for a person who supports woman's rights
Fatalist for one who believes in fate or chance
Honorary for an office for which no salary is paid
Incredible for that which can't be believed
Theist for one who believes in the existence of God
Atheist for one who does not believe in the existence of God
Illiterate for a person who is unable to read or write and so on.

Review the précis once again after writing it in the light of the following points to examine its accuracy and correctness that clearly state:

a. This is what was discussed.
b. This is how it was focused.
c. This is what was learned.
d. This is what it is important.

SAMPLE PRÉCIS

1. One day a crow was feeling very thirsty. On a hot summer day, it was flying to and fro in search of water but in

vain. It continued to search hard but it could not find any water to quench its thirst. Then after a long time it saw a pitcher. It flew there and saw that there was a little water at the bottom of it. The neck of the pitcher was too long and the water level too low. The crow could not reach the water with its beak. It saw many pebbles around. Suddenly the crow had an idea. It picked the pebbles one by one and dropped them in the pitcher. And lo! The level of water slowly rose to the top. The crow drank it thirstily. It was very happy.

Title of the Précis

A Thirsty Crow

A thirsty crow was looking for water. It saw a pitcher with a little water in it. Its beak was unable to reach the water level in the pitcher. Seeing many pebbles around, it dropped them one after another in the pitcher that rose the water level. Thus, it quenched its thirst.

Total no. of words in the passage – 136
Words used in the précis – 51

2. The best friend a man has in this world may turn against him and become his enemy. His son or his daughter that he has reared with loving care may prove ungrateful. Those who are nearest and dearest to us, those whom we trust with our happiness and our good name, may become traitors to their faith.

The one absolutely unselfish friend that man can have in this selfish world, the one that never deserts him, the one that never proves ungrateful or treacherous, is his dog.

The Dog

A man's best friend may become hostile. His son or daughter may turn ungrateful. His kith and kin may grow disloyal. But the dog remains unfailingly faithful to him.

Total no. of words in the passage – 87
Words used in the précis – 29

3. It is very easy to acquire bad habits, such as eating too much food, or drinking too much wine of any kind, or smoking cigarettes or taking tobacco. The more we do a thing, the more

we tend to like doing it: and, if we do not continue to do it, we feel unhappy. Such tendency should be fought against all odds.

Things which may be very good when only done from time to time tend to become very harmful when done too often and too much. This applies to even such good things as work or rest. Some people form a bad habit of working too much, and others of idling too much. The wise man always remembers that this is true about himself, and checks any bad habit. He says to himself, "I am now becoming idle," and then adds, "I will get myself out of this bad habit at once."

Bad Habits

Bad habits, such as over-eating, drinking and smoking, are very easy to acquire. One should fight against the force of habit. Even good things can be harmful when done to excess. The wise man always remembers this truth about himself and checks any bad habit at once.

Total no. of words in the passage – 152
Words used in the précis – 48

4. In every country people imagine that they are the best and the cleverest and the others are not good as they are. The English think that they and their country are the best: the French are very proud of France and everything French. The Germans and the Italians think no less of their countries and many Indians imagine that India in many ways is the greatest country in the world. This is wrong. Everybody wants to think well of himself and his country. But really there is no person who has some good and bad qualities. In the same way, there is no country which is not partly good and partly bad. We must take the good wherever we find it and try to remove the bad wherever it may be. We are, of course, most concerned with our own country, India. Unhappily, it is in a bad way today. Most of our people are poor and unhappy. They have no joy in their lives. We have to find out how we can make them happier. We have to see what is good in our ways and customs and try to keep it, and whatever is bad we have to throw away. If we find anything good in other countries, we should certainly take it.

Patriotism

People of every country—Englishmen, Frenchmen, Germans, Italians and many Indians—think too highly of themselves and consider their country the best and the greatest. No country can be absolutely good, just as no man can be thoroughly good. We have to eliminate poverty and misery from our country. We have to keep what is good in us and discard what is bad. We should accept whatever good we may find in other countries.

Total no. of words in the passage – 214
Words used in the précis – 74

5. One of the major problems we have to face is that of unemployment. It is a big problem, a human problem, which we cannot ignore. Yet in looking at it, it has to be remembered that merely giving some kind of occupation to a large number of people does not ultimately increase employment and lessen unemployment. Employment comes from newer and more effective means of wealth production. The whole experience and history of the past two hundred years shows that it comes through the growth of technological methods. Do not imagine that we can effectively deal with the problem of unemployment without technical progress. We can't. Every country which boasts of full employment today is a country which is technically advanced. Every country which is not technically advanced has unemployment or under employment. Therefore, if India is to advance, she must advance in science and technology. The fact is that our poverty is due to our backwardness in science and technology. If we remedy that backwardness we create not only wealth but also employment.

Technology: The Key to India's Problem

Unemployment is a burning problem. It can be easily solved through economic growth and not by providing some kind of jobs to large numbers of people. Experience shows that only technologically advanced countries have been able to achieve full employment. India's problems of poverty, backwardness and unemployment can also be remedied through advances in science and technology.

Total no. of words in the passage – 175
Words used in the précis – 57

Make a précis of the following passages

1. The future of English is very bright in India. It is not our national language. It is not our mother tongue. In our country hundreds of languages are spoken but English works as a link language among the people of India speaking various languages. We know that Indian private companies are getting global and international. They require English speaking people for their international trades. English is an international language. It is a language of international trade and commerce. Even the anti-English politicians have started recognizing its importance in the age of global market.

2. English is no longer being taught intensively in schools in India. Since independence, Hindi has been introduced as a compulsory subject in the lower classes and the teaching of English is begun later with the result that students come up to the university with inefficient grounding in English. Many of the great numbers of failures in examinations are due to this cause. Hence parents are more anxious than ever to get their children into the few schools where English is still well taught. They have no doubt about what they consider desirable. English they agree is a necessary world language for India. It is a key to international fellowship. It is the lingua franca of the educated all over the world.

3. The Ganges is a sacred river. Several towns are situated on its bank. She has seen many ups and downs. Several battles were also fought on the banks of the Ganges. The Ganges is a symbol of India's culture. She is the confluence of many rivers. Similarly our culture is the amalgam of many cultures. It is like the Ganges ever changing and yet ever the same. We are proud of our multi-faceted culture.

4. We have seen what a great part monsoon plays in providing our land with water without which little grow on it. That part is played in two ways, first by the rain by adding to the flow of rivers that come down from the mountains and flow through the plains. The first function is very important because rivers cannot and do not water all the land in our country. There are not enough rivers for that, and there are large areas which have no rivers at all. The rain from the cloud is in many places

the only water the dry land gets. There are parts of India such as upper Sindh where there is hardly any rain.

5. When we speak of the freedom of the press we usually mean freedom in a very technical and restricted sense—namely freedom from direction or censorship by the government. In this respect, the British press is, under ordinary conditions, free at large. It can affect foreign diplomacy, conduct campaigns to subvert constitution, incite citizen to discontent and rebellion, expose scandals and foment grievances. Likewise, it can function as an agency to bring reformative changes in the systems. It can become a weapon to coerce the government to conform to what it asserts to be the will of people.

6. Nobody can deny the achievements of science in the twentieth century. Its impact can be felt in every sphere of life. From the small pins and needles to the huge aeroplanes are the products of science. It has enabled man to have the same kind of control over the forces of nature. It has brought the distant parts of the world together. Remarkable cures for human diseases have been possible because of science. Our knowledge of the world has got widened and amplified because of science. No economic and industrial growth is possible without the helping hands of science.

7. Life without friendship is insipid and tiring and boring. Friendship is a precious thing to be treasured up by one and all. A friend in need is a friend indeed. A true friend appreciates our virtues but does not keep his eyes closed to our faults. He cares for us and shares our joys as well as sorrows. We turn to our friends for counsel and comfort. Blessed is the man or woman who is fortunate to have a true friend. Such friendship should be kept unbroken in all conditions.

8. Abraham Lincoln was born in 1809. He was a self made man. His father was a poor farmer. He worked first as a wood-cutter. But he wanted to make progress in life. He learnt how to read and write. He got a job as a clerk, then he was a storekeeper and then a postmaster. He studied law in spare time. He became a lawyer. He took up politics. Soon, he was well-known as an orator. In 1860, he made a famous speech against slavery. At that time slaves were kept in the southern

states of America. The same year he was elected president of the United States of America. He was a great man. He was one of the greatest presidents of America.

9. Child labour is a curse for our society. India is a democratic country. Here every child has been given right to education, good health and congenial social environment. However, it is ironical that there is estimated to be twenty million working children in India. Though our constitution prohibits under Article 24 the employment of children below fourteen in factories and hazardous jobs. It is a matter of national shame that even after sixty-five years of independence our country has not been able to eradicate the evil of child labour. The sight of small children working in hotels, factory units making carpets, slates, brass work and crackers is appalling. Children can be seen rag-picking and begging at railway platforms and bus-stands. Their life is miserable and most of them are homeless. The government and society should work together to do away with this evil of child labour.

10. Flood is an annual feature in many parts of India during the rainy season. If it rains cats and dogs, rivers, streams, ponds, etc. are not able to contain all the rain-water in their beds. As a result, the flood situation is created. Sometimes, it is caused by the melting of snow on the mountains, which increases the volume of water in the rivers. Now and then, breaches in embankment of a river also result in floods. Floods cause a heavy damage to men, animals, crops and houses. They render hundreds and thousands of people homeless. Animals and houses are washed away with the flood water. Floods also damage railway lines and roads which brings transportation to a standstill. The scarcity of food creates price-rise. Floods are frequent in Bihar. The water from Nepal creates flood in the Koshi river which is called the curse of Bihar. Both long-term and short-term measures are needed to tackle the menace of flood.

21

Letter Writing

What is Letter Writing?

Letter writing is an art of communicating facts and feelings in a transparent way.

In fact, a letter is an ambassador of thought and goodwill. It is a written or printed communication addressed to a person or organization. Nowadays, computer and email facilities have added grace to this art of writing.

Kind of Letters

Letters are broadly classified into two categories that include all the varieties of letters.

1. Personal letter (Informal letter): It is a kind of informal composition that is written to friends and relatives in a conversational style.
2. Formal letter: It is written with a practical purpose. So, it should be clear, courteous and to the point. It includes applications, business and office letters, reference letters, etc.

How to Write a Letter

In this fast changing world, we find considerable variations in the style and forms of letters and applications. In spite of it, some sort of uniformity is required to minimise the possibility of confusion. An attempt has been made here to present before you the latest styles and forms of letter writing which are in use these days. Let us have a look.

a. *Heading*: It includes address, date, designation of the recipient, subject and reference whichever is required in the letter.

Personal letter:	Sahjanand colony Bagdulhan, Hajipur 25.5.14, etc.
Formal letter:	To The Manager, Bharti Bhavan, Patna Subject—An order for grammar books, etc.

b. *Salutation*: It refers to the person or authority concerned.

Personal letter:	Respected Father/Mother, My Dear Sahil, Dear Raj, etc.
Formal letter:	Sir/Madam/Mr/Ms, Dear Sir, Dear Sirs, Messrs, etc.

c. *Body of the letter*: This is the main part of the letter that presents the gist of the letter.

Personal letter:	I just received your letter. I am fine here. How are you? I hope you are feeling better. I am pleased to hear that....... I was sorry to hear of your father's illness. Let me congratulate you on........, etc.
Formal letter:	Thank you for your letter of 7th May. In reply to your letter...... With reference to your letter........

I wish to draw your attention to the fact that....

I should be grateful if you would let me know..., etc.

d. *Complimentary close*: It is a courteous leave-taking before the letter ends. It must correspond to the salutation.

Personal letter:	With love, Yours affectionately, Yours sincerely, Your loving son/brother, etc.
Formal letter:	Yours faithfully/sincerely/ truly, etc.

Signature: The writer has to put his name or signature (with designation in business or official letters with stamp).

Personal letter:	Pratyush Raj, Priyanka, Jayant, etc.
Formal letter:	Raghubar Giri Section Officer, etc.

e. *Enclosures*: If the letter requires some additional papers to attach along with it, mention the exact number of papers under this heading.

Former letter	Enclosures - 4

Some tips for an effective letter

i. Leave a proper margin on the left.

ii. Try to write carefully, correctly and legibly.

iii. Avoid outdated expressions and out of date forms in all types of letters.

iv. Do not be formal with a friend and informal with a superior.

v. Make your approach logical and appropriate.

N.B. These days all parts of the letter are written preferably in left hand margin.

SAMPLE PERSONAL LETTERS

1. Letter from a daughter to her father about the coming examination.

Indian Public School

Paswan Chowk

Hajipur

25 May 2014

Dearest Father,

I have just received your letter. I am pleased to know that you are quite well.

My annual examination is at hand. It is only two weeks away. I have thoroughly prepared for the examination. Now I have enough time for revision. I am studying hard to get good marks.

I am taking care of my health also so that I may keep myself fit and fine during examination. The examination will be over on the 8th of June. I will reach home the next day and be there again with you all.

Your loving daughter,

Shreya

2. Letter to a friend advising him to take part in games.

Sitalpur

Saran

25.5.14

Dear Muskan,

I got your letter today and came to know all about your studies.

I think that reading is important. But, it is not good to read the whole day. More study will definitely affect your health. So try to spare an hour or two every day for games to keep yourself fit. You know that a healthy mind has a healthy body. The saying "All work and no play makes Jack a dull boy" gives us a hint to do both physical and mental work. So try to play some game everyday to keep your mind and body active and invigorating.

Remember me to everybody at home.

Your loving friend,
Ayush

3. Letter from an uncle to his niece with a birthday present.

Vidyanagar
Ranchi
22 April 2013

My dear Jolly,

I am well here with your cousin—Salini and Saloni. How are you? I think your birthday falls on the 28th of April. Many happy returns of the day! I hope the new year will bring happiness and success for you.

I am sending a laptop as a birthday present. I trust it will help you in studies.

With all good wishes,

Yours affectionately,
Mukul

SAMPLE FORMAL LETTER

1. A job application letter

Kankarbagh
Patna
20 June 2013

To
The Chief Editor,
The Hindustan Times
Patna

Dear Sir,

I wish to apply for the post of a computer operator which you advertised in your esteemed column of 18 June 2013.

I am a graduate with BCA Degree. I know how to operate a computer skilfully. I have been working in a computer institute for the last one year. I wish to improve my prospects in your firm.

I enclose two testimonials, one from the Principal of the college where I studied, and another from the computer institute.

If I get a chance to serve in your firm, I shall leave no stone unturned to satisfy you with my performance.

Yours faithfully,
Ravi

2. An order for books

Doctors colony
Gobarsahi
Muzaffarpur
20 Sept. 2013

Messrs Swarup and Sons,
New Delhi

Dear Sir,

I shall be obliged if you manage to send me one copy each of the following literary books at the earliest:

i. *The Waste Land*
ii. *Dr. Faustus*
iii. *Macbeth*
iv. *Pride and Prejudice*

Kindly send me the latest catalogue along with the books.

Yours faithfully,
Sarvdaman

3. Application for a transfer certificate

Gola Bazar
Sonpur
5 Jan. 2012

To
The Principal,
P.R. College
Sonpur

Subject: Request for transfer certificate

Sir,

With due respect, I have to state that my father has been transferred to Barauni as a railway employee. My entire family has settled down there except me. Now I am living alone here.

I, therefore, request you to issue me a transfer certificate so that I may join a college in Barauni.

For this kind act of yours, I shall feel highly obliged.

Yours faithfully,
Ahmed
Roll No. 224
I.Sc. 1st year
Session 2011-2013

4. A letter to the editor

Lalganj
Vaishali
10 May 2011

To
The Editor,
The Times of India
Patna

Sir,

Through the columns of your esteemed daily I wish to make the following facts known in the hope that something will get done.

Most of the roads are badly damaged under the jurisdiction of municipal area, Lalganj. They are out of repair for months. An accident a day has become the normal way. Filth and garbage continue to pile up on the road. There is a constant stink in our locality. This is due to the neglect of the municipal authority.

I hope that the authority concerned will take drastic steps to get the road repaired as soon as possible.

Yours faithfully,
Aman

EXERCISE-1

1. Write a letter to your friend telling him how you intend to spend your holidays.
2. Write a letter to your father asking him to send money for buying books.
3. Write a letter to your friend describing a train journey.
4. Write a letter to your sister congratulating her on her success.
5. Write a letter to your teacher inviting him to attend the wedding party.
6. Write a letter to your mother asking her to knit a sweater.
7. Write to your uncle on his 55th birthday.

EXERCISE-2

1. Write an application to your principal requesting a day's leave.
2. Write to the editor of a newspaper on the frequent power cut in your locality.
3. Write an application for a post of clerk in an institute.
4. Write to the manager of a factory asking permission to visit it.
5. Write to a firm ordering goods.

6. Write to the editor of a newspaper calling attention to the bad conditions in government hospitals.
7. Write an application to your principal requesting him to issue a character certificate.
8. Write to your landlord requesting him to carry out repair work in your flat.
9. Write an application to your principal requesting him to grant free-studentship.
10. Write to the postmaster informing him about the change in your address.

22

Reading Comprehension

What is Reading Comprehension?

Reading comprehension is an active process of interpretation and understanding of a passage or text.

The object of reading comprehension is to test a candidate's ability to grasp exactly the meaning of the passage. Its main purpose is to examine the ability of a candidate whether he/she is capable of constructing meaning from the passage and using it in a correct, clear and coherent manner or not. Basically, reading comprehension is a kind of intelligence test that collectively involves reading and thinking with reasoning.

Primarily, word meaning and text apprehension are the two basic tools of reading comprehension. Each passage has a set of questions. It may also have multiple-choice questions such as antonyms, synonyms, true or false statements, vocabulary test, matching test and alternative choice questions. Each question is really a test checking of either vocabulary items or compositional skill of the candidate.

In order to be good at reading comprehension, one should have a clear view about the basic information of the passage. One should also have the ability to answer the question in one's own words briefly and to the point.

How to go about a Reading Comprehension Passage

There are various points that should be kept in mind in order to develop the proper understanding of a passage. They are as follows:

Context of Questions: One needs to read the entire passage carefully so that one can comprehend the context to communicate the intended meaning.

Information: It is simply a message of the passage. It depicts a lot of information in the form of events, incidents and situations.

Fact: The point of facts can be had with the help of question words like *who?, why?, where?, what?*, etc. to understand the importance of the passage.

Point of View: The point of view of the writer can be noticed in terms of analysis of the passage.

Analysis: The passage may analyze any kind of situation and the questions related to it may form the basis of that analysis itself.

Conclusion: Obviously, it sums up the whole passage in a concrete way.

Tips for Solving Questions Based on Reading Comprehension

The following are the important points to bear in mind while answering a comprehension passage.

1. Read the passage carefully two to three times to understand the central idea.
2. Read the questions based on the passage.
3. Reread the passage to construct the answer from the passage.
4. Answer the main idea of the question.
5. Answer the questions in your own words.
6. Answer the question correctly and to the point.
7. Answer the questions in short and simple sentences.
8. Never use the language of the passage.
9. Never give additional information.
10. Maintain the verbal form of the question.
11. Try to use indirect method of narration.

Sample of Reading Comprehension Passages

1. Read the passage given below and answer the questions that follow.

I have a dream that one day this nation will rise up and live out meaning of its creed. "We hold these truths to be self-evident that all men are created equal." I have a dream that one day on the red hills of Georgia the sons of former slaves and the sons of former slave owners will be able to sit down together at the table of brotherhood. I have a dream that one day the state of Mississippi, a desert state, sweltering with the heat of injustice and oppression, will be transformed into an oasis of freedom and justice. I have a dream that my four children will one day live in a nation where they will not be judged by the colour of their skin but by the content of their character.

Questions:

1. What does 'one day' mean in the passage?
2. What kind of message does the writer wish to convey?
3. How will the children be judged in the writer's nation of dream?
4. Which has been called 'a desert state'?
5. What is Mississippi sweltering with?
6. Where will the sons of former slaves and the sons of former slave owners sit together?
7. What idea does 'I have a dream' signify?
8. What does the writer want to communicate through the passage?
9. Use the following phrases in the sentences of your own.

   rise up, live out, sit down
10. Choose a suitable alternative from the given words in the bracket to make a meaningful statement.

   a. The passage conveys the message of......................

   (equality, brotherhood, love)

b. A desert state refers to......................
(Georgia, Mississippi, Africa)

c. The nation was sweltering with injustice and ....
(suppression, oppression, depression)

Answers:

1. 'One day' refers to future course of action towards justice.
2. The writer wants to convey the message of equality and brotherhood.
3. The children will be judged not by the colour of their skin but by the content of their character in the speaker's nation of dream.
4. Mississippi has been called 'a desert state'.
5. Mississippi is sweltering with the heat of injustice and oppression.
6. The sons of former slaves and the sons of former slave owners will sit down together at a table of brotherhood.
7. 'I have a dream' signifies the hope of good governance and equal participation.
8. The writer wants to communicate the feeling that one day the high and the low will have equal right and live with love and brotherhood.
9. Rise up – India will rise up in Modi's regime and live up to the expectations of the people.

   Live out – He lives out a village life.

   Sit down – Sit down, please.
10. a – equality, b – Mississippi, c - oppression

2. *Read the passage to choose the best answer to the question. Answer the question on the basis of what is stated or implied in the passage.*

One day a father asked his daughters, "What is the sweetest thing in the world?" "Sugar" said the elder daughter. "Salt," said his younger daughter. Her father thought that his younger daughter was making fun of him, but she stuck to her opinion. The father was obstinate, and so was his daughter. A quarrel broke out between them over this small matter, and he drove her out of the house, saying: "As you think that salt is sweeter than sugar, you had better find another home where the cooking is more to your taste."

It was a beautiful summer night, and as the pretty maiden sat singly sadly in the forest around her father's cottage, a young prince, who had lost himself while hunting the deer, heard her voice and came to ask her the way. Then, struck by her beauty, he fell in love with her, took her home to his beautiful palace and married her.

The bride invited her father to the wedding feast, without telling him that she was his daughter. All the dishes were prepared without salt, and the guests began to complain as they ate the tasteless food. "There is no salt in the meat" they said angrily.

Ah! said the bride's father, "Salt is truly the sweetest thing in the world". But when my daughter said so, I turned her out of my house. If only I could see her again and tell her how sorry I am!

Drawing the bridal veil aside from her face, the happy girl went to her father and kissed him. Now properly salted dishes were brought in and all the guests were satisfied.

Questions:

1. What question did the father put to his daughters?
2. What answers did the daughters give?
3. Whose answer did the father think to be correct?
4. Why did the younger daughter stick to her opinion?
5. Who was wrong in making a logical opinion?
6. How did the bride prove her opinion?
7. Read the following statements and write T for true and F for false.

   a. The father thought that the younger daughter was making fun of him.

b. The father drove the younger daughter out of the house because she had disobeyed him.

c. The younger daughter was as obstinate as her father.

d. The prince married the girl because he took pity on her.

e. Salt is the sweetest thing in the world because it adds taste to the dishes we eat.

8. What is the antonym of the following words?

   Obstinate, satisfied, bride, sweet, tasteless, pretty

9. Underline the word which is almost the same in meaning and use them in sentences of your own.

   Dishes – soup, salad, meal, items

   Quarrel – talk, altercation, discourse

   Angrily – disappointingly, seriously, horribly, furiously

10. Match the words from A with the meaning of B.

A	B
i. Pretty	a. an unmarried girl
ii. Complain	b. stately mansion
iii. Palace	c. grievance
iv. Maiden	d. contented
v. Satisfied	e. mask
vi. Veil	f. beautiful

Answers:

1. The father asked the two daughters what was the sweetest thing in the world.
2. The elder daughter said it was sugar; the younger daughter said it was salt.
3. The father agreed with the elder daughter.
4. The younger daughter was as rigid as her father.
5. The father was wrong in making a logical opinion.

6. The bride proved her statement correct by offering dishes without salt to make her father realize the importance of salt.
7. True or False statements

   a – T, b – F, c – T, d – F, e – T
8. Antonyms:

   obstinate flexible

   satisfied dissatisfied

   bride groom

   tasteless tasty

   pretty ugly
9. Synonyms

   Dishes – Meal – We had good dishes in the wedding party.

   Quarrel – Altercation – The naughty students entered into an altercation in my class.

   Angrily – Furiously – The dog attacked the beggar furiously.
10. Matching test

    A – B

    i – f

    ii – c

    iii – b

    iv – a

    v – d

    vi – e

EXERCISE–1

Read the passage given below and answer the questions that follow.

1. It would be fatal for a nation to overlook the urgency of the moment and underestimate the determination of the Negro. This sweltering summer of the Negro's legitimate discontent

will not pass until there is an invigorating autumn of freedom and equality. 1963 is not an end but a beginning.

Those who hope that the Negro needed to blow off steam and will now be content will have a rude awakening as the nation returns to business as usual. Negro is granted his citizenship rights, the feeling of revolt will continue to shake the foundations of our nation until the bright day of justice emerges.

Questions:

1. What would be fatal for the nation?
2. What will happen when the nation returns to business as usual?
3. How long will the revolt continue to shake the foundation of the nation?
4. What does the writer want to convey through the sweltering summer of the Negro's legitimate discontent?
5. Match the words from A with the meaning of B.

A	B
I. sweltering	determination
II. legitimate	base
III. foundation	hot and perspiring
IV. overlook	justifiable
V. dedication	ignore

EXERCISE-2

Read the text and answer the questions that follow.

There was a king. He wanted to know the answers to his three questions. The three questions were what was the right time for him to start something? What people he ought to pay attention to? What was the most important thing for him to do? The king sent messengers throughout his kingdom promising a huge reward for the man who would give the right answers to his three questions. Many people came to the king with their different answers but the king was not satisfied with their answers. So, he did not give the promised reward to anyone. The king decided to seek the advice of a hermit who was widely famous for his wisdom. The hermit lived in a wood and met only with ordinary people. The king put off his royal clothes and bodyguards and went to the hermit as an ordinary person. The hermit at that time was digging the earth. He greeted the king. The king took pity on him and began to work in place of him and put his three questions before him.

Questions:

1. What were the three questions of the king?
2. Why did he want to know?
3. Was the king satisfied with the answers of different people?
4. What was the final decision of the king to know the right answer?
5. Where did the hermit live and what type of people did he meet?
6. What was the hermit doing when the king reached there?
7. Which of the alternatives best completes the statements?
   (i) The king was very eager to know three things because
      a. he wished to be famous.
      b. he wished to succeed in life.
      c. he wished to please his subjects.

   (ii) The king went to the hermit because
      a. he was wise.
      b. he knew the answer.
      c. he knew the art of magic.

   (iii) The king helped the hermit because
      a. he felt pity on him.
      b. the hermit asked him to do so.
      c. he wanted to do him a favour.

8. Say whether the following statements are true or false.
   (i) All the wise men gave the same answer.
   (ii) The king had no faith in the hermit.
   (iii) All the wise men answered the king's questions differently.
   (iv) The king did not get any answer from the hermit.
   (v) The king had great faith in the hermit.
9. Choose the right group of word or words from the following sentences.
   (i) The king went to the hermit

      a. with the bodyguard, b. all alone, c. with his son
   (ii) The hermit lived in

      a. hotel, b. forest, c. palace
10. Choose the similar word from the given alternatives.
    a. Kingdom – state, country, realm
    b. Advice – idea, notion, suggestion
    c. Greet – thank, salute, adore
    d. In place of – by dint of, in lieu of, in search of

EXERCISE-3

Read the passage and answer the questions.

Arundhati Roy, the famous novelist and activist who won the Booker Prize in 1997 for her novel *The God of Small Things*, was born in Shillong on September 24, 1961. She was an issue of a Keralite mother and a Bengali father. She spent her childhood in Aymanam, in Kerala with her mother. She left Kerala for Delhi at the age of 16 and made a living by selling empty bottles. She studied architecture in Delhi but did not take it up as a profession. In 1984, she began a brief career in films under the influence of her husband, who was a film-maker. She played the role of a village girl in the award winning movie *Massey Sahib*. She began writing her novel in 1992 and finished it in 1996. She received half a million pounds as an advance from the publisher.

Questions:

1. What is Arundhati Roy famous for?
2. Where was she born?
3. Where did she spend her childhood?
4. When did she come to Delhi and what did she study there?
5. How much money did she receive as an advance for her novel?
6. Name the film in which she played the role of a village girl?

EXERCISE-4

Read the passage given below and answer the questions that follow.

Midas, the king of Phrygia was foolish enough to make Apollo, the sun-god, jealous. Apollo was a fine musician, but Midas said one day that he thought the goat-god, Pan was a better musician than Apollo. This made the sun-god very angry, and he revenged himself by giving the king donkey's ears in place of his ordinary ones; "because" said Apollo, "he must have donkey's ears if he cannot hear that my music is the most beautiful in the world."

Midas was filled with shame and tried to hide his donkey's ears under his hair. But his barber found out his secret. Midas made him promise never to tell anyone the secret, but the barber could not keep it to himself. "I must tell someone or I will burst." He thought, and at last he went out into a field. Here he dug a deep hole, and spoke softly into it. "Midas has donkey's ears." He said, and then went home again.

Time passed. The hole was filled with earth, and grass grew there. The wind whistled through the tall grasses, and they were heard to say: "Midas has donkey's ears! Midas has donkey's ears!"

And so Midas's secret was a secret no longer.

Questions:

1. Who was Apollo and why did he become angry with the king?
2. Where did the barber dig the hole?
3. How did the king try to hide his hair?
4. Which of the given alternatives completes the sentences?
   (i) The king wanted the barber not to
   a. tell the secret b. trim his moustache c. come again
   (ii) Apollo gave the king
   a. sermon b. goat's ears c. donkey's ears
   (iii) The goat-god was
   a. Zeus b. Pan c. Aphrodite
5. Fill in the blanks with a suitable word given in brackets.
   a. The hole was filled with........... (water, earth, stone)
   b. Lastly, all knew Midas's........... (address, secret, plan)
   c. The barber dug a deep........... (pit, well, hole)
6. Say whether the statements given below are true or false.
   a. Apollo was pleased with the king.
   b. Midas was a wise man.
   c. Apollo was very angry with the king.
   d. Apollo was the god of the sun.
   e. Midas was a foolish man.

EXERCISE-5

Read the passage and answer the questions.

While going to visit Ganymede, Orlando saw a man lying asleep on the ground. A large green snake had twisted itself around his neck. The snake, seeing Orlando come near, slid off among the bushes. Orlando went closer, and then discovered a lioness lying with her head on the ground, watching like a cat for the sleeping man to awake.

Orlando saw that the man lying on the ground was his own brother, Oliver. For an instant he was tempted to leave him to the lioness, but the gentleness of his nature overcame his first anger against his brother and he drew his sword. He leapt to attack the lioness and with some difficulty, succeeded in killing her, although not before she had torn one of his arms with her sharp claws.

Oliver awakened during the fight and saw that his brother whom he had so cruelly treated, had saved him at the risk of his own life. He was filled with shame and sorrow, and begged Orlando to forgive him to the injuries he had done him. Orlando readily forgave him. From that hour Oliver loved Orlando with a true brotherly love, although he had come to the forest to kill him.

Questions:

1. What did Orlando see while going to visit Ganymede?
2. Who was the man sleeping there?
3. How did the enmity between the two brothers come to an end?
4. Why did Orlando take risk to save his brother?
5. Which of the given alternatives completes the sentences?
   a. Lioness does not attack anything that is.......... (alive, dead, wounded)
   b. The snake slid off among the.......... (grasses, bushes, trees)
   c. The lioness was watching like a.......... (dog, crow, cat)
6. Write true or false against each of the following:
   (i) Oliver had come to the forest to help Orlando.
   (ii) Orlando recognised his brother.

(iii) The lioness tore one of the arms of Oliver.

(iv) Oliver came to the forest to kill Orlando.

7. Choose the right group of words to make a correct sentence:

   a. Oliver begged Orlando to..........

      help him, support him, forgive him

   b. The lioness tore Orlando's arms with her..........

      sharp teeth, sharp claws, sharp nails

   c. The relationship was that of..........

      brother and brother, father and son, master and servant

Bibliography

Adger, D. (2003). *Core Syntax: A Minimalist Approach*, Oxford University Press: Oxford.

Aarts, F. and J. Aarts (1982). *English Syntactic Structures: Functions and Categories in Sentence Analysis*, Pergamon Press: Oxford.

Baker, A. (1982). *Introducing English Pronunciation*, Cambridge University Press: Cambridge.

Baltin, M. and C. Collins (2001). *The Handbook of Contemporary Syntactic Theory* (edited), Blackwell: Oxford.

Bauer, L. (1988). *Introducing Linguistic Morphology*, Edinburgh University Press: Edinburgh.

Blakemore, D. (1992). *Understanding Utterances*, Blackwell: Oxford.

Balasubramanian, T. (1996). *A Textbook of Phonetics*, Macmillan India Press.

Black, B. (1990). *Relational Grammar*, Routledge: New York.

Carter, R. and Michael McCarthy (2006). *Cambridge Grammar of English*, Cambridge University Press.

Catford, J.C. (1988). *A Practical Introduction to Phonetics*, Oxford University Press.

Chomsky, N. (1965). *Aspects of the Theory of Syntax*, MIT Press: Massachusetts.

—— (1980). *Rules and Representations*, Blackwell: Oxford.

—— (1986). *Barriers*, MIT Press: Cambridge.

—— (1995). *Minimalist Programme*, MIT Press: Cambridge.

Cook, V.J. and Mark Newson (1988). *Chomsky's Universal Grammar: An Introduction*, Blackwell Publishers: Oxford.

Cowan, R. (2008). *The Teacher's Grammar of English*, Cambridge University Press.

Cruttenden, A. (1994). *Gimson's Pronunciation of English*, 5th edition, Gimson's original book revised and edited, Edward Arnold: London.

Crystal, David (1989). *Linguistics,* Pelican Books.

—— (1988). *Cambridge Encyclopaedia of Language*, Cambridge University Press.

Formkin, V. and Robert Rodman (1993). *An Introduction to Language*, Harcourt Brace College Publishers: New York.

Giegerich, H.J. (1992). *English Phonology: An Introduction*, Cambridge University Press: Cambridge.

Griffiths, P. (2006). *An Introduction to English Semantics and Pragmatics*, Edinburgh University Press.

Harris, J. (1994). *English Sound Structure*, Blackwell: Oxford.

Heageman, L. (1991). *An Introduction to Government and Binding Theory*, Blackwell: Oxford.

Horrocks, G. (1987). *Generative Grammar*, Longman: London.

Hurford, J.R. and B. Heasley (1983). *Semantics: A Coursebook*, Cambridge University Press.

International Phonetic Association (1999). *Handbook of the International Phonetic Association*, Cambridge University Press: Cambridge.

Ladefoged, P. (2000). *Vowels and Consonants*, Blackwell: Oxford.

Leech, Geoffrey (1974). *Semantics*, Penguin Books.

Lyons, John (1992). *Language and Linguistics: An Introduction*, Cambridge University Press.

Matthews, P.H. (1974). *Morphology*, Cambridge University Press.

O'Connor, J.D. (1991). *Phonetics*, Penguin: London.

Ostler, Nicholas (2005). *Empires of the Word: A Language History of the World*, Harper-Collins: London.

Poole, S.C. (1999). *An Introduction to Linguistics*, Macmillan Press Ltd: London.

Quirk, Randolph and Sidney Greenbaum (1973). *A University Grammar of English*, Longman: London.

Radford, A., A. Martin and B. David (1999). *Linguistics: An Introduction*, Cambridge University Press.

Radford, Andrew (1988). *Transformational Grammar: A First Course,* Cambridge University Press.

—— (1997). *Syntax: A Minimalist Introduction*, Cambridge University Press.

Roach, P. (1983). *English Phonetics and Phonology*, Cambridge University Press.

Sinha, R.P. (2002). *Current English Grammar and Usage*, Oxford University Press: Delhi.

Spencer, A.J. (1991). *Morphological Theory*, Blackwell: Oxford.

Tallerman, M. (1998). *Understanding Syntax*, Edward Arnold: London.

Thomas, L. (1993). *Beginning Syntax*, Blackwell Publishers: Oxford.

Verma, S.K. and N. Krishnaswamy (1989). *Modern Linguistics*, Oxford University Press: Delhi.

Williams, E. (1994). *Thematic Structures in Syntax*, MIT Press: Cambridge.

Yule, George (1996). *Pragmatics*, Oxford University Press.

—— (1985). *The Study of Language: An Introduction*, Cambridge University Press.